SIP Trunking

Christina Hattingh

Darryl Sladden

ATM Zakaria Swapan

Cisco Press

800 East 96th Street

Indianapolis, IN 46240

SIP Trunking

Christina Hattingh, Darryl Sladden, and ATM Zakaria Swapan

Copyright © 2010 Cisco Systems, Inc.

Published by:
Cisco Press
800 East 96th Street
Indianapolis, IN 46240 USA

Printed in the United States of America

Second Printing November 2011

Library of Congress Cataloging-in-Publication Data is on file.

ISBN-13: 978-1-58705-944-5

ISBN-10: 1-58705-944-4

Warning and Disclaimer

This book is designed to provide information about Session Initiation Protocol (SIP) networking technology. Every effort has been made to make this book as complete and as accurate as possible, but no warranty or fitness is implied.

The information is provided on an "as is" basis. The authors, Cisco Press, and Cisco Systems, Inc. shall have neither liability nor responsibility to any person or entity with respect to any loss or damages arising from the information contained in this book or from the use of the discs or programs that may accompany it.

The opinions expressed in this book belong to the authors and are not necessarily those of Cisco Systems, Inc.

Trademark Acknowledgments

All terms mentioned in this book that are known to be trademarks or service marks have been appropriately capitalized. Cisco Press or Cisco Systems, Inc., cannot attest to the accuracy of this information. Use of a term in this book should not be regarded as affecting the validity of any trademark or service mark.

Corporate and Government Sales

The publisher offers excellent discounts on this book when ordered in quantity for bulk purchases or special sales, which may include electronic versions and/or custom covers and content particular to your business, training goals, marketing focus, and branding interests. For more information, please contact:
U.S. Corporate and Government Sales   1-800-382-3419   corpsales@pearsontechgroup.com

For sales outside the United States please contact: **International Sales**   international@pearsoned.com

Feedback Information

At Cisco Press, our goal is to create in-depth technical books of the highest quality and value. Each book is crafted with care and precision, undergoing rigorous development that involves the unique expertise of members from the professional technical community.

Readers' feedback is a natural continuation of this process. If you have any comments regarding how we could improve the quality of this book, or otherwise alter it to better suit your needs, you can contact us through email at feedback@ciscopress.com. Please make sure to include the book title and ISBN in your message.

We greatly appreciate your assistance.

Publisher: Paul Boger

Associate Publisher: Dave Dusthimer

Executive Editor: Brett Bartow

Managing Editor: Patrick Kanouse

Project Editor: Mandie Frank

Editorial Assistant: Vanessa Evans

Cover Designer: Louisa Adair

Composition: Mark Shirar

Indexer: Tim Wright

Business Operation Manager, Cisco Press: Anand Sundaram

Manager Global Certification: Erik Ullanderson

Development Editor: Deadline Driven

Copy Editor: Apostrophe Editing Services

Technical Editors: Maulik Shah and Vinay Pande

Proofreader: Jovana San Nicolas-Shirley

CISCO.

Americas Headquarters	Asia Pacific Headquarters	Europe Headquarters
Cisco Systems, Inc.	Cisco Systems (USA) Pte. Ltd.	Cisco Systems International BV
San Jose, CA	Singapore	Amsterdam, The Netherlands

Cisco has more than 200 offices worldwide. Addresses, phone numbers, and fax numbers are listed on the Cisco Website at **www.cisco.com/go/offices**.

CCDE, CCENT, Cisco Eos, Cisco HealthPresence, the Cisco logo, Cisco Lumin, Cisco Nexus, Cisco StadiumVision, Cisco TelePresence, Cisco WebEx, DCE, and Welcome to the Human Network are trademarks; Changing the Way We Work, Live, Play, and Learn and Cisco Store are service marks; and Access Registrar, Aironet, AsyncOS, Bringing the Meeting To You, Catalyst, CCDA, CCDP, CCIE, CCIP, CCNA, CCNP, CCSP, CCVP, Cisco, the Cisco Certified Internetwork Expert logo, Cisco IOS, Cisco Press, Cisco Systems, Cisco Systems Capital, the Cisco Systems logo, Cisco Unity, Collaboration Without Limitation, EtherFast, EtherSwitch, Event Center, Fast Step, Follow Me Browsing, FormShare, GigaDrive, HomeLink, Internet Quotient, IOS, iPhone, iQuick Study, IronPort, the IronPort logo, LightStream, Linksys, MediaTone, MeetingPlace, MeetingPlace Chime Sound, MGX, Networkers, Networking Academy, Network Registrar, PCNow, PIX, PowerPanels, ProConnect, ScriptShare, SenderBase, SMARTnet, Spectrum Expert, StackWise, The Fastest Way to Increase Your Internet Quotient, TransPath, WebEx, and the WebEx logo are registered trademarks of Cisco Systems, Inc. and/or its affiliates in the United States and certain other countries.

All other trademarks mentioned in this document or website are the property of their respective owners. The use of the word partner does not imply a partnership relationship between Cisco and any other company. (0812R)

About the Authors

Christina Hattingh is a member of the technical staff in the Access Routing Technology Group (ARTG) of Cisco. The ARTG router product portfolio, including the Cisco 2800, 3800, 2900, and 3900 Series integrated services routers and their predecessors, was one of the first Cisco platforms to converge voice and data starting in the late 1990s by offering TDM voice interfaces, WAN interfaces, and critical QoS features. Over time sophisticated call control and routing elements were integrated into the router-based platform making stand-alone VoIP deployments and wide inter-vendor VoIP network interoperability possible. In this role, Christina trains Cisco sales staff and customers and consults widely on voice network deployment and design. She is a long-time speaker of the Cisco Networkers and CiscoLive conferences. Christina holds a graduate degree in mathematical statistics and computer science from the University of Pretoria, South Africa.

Darryl Sladden is a product manager at Cisco and has been with Cisco for more than ten years. Currently, Darryl is a member of the ARTG at Cisco. The ARTG responsibilities include the Cisco ISR and ISR G2, AS5000, and the Cisco Unified Border Element (CUBE). Darryl has been a key contributor to the AS5000 product, CUBE, and several other VoIP technologies at Cisco for several years. The CUBE and the AS5000 product lines are widely used by service providers and enterprise customers as border elements between SIP, H.323, and TDM networks. Darryl has worked with many service provider and enterprise customers who use CUBE to implement SIP Trunks into both Cisco Unified Communications Manager (CUCM) and Cisco Unified Communications Manager Express (CUCME) solutions. Darryl has a degree in mathematics from the University of Waterloo and holds a patent in the use of voice-based network management, and several other patents are under consideration.

ATM Zakaria Swapan is a member of the technical staff in the ARTG at Cisco. The ARTG responsibilities include the Cisco 2800, 3800, 2900, and 3900 Series integrated services routers and the CUBE. ATM has been a key contributor to SIP, Secure Unified Communications, Wireless Voice, Network Intelligence, Network Virtualization, RSVP, and many other developments. ATM has also worked with service providers and enterprise customers who use CUBE to implement SIP Trunks into both CUCM and CUCME solutions. ATM holds an M.S. degree in computer science from Texas A&M University and a B.S. degree in computer science and engineering from Bangladesh University of Engineering and Technology (BUET).

About the Technical Reviewers

Maulik Shah has been with Cisco Systems for the past nine years. He has worked with Unified Communications and Voice over IP (VoIP) systems for the last seven years as part of the Cisco Technical Assistance Center and Technical Marketing Team. He has helped design, deploy, and troubleshoot multiple customer VoIP networks. In his current role as Technical Marketing Engineer, he is focused on Cisco Small Business Solutions including Cisco SBCS and SIP trunking deployments. He also is a CCIE in Routing and Switching and Voice.

Vinay Pande is a technical leader at Cisco, where he is the subject matter expert for SIP trunking architectures. He works with customers to identify new features and designs network architectures with a focus on delivering end-to-end solutions. Prior to joining Cisco, Vinay was a VoIP interop and test lead for Lucent Technologies. He has filed seven patents in the areas of SIP and NAT transversal for SIP. He has over 12 years of experience in the field of voice, data, and video network integration.

Dedications

From Christina Hattingh: To Robert Verkroost and my parents for their unfailing encouragement and support.

From Darryl Sladden: To Melissa Brown and my mom, sisters, and friends for their patience and support.

From ATM Zakaria Swapan: To my parents for their great contribution that brings me here today.

Acknowledgments

We would like to extend special thanks to Mike Wood, Sibrina Shafique, and Syed Rahman who were coauthors on some early SIP trunk white papers, the content of which were adjusted, updated, and reused in this book. These white papers, available on Cisco.com as of early 2008, represent some of the earliest writing on the start of the industry transition from TDM to SIP trunking.

We would also like to extend special thanks to the many Cisco employees on whose expertise, advice, laboratory work, configurations, and examples we drew from for the technical accuracy of this book. Specifically, to Vinay Pande who is an undisputed expert in the area of SIP trunking and Francisco Sedano Crippa, one of the many enterprising Cisco engineers who developed a novel Tcl-based Cisco Unified Border Element (CUBE) script solution for his customer, which is reused in this book.

Special thanks also go to Tony Banuelos of the Cisco Unified Communication interoperability laboratory, whose unfailing dedication generates countless working configurations to ease customer network implementations and to the unfailing support and cooperation of Patty Mertz Medberry who manages the interoperability lab.

Special thanks also go to David Hanes for his expertise on topics involving fax and modem traffic; to Charles Ganzhorn for video expertise; to Dan Wing and Paul Kyzivat for their knowledge of SIP and the SIP standards; and to Ed Curry, Charles Demaret, and Tim Cabeceiras for their expertise on specific SP SIP trunk service offerings.

Thanks also go to various experts who helped with the case studies contained in this book, including Kees Gerritsen, Zulfi Anees, Kevin Whelan, Mike Haag, and Spencer Lawes. Thanks also to Kim Haugan Cook for documentation support; to John Heaton for help in the cost analyses; and to Vivek Bhargava and James Stormes for general expertise in enterprise SIP trunk design.

Lastly, thanks go to Mike Wood, David Sauerhaft, and Teresa Newell for their leadership and executive support.

Contents at a Glance

Contents

Icons Used in This Book

Communication Server | PC | PC with Software | Sun Workstation | Macintosh | Access Server | ISDN/Frame Relay Switch

Token Ring | Terminal | File Server | Web Server | Ciscoworks Workstation | ATM Switch | Modem

Printer | Laptop | IBM Mainframe | Front End Processor | Cluster Controller | Multilayer Switch

Gateway | Router | Bridge | Hub | DSU/CSU | FDDI | Catalyst Switch

Network Cloud | Line: Ethernet | Line: Serial | Line: Switched Serial

Command Syntax Conventions

The conventions used to present command syntax in this book are the same conventions used in the IOS Command Reference. The Command Reference describes these conventions as follows:

- **Boldface** indicates commands and keywords that are entered literally as shown. In actual configuration examples and output (not general command syntax), boldface indicates commands that are manually input by the user (such as a **show** command).

- *Italic* indicates arguments for which you supply actual values.

- Vertical bars (|) separate alternative, mutually exclusive elements.

- Square brackets ([ ]) indicate an optional element.

- Braces ({ }) indicate a required choice.

- Braces within brackets ([{ }]) indicate a required choice within an optional element.

Introduction

Today is an unusually interesting time in the field of unified communications as we stand at the dawn of a major industry transition in how communications flow between businesses. The network implementation to enable this communications flow is drastically changing in terms of technology, products, connectivity, service provider offerings, and cost. One of these changes is the transition to Public Switched Telephone Network (PSTN) trunking technology.

The industry is active with discussions of Session Initiation Protocol (SIP) trunking, but the appreciation of its real implications is just beginning. This book is written to help you understand and navigate these uncertain and fast-changing waters. Deciding when to change your network to take advantage of SIP trunking, how much of your network to change, and at what pace are all daunting decisions, and there might not be a single answer for all. The decisions you make today can have far-reaching effects on the productivity and cost-effectiveness of your company's communications. As an equipment vendor, we advise numerous customers on the available options and network designs and provide anecdotes as to what has worked and warnings to what has not in this epic journey to end-to-end rich media communications.

This book lays out charts and navigational assistance to help you sail these waters successfully. A variety of decision makers can benefit from this book, whether you are interested in the details of the industry transition from Time Division Multiplexing (TDM) to SIP, you are an executive who has to decide where to direct the communications investments of your company, or you are an IT staff member or consultant challenged with implementing these technologies.

The book is divided into three easy-to-use sections to address each of these interest groups:

- Part I, "From TDM Trunking to SIP Trunking," is for the beginner or executive reader and covers an overview of the industry transition, trends in the communications industry, an introduction to transitioning your network from TDM to SIP trunking, and a sample cost analysis.

- Part II, "Planning Your Network for SIP Trunking," is for the IT staff member or consultant responsible for the planning, architecture, design, and rollout logistics of the network transition. This section provides information on the network design considerations, dial plan operation, phases of rollout, service provider offering evaluation, and much more.

- Part III, "Deploying SIP Trunking," is for the network engineer who implements the changes and configures the equipment. This section provides information on network deployments and configuration examples including several case studies.

Goals and Methods

The goal of this book is to help you understand, decide, and execute the transition from using TDM trunking to SIP trunking in your network for PSTN access. If you have already made the decision to go forward with this transition, this book will help you implement it.

The organization of the book arranges the content into three easy-to-use sections at successive levels of detail and an increasingly closer look at the actual implementation of the network. The first part provides guidance and overview material, the second part offers hands-on, in-the-trenches planning information, and the last part provides configuration examples for network implementation.

This book is a practical guide for migrating your network to incorporate SIP trunking for PSTN access. It addresses questions such as:

- What is a SIP trunk, and why should I care about it for my network?

- What are the components of a SIP trunk solution?

- How much can I expect a SIP trunk to save me on my communications bill?

- How do I determine which service provider's offering to go with?

- What does SIP trunking mean to the way calls flow in my network between my data centers and remote offices?

- What does SIP trunking mean to my dial plan?

- What security issues does a SIP trunk expose my network to?

- How do I configure the extensive features required to implement a successful SIP trunk?

Who Should Read This Book?

This book is a roadmap to help you understand the path toward rich end-to-end communications using SIP.

Part I of this book is helpful if you want to learn about the communications industry trends and direction. It provides an overview of the TDM to SIP transition at a high, easy-to-grasp level with a handy cost-analysis right up front.

Part II should be read if you are responsible for the planning and design of a network migration for your company or for your customer's network. It is also helpful if you are doing the service provider evaluation for bringing in a SIP trunk.

Part III is helpful to the network engineers and implementers who configure the network equipment that carries calls to and from SIP trunks.

This book is not designed to be a general networking topic book; a certain familiarity and level of experience with SIP and unified communications are assumed.

How This Book Is Organized

Although this book can be read cover-to-cover, it is designed with increasing levels of technical depth and practical network implementation as the chapters progress, geared toward readers of different interest levels. If you are an overview or trends reader, the chapters in Part I are for you:

- Chapter 1, "Overview of IP Telephony": Provides the introduction to IP Telephony and its essential components such as voice compression technologies, multiple voice signaling protocols, PBXs, Digital Signal Processing (DSPs) and TDM trunks, including an introduction to the latest development in IP Telephony and SIP Trunks.

- Chapter 2, "Trends in IP Telephony": IP telephony has traditionally been about connecting new IP endpoints, such as IP PBXs from businesses or IP phones for consumers, to the traditional TDM-based PSTN. The latest trend is for the service providers (SP) to offer IP-based PSTN connectivity services or trunks. This enables traditional IP PBX customers, in both large and small businesses, to purchase IP trunking services as opposed to traditional TDM trunking services. This chapter provides an overview of these industry migrations.

- Chapter 3, "Transitioning to SIP Trunks": Explains the stages that a company needs to plan or execute when transitioning its current systems from one that uses TDM or H.323 trunks to a system that uses SIP trunks, either for intra-application connections or for PSTN access connectivity.

- Chapter 4, "Cost Analysis": Focuses on the cost structure of deploying the SIP trunks, one of the major criteria to select the SIP trunk service provider.

If you are a network planner or designer, Part II's chapters are appropriate reading, with or without necessarily having read Part I, or perhaps reading them out of sequence:

- Chapter 5, "Components of SIP Trunks": Describes the major components used to deploy SIP trunks including call agents, session managers, session border controllers, billing servers, network infrastructure components, media gateways, and monitoring equipment. This chapter also describes the differences in components for SIP trunks into large enterprises, medium-sized enterprises, and small-medium businesses.

- Chapter 6, "SIP Trunking Models": Explains the centralized, distributed, and hybrid network topology alternatives for connecting a SIP trunk from an SP into an enterprise network for PSTN access.

- Chapter 7, "Design and Implementation Considerations": Focuses on network design and implementation considerations after a decision has been reached to connect to an SP via a SIP trunk, including geographic and regulatory considerations, IP connectivity options, dial plans and call routing, supplementary services, network demarcation and security, call traffic capacity and bandwidth control, and scalability and high availability.

- Chapter 8, "Interworking": Explores an additional set of interworking network design considerations, including dual-tone multi-frequency (DTMF) conversion, fax and modem traffic, and connecting different H.323 and SIP variations.

- Chapter 9, "Questions to Ask of a Service Provider Offering and an SBC Vendor": Explains the questions you should ask and appropriate answers you should seek from your SPs and SBC vendors before you deploy a SIP trunk into your network.

Part III is for the network implementer. If you are familiar with the material in Part II, you can dive straight into this, but for most readers it would make more sense to cover Part II first before starting on Part III's chapters.

- Chapter 10, "Deployment Scenarios": Covers configurations for the typical SIP trunk deployment scenarios, including enterprise to SP deployments, SMB to SP deployments, and configurations with SRST, transcoding, a collocated firewall, Tcl scripting, and many more.

- Chapter 11, "Deployment Steps and Best Practices": Pulls together the detailed information from preceding chapters on network design considerations and deployment scenarios into an easy-to-use, step-by-step guide to implementing SIP trunking and a summary of best practices to follow.

- Chapter 12, "Case Studies": Covers a few case studies of real-life SIP trunk deployments, including the challenges faced and overcome.

- Chapter 13, "Future of Unified Communications": Shows some of the examples of how Unified Communications might develop in the next 40 years based on roadmaps of current products and technologies.

Chapter 1

Overview of IP Telephony

This chapter covers the following topics:

- History and overview of IP Telephony

- Basic components of IP Telephony

- Comparision of VoIP signaling protocols

The technology of communications has always been a great area of innovation. Since the invention of the telephone in the 1890s to the latest advancements in Telepresence technologies today, communications have been an important area of development. Since late 1990, the major development in communications has been the shift from many different protocols to the use of Internet Protocol (IP) for communications. Overall, this is known as IP Telephony.

This chapter provides the introduction to IP Telephony and its essential components, including an introduction to the latest development in IP Telephony, Session Initiation Protocol (SIP) trunks. This chapter covers LAN solutions; WAN solutions; voice compression technologies; multiple signaling protocols; quality of service (QoS), bandwidth requirement; Digital Signal Processors (DSP); Internet Protocol Public Branch Exchanges (IP-PBX); Cisco Unified Communications Manager (CUCM); Time-Division Multiplexing (TDM) to IP conversion gateways; dial plans; supplementary services, and so on, and it provides some of the basic information that a service provider, systems integrator, and enterprise employees need to have to architect, design, and implement an IP Telephony system and SIP trunks.

History of IP Telephony

The first Voice over IP (VoIP) technology trials occurred in university and nontraditional company research labs in the late 1980s. Users wanted to take advantage of the growth in networked computer systems that included the capability of encoding and decoding audio. Using basic components such as a networked computer, microphone, and speaker, the VoIP equivalent of "Hello, Watson. Come here. I need you." was achieved.

Traditional telecommunications companies had the equivalent of VoIP for many years in the form of the Primary Rate Interface (PRI) Integrated Services Digital Network (ISDN) circuit. The PRI ISDN circuit takes a TDM voice channel and breaks it into segments that are multiplexed down a single physical wire. The idea that was going to dramatically change the world of communications was that the protocol stack that voice communications travel on was not specifically designed for predictable voice traffic. IP had no underlying expectation of the traffic that flows across it, so the idea of sending VoIP was not envisioned when the protocol was created. Instead, the wide adoption of networked computers using a standard TCP/IP stack enabled the advancements in technology that have lead to more development of communications technology and ultimately widespread adoption of Unified Communications.

These first basic experiments in telephony quickly created a movement, and what is currently seen as IP Telephony emerged around 1996. Since then, IP Telephony systems, hardware, and software have matured and become more sophisticated, but many of the basic components remain the same.

Basic Components of IP Telephony

The primary data that travels over IP Telephony is voice communications, so the first component required is a microphone to record the voice and a speaker to play back the audio. The technology that was widely deployed in these components changed little between 1996 and 2006; however, since 2006, new advancements have occurred.

Microphones and Speakers

Standard microphones and speakers that have historically been used in telephony are able to capture and transmit audio fidelity from 200 to 2000 khz. This is referred to as narrowband audio and matches what can be transmitted over the Public Switched Telephone Network (STN). The limitations of narrowband audio can be removed when transitioning to all IP communications, as such a need arose for widerband codecs. Wideband codecs capture and encode sound from 20 kz to 20,000 hkz. With the advent of widerband codecs, there is a requirement to ensure that the microphones can accurately record these wider fidelity sounds and that the speakers used can accurately reproduce this wider fidelity audio. Equipment that is designed for wideband capture and reproduction has been used by professional audio recorders, but the use of this professional level equipment has only just started in IP Telephony. The most widely used wideband codecs are G.722 and AMR-WB. These wideband codecs require that the microphone and speaker have the ability to accurately records and play back 20 kz to 20,000 kHz sound frequencies.

After the sounds are accurately recorded with the a high-quality microphone that is required for wideband codecs, a digital signal processing must be performed to encode the audio.

Digital Signal Processors

Architecturally, the requirements of Digital Signaling Processing (DSP) can be done in one of two methods. The first is widely used in dedicated IP Telephony devices such as IP Phone or IP Video endpoints. This method uses a DSP chip that is optimized for receiving analog signals and encoding them into digital signals in real time from the analog source to the digital stream and from the digital stream to the analog source. This capability requires that the DSP chip has buffers to accept the incoming packets, a set of processors that keep the mathematical formulas to decode or encode the packets, and analog encoding circuitry to play back or sample the real-time media feed. The real-time media is either audio, video, or both.

The second method of encoding these signals is called Host Media Processing (HMP). This solution uses the central CPU of a general processing device (normally a personal computer) to encode and decode the real-time signals. The benefits of a dedicated DSP for media processing are that the real-time encoding of the media streams do not have to compete against other processes for the resources, and as such, less jitter occurs in the signaling. The benefits of sharing the host processor are that the costs of the capability can be spread across the larger centralized components. Most HMP-based systems are either larger room-dedicated systems that utilize the central CPU as a replacement for the DSP, or much more commonly, HMP is used for software-based IP Telephony clients. Table 1-1 lists the strengths and weaknesses of DSPs versus HMPs.

The next important component in IP Telephony is the user agent. The user agent is the software application that receives and interprets the signaling messages and determines how the various components of the system should be programmed to process the media. The signaling messages can come in a variety of formats, including MGCP, H.323, XMPP, and SIP. However, the protocol that has the most new features and highest amount of development focus today is SIP. User agents come in many forms according to the SIP standards (RFC-3261); however, they all perform some basic functions. A user agent must receive, interpret, and process SIP messages. As such, it must have, as a basic, minimum connectivity to and IP network and an IP stack.

Table 1-1   *Strengths and Weaknesses of DSPs Versus HMP for VoIP Call Processing*

Device Type	Digital Signaling Processors (DSP)	Host Media Processors (HMP)
Strengths	Real-time encoding of audio does not affect other processes. Unlimited scalability. Lower heat dissipation. Can be optimized for the type of decoding required.	Flexible architecture to support new codecs. High amount of processing power.
Weaknesses	Embedded architecture makes implementation of new features more difficult. Fewer programming tools. Higher initial costs for development. Not as flexible as host-based systems.	Real-time encoding of media affects other systems. Cost of deployments is high. Low-energy efficiency.

Comparing VoIP Signaling Protocols

Any protocol that communicates messages can be used for IP Telephony. However, having a standard protocol that many people use has the following great benefits:

- Interoperability between vendors is easily accomplished.

- A wider base of training for talent exists in the field.

- A guideline for tools expected to work with these protocols exists.

The primary protocols used for VoIP are the following:

- **H.323:** This is the longest running VoIP standard. Implemented to help solve the problem of mapping traditional telephony features from TDM signaling that had existed for years to IP based signaling. This standard was implemented and ratified by the Internal Telecommunications Union (ITU). One of the major objectives to the early version of this protocol was to minimize signaling overhead. To accomplish this, it mandated that the signaling messages be encoded in a binary format called ASN.1 encoding. This required the messages be decoded in a specific order to be read and could not be read without running the packet trace of a call through a decoder. This encoding requirement was relaxed in subsequent versions of the protocol but is still the primary method used for encapsulating H.323 messages in most networks today. H.323 is currently on Version 6 of the standard protocol, but the most widely deployed versions are H.323v2 and H.323v6.

- **SIP:** SIP was first proposed as RFC-2543 in 1999 to the International Engineering Task Force (IETF) by E. Scholler and Jonathan Rosenberg and has since been updated to RFC-3261. You can view the current draft recommendation at http://www.ietf.org/rfc/rfc3261.txt.

This protocol, because it is authored and standardized at the IEFT, is more similar to other protocols that have built the Internet, such as HTTP and SMTP, and less similar to the protocols that built the large TDM-based networks, such as ISDN that were standardized in the ITU. One of the major differences between the protocols developed in the ITU and the protocols developed in the IETF is that the protocols developed in the IETF are often ASCII-based and do not require any encoding to be read. The other major difference is that SIP is a more flexible protocol, designed to deal with different types of media, including voice, video, and chat from initial conception. Because of this flexibility, many different methods often are used to implement the same functionality; for example, putting a voice call on hold can be accomplished by many different methods, though there is a recommended method for this. This flexibility causes many problems with interoperability but does provide the capability for the protocol to be adopted for many different purposes.

H.325 is being proposed at the ITU as a third generation protocol that supports distributed and media rich collaboration environments for initiating real-time communications as an alternative for SIP and H.323. The goal of this protocol is to quickly and reliably establish communications. The design goal of this protocol is to take the strengths of both SIP and H.323 to create a protocol that should be used for many different purposes. To date, no one has implemented this protocol, and at this time, there has been limited movement toward its standardization.

Call Control Elements of IP Telephony

The call control component of IP Telephony is usually one of the following:

■ Endpoint-based user agents (such as IP Phones and analog to TDM gateways)

■ Back-to-Back User Agents that contain the central call control component.

Cisco Unified Communications Manager (Cisco UCM) is a back-to-back user agent that, as one of its functions, is to receive and interpret messages from IP Phones, generate SIP messages to other entities such as SIP gateways, and send messages to control a SIP Trunk to another device. Cisco UCM also provides the function of interworking with other call control protocols such as Media Gateway Control Protocol (MGCP) and H.323. The most common devices that Cisco UCM controls are Cisco IP Phones that contain an operating system and respond to control messages in the format of SCCP packets, often called *Skinny Packets*, or respond to SIP packets when they run a version of code that contains a SIP User Agent. *Call Control* is considered the heart of any IP Telephony system because all signaling passes through the call control element, and calls fail if the central call control element does not completely understand the context and content of all messages.

Other Physical Components of IP Telephony

Some of the other physical components of an IP Telephony solution include LAN cabling and WAN connectivity. In today's modern solutions, the LAN connectivity is most often provided by a 10/100/1000 auto-sensing LAN Ethernet switch.

Following are two items often deployed in Ethernet switches used for IP Telephony:

■ Gigabit Ethernet (GigE) connectivity

■ Power of Ethernet (PoE)

GigE is deployed in less than 10 percent of the total number of physical Ethernet ports (as of late 2009), but most newly deployed Ethernet ports use Gigabit because of the low cost. PoE supplies electrical power to IP Telephony endpoints such as IP Phones and is a great solution because one cable provides power and a connection to the network, resulting in fewer cables for the same number of IP devices. However, sending PoE cables is one of the definite determinations of the length of cable supported. PoE cables cannot generally extend past 1500 meters.

IP Phones

IP Phones vary widely in IP Telephony deployments from very basic phones that replicate the capability of POTS phones to complex phones that are closer to personal computing devices. The basic components of all IP Phones include a speaker, microphone, user agent, and DSP.

IP-PBX

An IP Public Branch Exchange (PBX) is the primarily call control agent for most IP Telephony deployments.

Ethernet Switches

An often overlooked component of IP Telephony is the Ethernet switches that connect all of the end devices together and provide the basic connectivity and power for end devices. Ethernet switches that are badly implemented with loops or that have a great deal of congestion can negatively affect IP Telephony deployments, including the quality PSTN access via a SIP Trunk.

Non-IP Phone IP Telephony Devices

Non-IP Phone IP Telephony devices usually include video. The two basic types of video endpoints are Standard Definition (SD) Video endpoints and High Definition (HD) Video endpoints. A subset of HD video endpoints include Telepresence video endpoints. As a component of IP Telephony, these endpoints normally share the dialplan of other IP Telephony devices, meaning that they can be accessed with a phone number and normally share the bandwidth when calls are made between sites. When considering a SIP Trunk solution, it is important to consider how non-IP Phone devices will be able to consume the SIP Trunk services that are provided.

WAN Connectivity Device

All IP Telephony solutions that connect across long distances must have some type of WAN connectivity solution. The most standard types follow

- T1
- DS3
- Metro Ethernet
- WiMax
- Cable (for example, DOCSIS)
- DSL

For each of these connectivity solutions, a physical device sits on the customer's premises and connects to the service provider (SP). These SPs, in turn, connect to other SPs, ultimately forming a mesh that enables all SPs that use PSTN routing technology— specifically, the E.164 phone number—to communicate with each other.

The size and capabilities of an enterprises' connection method with their SP determine which type of SIP Trunk solutions are possible. The bandwidth provided by the SP has two important components. First is *raw* bandwidth. This is an important measure of the number of packets per second and the size of the packets that can be sent from the enterprise to the SP. The bandwidth provided by the SP is the ultimate determination of the number of simultaneous conversations that occur between the SP and enterprise and the number calls and size of the SIP Trunk. The second consideration is the quality of the connection. The number of packets that the SP drops in each link of the connection is the ultimate determination of the quality of a call. A voice or video call deteriorates only in quality if the numbers of packets received are fewer than the number of packets sent. The other determination of quality is the latency of the connection. Latency is the measure of the time a packet takes to traverse a network; if the SP network has a long latency, the quality of the connection deteriorates.

Voice Gateways

The component of an IP Telephony system that converts the TDM connection from a traditional telephony system, either a Private Branch Exchange (PBX) or a Public Switch Telephone Network (PSTN) connection to an IP connection, is known as a *voice gateway*. Voice gateways include several essential components including a central CPU that supports the signaling required to connect to the IP network and the TDM network and a DSP to convert the TDM connection to an IP connection.

Voice gateways can generally be divided into three groups. Initially, voice gateways were created as add-on cards to PC- or server-based systems. This was convenient during the time when a rapid expansion of the features was provided by voice gateways. At this time, having a CPU-based system that allowed for independent updating of individual software components, such as the IP signaling method and the TDM signaling stack, while leveraging the add-on card that included the DSPs to allow for higher density, was the most efficient method to create a feature rich voice gateway.

The second iteration of voice gateways is the form that is most popular in enterprise and small businesses today: standalone dedicated devices or a feature integrated into a router with many capabilities. These devices simultaneously provide connectivity to the PSTN, a central CPU for call processing, connectivity to the LAN or WAN, and DSPs for media processing. The important distinction is that a general purpose PC is not used as the basis for the device. Instead, the system is designed and built from the ground up to support VoIP connections. The scale of these dedicated voice gateways ranges from one to approximately 4,000 channels on a single dedicated chassis.

The last version of voice gateways is one that does not contain all the signaling elements in a single box and instead relies on distributed processing of the media in the voice gateways and the signaling aspects in a separate device. These devices then communicate via a standards-based protocol to enable the Media Gateway to be controlled by the Media Gateway Controller. The most prevalent protocols used to exchange information between the Media Gateway and the Media Gateway Controller are MGCP and H.248. MGCP was never standardized by the IETF and instead was left in a draft state. However, Cisco and other companies built and deployed many high-density media gateways that used this protocol. H.248, which has some heritage from MGCP in that it is a master/slave protocol, was ratified by the ITU and standardized. This standardization was encouraged by the large, traditional national telecommunications companies to enable interoperability between vendors.

Currently, state-of-the-art voice gateways combine many features to enable connections to both TDM trunks and SIP trunks. This dual termination capability enables service providers to reuse much of their large investment in in TDM to IP gateways. However, there is no consistency or standardization as it relates to the dual use of a voice gateway to terminate both TDM and SIP Trunks. The H.248 standard does enable both TDM and IP call contexts to be created, but generally devices are not simultaneously used for both IP and TDM termination of calls.

The other capability of advanced TDM to IP voice gateways is the capability to handle several protocols. The majority of deployed voice gateways in 2009 use H.323 connections; however, the majority of new installations use the SIP protocol. The expectation is that the industry will standardize around the SIP protocol with fewer requirements to support multiple protocols. However, SIP is a complex protocol that allows for many different implementations of similar functionality, and, as such, a great deal of interworking issues need to be resolved within this protocol.

When attempting to determine which voice gateways to use for a deployment, you need to understand that the primary goal of a voice gateway is to accurately reproduce voice with as little negative effects as possible while performing as many interworking functions as possible. A well-designed VoIP gateway should add no more than 5 milliseconds of delay to a solution and should also enhance the overall voice experience by providing the following:

- A high-quality conversion from PCM to IP voice with a fast and accurate sampling rate.

- The capability to detect and cancel echo that exists on the TDM connection (known as Echo Cancellation). A high-quality voice gateway has the capability to cancel echo that occurs as much as 128 ms after the initial voice sample.

- The capability to detect and suppress silence, which is an important capability that enables fewer packets and thus uses less bandwidth on the IP connection when silence is detected. The downside of any Voice Activity Detection (VAD) system is that the time between the DSP detecting a voice packet and the voice being sent can result in words being clipped. A high-quality voice gateway has a minimal amount of clipping, but all voice gateways employing VAD will have some amount of clipping.

Finally, voice gateways need to have a great deal of flexibility as to the TDM connections they connect to. TDM connections vary greatly by region and are something that is dependent on location. In North America, the primary analog connection is a Foreign Exchange Office (FXO) connection, and the primary digital connection is a T1, which multiplexes 23 or 24 audio changes into a single connection. A T1 can either utilize the older Channel Associated Signaling (CAS) system, in which the signaling information about a call, such as the number that is called and the caller ID, is incorporated into the same channel as the media, or a Primary Rate Interface (PRI) that uses a common signaling channel for all voice channels in that T1. A T1 PRI multiplex, 23 audio channels, called B channels, and a single signaling channel, called a D channel, into a single connection are referred to as 23B+D. In Europe and most of the rest of the world, the primary digital connection is an E1 that contains 30 audio channels and one signaling channel, known as 30B+D. There is also a standard in Japan that is referred to as a J1 interface. State-of-the-art voice gateways, such as Cisco Voice Gateways, support modular interface cards that can support many different types of interfaces. When making the transition to SIP trunking, you need to know these different solutions because much of the complexity involved in the solution is mapping the TDM signaling to SIP. Transitioning to SIP trunking can be analogous to outsourcing your TDM gateways to the service provider. Finally, Signaling System 7 (SS7) is another form of signaling used primarily by carriers and has separate messages that can be mapped to SIP in a SIP-T protocol.

Supplementary Services

The term *supplementary services* is often used without a good explanation of what it means. Generally, supplementary services is a blanket term that covers any change that occurs in a voice call outside of most basic SETUP, RING, TALK, and DISCONNECT that occurs. The best example of a supplementary service is putting a call on HOLD so that the person initiating the hold no longer transmits audio to the person ON HOLD. This basic feature also requires that a call can be resumed when it is resumed from hold. This means that while a call is on hold, the receiver does not hear the caller. When taken off hold, the receiver transitions back to a standard call in which the caller and called party can talk.

Following is a list of the most common supplementary services:

- Hold

- Resume

- Music on Hold

- Blind Transfer

- Attended Transfer

- Three-Party Conferencing

- Call Forward on Busy

- Call Forward All

Each of these supplementary services requires a complex call flow, and as such, this capability of the PSTN and TDM network can cause a great deal of interworking issues when transitioned to SIP trunks. The most basic capability of HOLD and RESUME in SIP requires changing the media parameters of a call. The standard method for changing the media parameters for a call is to use a REINVITE that changes the call state from SEND RECEIVE to a state of RECEIVE only. Placing a call on HOLD is an example of a basic supplementary feature changed from having no standard method for implementation in the original SIP RFC to one that does have a standard method for innovation in the latest RFC-3261. However, many supplementary services do not have a standard SIP implementation, and a great deal of interworking problems occur as customers transition from TDM trunks to SIP trunks with the expectation of these supplementary services working as efficiently and smoothly as they did in TDM networks.

Summary

IP Telephony can be viewed in two distinct ways. One is as an exact replacement for traditional telephony with the change of using packet-based networks as a replacement for the traditional TDM networks. This initial but limited view of IP Telephony is the first way that most users look at this transition. The second and more dramatic way to look at IP Telephony is as a wholesale change in the method of using communications technologies.

The phone transitions from a device that is only about speech to a device that can be used to initiate and manage many different methods of communications.

Finally, the ultimate transition of IP Telephony might be to a world in which little distinction exists between a standard phone and any other general purpose communicating device. The future of communications will allow for endless possibilities, but the basics of telephony will always be about communications.

Chapter 2

Trends in IP Telephony

This chapter covers the following topics:

- Major trends in IP communications

- Enterprise IP communications endpoints

- Endpoint trends in enterprises and their effects on SIP trunk

- Feature trends in SIP trunking within the enterprise

- Feature trends in SIP trunking between enterprises

- Feature trends in SIP trunk for PSTN access

- Feature trends in advanced SIP trunking features from service providers

- Feature trends for call center services from SIP trunk providers

Internet Protocol (IP) telephony has become a widespread and standard means of communication. Prior to 2000, IP telephony was the choice of only a select few. Now, in 2010, more and more people and businesses are adopting Voice over IP (VoIP) solutions. In many areas VoIP solutions is the dominant method of communications.

In large-scale business telephony solutions, the transition is almost complete with the vast majority of all new telecommunications installations utilizing IP telephony. As the demand for IP telephony has increased, the number of vendors, implementers, and providers in this field has also increased, and this trend is expected to continue. The heavy competition prevalent in the IP telephony market has resulted in the greatest benefits for consumers. Competition has driven service providers (SP) to slash their prices and offer a wide range of features. Aggressive competition has also lead to major reductions in costs from equipment providers. Finally, there has been an explosion in capabilities of IP telephony and the term Unified Communications (UC) has been adopted to include the expansion of all these services to include voice, voice mail, video, email, faxes, SMS, and just about any other type of communications that can be coupled with IP telephony.

Per the laws of economics, the increases in IP telephony usage have brought down prices and increased choice to the consumers. There is also a major technological trend toward end-to-end IP communications. IP telephony has traditionally been about connecting new IP endpoints, such as IP-PBXs from businesses or IP Phones for consumers to the traditional time division multiplexing (TDM)-based PSTN. In the consumer world, the transition from TDM to IP occurred at the handset using a device such as an Analog Telephony Adaptor (ATA) voice, which was converted from TDM signals into IP. In the business world, the traditional method was to have IP handsets and the conversion to TDM occur at the edge of the network. This enabled businesses to continue to purchase traditional TDM connectivity services. The latest trend is for the SPs to offer IP-based PSTN connectivity services or trunks. This enables traditional IP-PBX customers in both large and small business to purchase IP trunking services as opposed to traditional TDM trunking services.

Approximately three-quarters of large companies in the United States have already made the switch to IP telephony, initially to the dismay of the traditional phone companies; although many of the traditional phone companies have transformed themselves into Tier-1 VoIP SPs. Companies who have made the switch from TDM to IP telephony have lowered their bandwidth costs, reduced personnel requirements, saved on taxes, and spent less on moving, adding, and changing phone lines.

This chapter covers the trends in Enterprise Unified Communications, endpoints, and call centers.

Major Trends in IP Communications

IP communication has gone through many changes in the 15 years since the first VoIP solutions were created. However, even after 15 years of development, there is a bright future. The trends that occurred over those 15 years have been in several areas focused around creating a better and lower-cost alternative to the traditional phone. However, some of the overall themes of these trends have been consistent.

Traditional telephony includes a fixed number of protocols, endpoints, and applications. SS7, ISDN, and CAS are the primary protocols; TDM base phones are the primary endpoints; and the primary applications are voice devices. Figure 2-1 shows how the traditional telephony protocols, endpoints, and applications are distributed.

With IP communications, a few numbers of distinct protocols still exist; however, to date these protocols are still in the early stage of development, and their implementation varies by vendor. This is most likely a short-term issue. Long term, the expectation is that the industry will resolve to a use a few well-defined protocols.

In the area of endpoints, the trend toward diversity goes beyond just protocols. The communications methods between the endpoints expand with IP communications. These methods for communicating between endpoints over IP include voice, video, chat, photos, and even the capability to provide remote haptic feedback. Finally, the true value of IP communications is in the applications. The number, value, and variety of applications in IP communications explode. Figure 2-2 shows how IP communication is distributed.

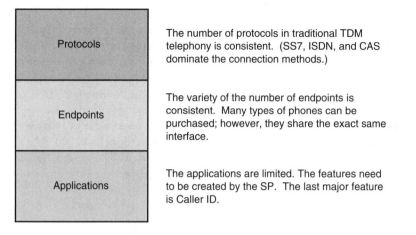

Figure 2-1 *Historical Distribution of Telephony*

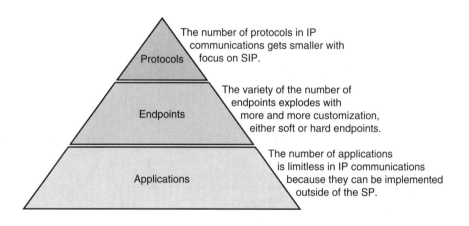

Figure 2-2 *Distribution of IP Communication*

Enterprise IP Communications Endpoints

Several accepted definitions for *enterprise* scale deployments exist, ranging from 10 to millions of users. The definition we use for enterprise is a large-scale deployment of more than 500 phones controlled by a single large-dial plan, with features above and beyond the current TDM-based telephony that can be used only within the enterprise. Using this definition, enterprise phones were 100 percent TDM-based just more than 15 years ago. During a 10-year period from 1996 to 2006, the trend to IP Phones resulted in the tipping point of phones deployed transitioning from 100 percent TDM to more than

50 percent being IP-based. The trend for new phone deployments (see Figure 2-3) is now that more than 90 percent of new enterprise phone deployments use IP Phones. This trend from 1996 to 2006 was based upon the greatest value in the company occurring at the transition point of the handsets. More handsets exist than any other component of IP telephony, and this important touch point is an early part of the conversions from TDM- to IP-based telephony. A second point to understand about the enterprise IP Phone is that the IP Phone has traditionally been a hard endpoint, specifically a device that is a stand-alone with a physical link to the central site for power and connectivity. This is changing with the adoption of softphones installed on PC devices and 802.11 wireless WiFi phones that connect in any location where there is WiFi in the enterprise. Hardphones still make up the majority of the phones in the enterprise, but the growth rate for softphones is significant.

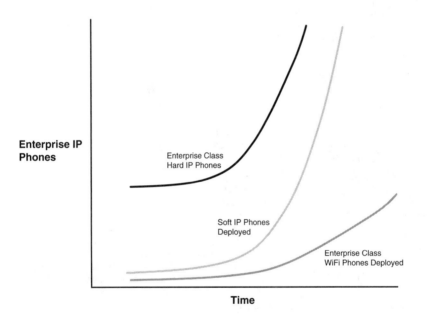

Figure 2-3   *Enterprise Phone Growth*

Over the last 10 years, the enterprise class hard IP phone has gone through many changes. Initially, little difference existed between the IP Phones and the traditional TDM-based phones. One of the goals in the initial transition to IP Communications was to have the transition be as seamless as possible so that the end users would not have to make any changes in behavior. This led to the rapid increase in adoption but limited the features that could be delivered. The basics of a handset with at least 10 keys and lighted buttons to indicate the active lines have remained the same, but the trends in the enterprise handsets over the next 10 years should be dramatically different.

Desktop Handset Trends

The current desktop handset for IP Telephony has a few distinct differences from the older versions. The first major difference is the power of the platform. With the advent of cheaper and faster Digital Signaling Processors (DSP), faster and cheaper memory, and System on Chip (SoC) technologies, the basic handset has a great deal more power today than when it was first introduced. As this trend continues, you should see desktop handsets get more and more CPU power. The most advanced desktop handsets today have a full CPU that would be the equivalent to the fastest desktop computers of 1999 with as much memory as most computers in 1999 (1.6 Ghz ATOM chip with 512 MB of RAM).

The second change in the desktop phones is in the area of display. The state of the art today is a touch screen combined with a full-color display that enables for full motion video to be displayed. These displays blur the line between a phone and a computer.

The next trend in the handset market is to improve acoustics through a combination of higher fidelity headsets and better audio compression techniques. Modern headsets have the capability to support wideband audio. The other trend in headsets is the integration of Bluetooth to support industry-standard headsets. Historically, the headsets included in desk phones have been expensive propriety wireless devices or wired devices that have not been that functional.

The biggest trends to date in IP Phones can be summarized as:

- Higher speed central processors (DSP- or CPU-based)

- Larger and better screens, including touch-screen capabilities

- Better audio capabilities

- Built-in Bluetooth support

In the future, the primary trends in desktop IP Telephony will be in the following areas:

- Conversion of signaling methods to SIP

- Inclusion of some real-time video capabilities

- Expandability via USB

These future capabilities should be taken into account when considering SIP trunking solutions. Current SIP trunking solutions that are limited to narrow-band PSTN voice will not be successful when the next major upgrade of enterprise IP Phones occurs and enables for a wider range of features. Enterprise customers need to consider the requirements imposed on a SIP Trunking solution when endpoints become more advanced.

The summary of the requirements is as follows:

- More complex endpoints with greater capability result in more complex use cases for SIP trunking, outside of basic voice.

- Increase in use of wideband codec and video calls require the solution to support higher bandwidth sessions.

- Complex features, such as location-aware calling, advanced caller-id, and presence are demanded by end users, and the SIP trunking solution needs to adapt to these new features.

Enterprise Softphone IP Phone Trends

Softphones are clients installed on laptops, desktops, netbooks, or any other devices that weren't originally designed as phones. They are an IP communications endpoint. Softphone deployments have exploded in enterprise telephony as secondary communications options for most and as a primary communications option for a few.

Softphones benefit workers who are remote or teleworkers who can work from anywhere as if they were in the office provided they have secure IP connectivity to the central call-control entity.

With the increase in speed and fidelity of the integrated microphones and speakers included in most PCs, it is a safe bet for most companies to assume the PC devices their employees have include the basic capabilities to enable them to run as softphones. Because the cost model shifts dramatically with the use of softphones from the traditional cost of a $300 to $500 handset per person in an enterprise to a software cost model of generally less than $200 per person, the telecommunications departments have a great incentive to adopt softphones, which is the primary reason for the trend of the dramatic increase in the number of softphones.

The major inhibitor to the increased adoption of softphones is end-user behavior. End users often have frustrating experiences with softphones because of the lack of correct utilization. When softphones are used with a high-quality headset, in an environment in which the IP connectivity is high quality and consistent, the user experience is usually excellent. Unfortunately, many users turn to softphones in less than ideal conditions, such as hotel rooms, while downloading a large amount of other traffic, or in noisy environments. Any of these, or similar, situations often results in a negative user experience.

However, an important component of this trend is that SIP trunking solutions need to accommodate endpoints such as softphones with features where the network components of SIP trunking, such as DSPs, compensate for the lack of the feature at the end user. Secondly, SIP trunking solutions should adapt to the variable bandwidth availability of these types of devices and support a wider variety of codecs, such as iLBC or G.722.

The summary of softphone trends is as follows:

- Lower-cost endpoints

- Wider adoption of softphones in business environments

- More reliance on network components providing the role that was traditionally done in the hard phone

- More robust codec support as a requirement of SIP trunking services

Enterprise WiFi IP Phone Trends

The WiFi phone is a unique combination of technologies that has yet to establish itself as a prevailing force in enterprise telecommunications. However, it plays an essential role in enterprise locations where staff is homed to a physical location, yet are required to roam within it. Specific examples of this type of enterprise are hospitals and retail locations where WiFi enterprise IP Phones have been successful.

The WiFi IP Phone is distinct from a cellular phone in two major areas:

- WiFi phones run over 802.11a, b, g, or n WiFi frequencies instead of the traditional GSM or CDMA bands. This physical difference limits the long-range capabilities and deterministic quality of WiFi phones.

- WiFi phones are homed or controlled by the enterprise IP-PBX and not an SP. This enables for much greater flexibility in terms of endpoint features.

Other than these two unique capabilities of WiFi phones, their advancement is moving in the same general direction of mobile phones. That is, they are becoming lighter, rugged, and longer lasting as technology advances. WiFi phones have better screens for displaying information about a call and are improving their integration with Bluetooth as a method to offload the audio playback to another device, gaining a great deal of nontraditional phone features. These nontraditional phone features generally relate to the use of the phone as a mobile application platform. As an application platform, one of the unique capabilities of a phone is that it is locations-aware. This leads to advanced applications, such as the capability to display ads for stores that you are physically close to.

These trends require that SIP trunk providers and consumers take into account that some of their endpoints might be WiFi phones because they have different capabilities that must be considered, such as the following:

- Being mobile, they have a tendency to change audio characteristics within a call. This would mean that to take advantage of this, the SIP trunk might need the capability to read and determine that the signal strength is weakening and switch over to a lower bandwidth codec. This is done in the cellular world but has not been adopted in the SIP trunking area. However, this adaptation could occur at either the premise IP-PBX or the SP network.

- The IP endpoint is no longer likely to be stationary; as such, the capability to receive the location along with the call setup should be something that is offered. This is essential for emergency services but also can be helpful when routing calls for things such as dispatching repair services. If the location of the endpoint is known, SIP trunk providers could do a better job in optimizing the call for the location.

- One of the important capabilities that SPs have not taken advantage of is the multiplicity of services. Many SPs have to pay for use of a WiFi network as a service along with their SIP trunking service. A trend that should become relevant is to enable Enterprise WiFi phones from a company that has subscribed to the SIP trunking service access to the WiFi network. This allows an SP to provide a unique combination of capabilities of WiFi access to the physical devices and SIP trunking as a service for this device.

In summary, the capabilities of enterprise WiFi devices will continue to get better by taking advantage of the technology that is constantly improving in cellular phones. However, there will always remain a distinct difference in WiFi phones and cellular phones. SIP trunking providers can take advantage of these differences by offering unique services, such as enterprise WiFi phone roaming, location-based services, and bandwidth adaptation to effectively take advantage of the unique characteristics of WiFi phones in a SIP trunking environment.

Cellular Phone Trends Within Enterprises and Their Effects on SIP Trunking

Cellular phones for most business users have become ubiquitous. In the enterprise, they have also become a major factor with more than 60 percent of business users having a desk or hard phone and a cellular phone. This has resulted in an explosion of overlapping features and billing of enterprise locations for both a desk and cellular phone. With the increasing mobility of today's workers, the number of minutes on the cellular network is also growing faster than the number of minutes on the enterprise TDM network.

This creates a dilemma for enterprise telecommunications managers. To better service employees in the enterprise, they need to expand the use of cellular services, but to better contain costs there is a need to expand their internal communications network.

One of the direct effects is the increased use of Single Number Reach (SNR) solutions in enterprise locations. With SNR solutions, when a call comes into the enterprise, the signal is duplicated so that both the person's desktop phone and cellular phone ring at the same time. This forking of calls requires that a single call into an enterprise can potentially use two trunks or channels for both signaling and media.

When the enterprise primarily used TDM trunking, this was expensive and required a wholesale update of all the TDM trunking capabilities to double the number of trunks that a location would use as it adopted the SNR service across a wider number of endpoints.

Adopting SIP trunking as a connection to the SP to replace the TDM connection has resulted in a change of some of these architectures. The changes can be seen as phases in the development of the services of integrating enterprise and cellular networks:

- **Phase I:** SNR service enabled via an outbound call on the TDM network. Currently, this is most-widely deployed and can require a major update of all the TDM connection to handle the doubled load.

- **Phase II:** SNR service-enabled via an outbound call to the TDM network via a SIP trunk service. This is made available by a few SPs and offers the unique advantage of the physical medium not being the limiting factor. Calls are not channelized over a TDM connection, so the number of calls can grow to fill the IP pipe, and the IP pipe can grow at a much larger pace than the TDM pipes.

- **Phase III:** SNR service-enabled via an outbound call to the TDM network via a SIP trunk service, but the signaling is the only component that goes to the enterprise. The media is optimized and stays at the SP. This optimization enables the IP-PBX to stay in control of when the call is sent to the SP cellular network and maintains billing for these types of calls; however, instead of the media being hairpinned at the enterprise location, it is optimized in the network. This optimization leads to better call quality (lower latency) and lower bandwidth utilization.

- **Phase IV:** SNR services enabled at the SP. This phase is more controversial because it changes the place in the network where the forking occurs from the enterprise control to the SP. At this phase, the SP knows that a certain cellular phone is the same as a certain enterprise phone number and rings both. This service is popular among smaller deployments in which the power and control of the enterprise dialing plan is easy to move into the SP, but as companies grow larger, it is controversial as to whether to allow the SP to make the decision to fork the call before it comes into the enterprise.

In summary, the use of cellular phones as an alternative to desk phones will continue, and the major effect on the trunking solutions is how this SNR capability will be implemented.

Endpoint Trends in Enterprises and Their Effects on SIP Trunk

The changes in the endpoints at enterprises will have a direct and significant impact on the SIP trunking services that SPs will offer and customers will consider purchasing. Table 2-1 summarizes these trends.

Table 2-1 *Endpoint Trends and Effects on SIP Trunking*

Endpoint Type	Trend	Effect on SIP Trunking Service Offered by SPs
Desktop handset	Advanced functionality and new features that take advantage of the faster CPU and advanced screen capabilities. Color phones, touch screens, and more PC-like capabilities have become the norm in desktop phones.	Advanced services need to be offered to take advantage of the advanced capabilities of the endpoints. Calls with subject lines, video calls, and wideband codecs.
Softphones	Softphones become more widely adopted because of lower cost and wide availability of PCs.	New features are offered that take advantage of these capabilities. Codec selection based on available bandwidth, location-based services, and wide and narrow band codecs.
WiFi phones	WiFi phones have a high adoption at niche locations. Their capabilities follow suit with the advancement of cellular phones.	New features need to be offered to take advantage of WiFi phone capabilities such as location-based services and WiFi roaming.
Cellular phone adoption	Cell phones continue to be adopted as an alternative to enterprise phones.	SIP trunk providers and consumers respond to this trend by requiring services that take into account how the trunking changes with SNR capabilities. First, the services that offer basic connectivity with hairpinning are made available; the subsequent features are for SNR with optimized media. The final new feature is for SNR capabilities to occur within the network, under control of the SP instead of the enterprise.

Feature Trends in SIP Trunking Within the Enterprise

Trunking solutions are used extensively within an enterprise to connect to distinct realms of Unified Communications that are under the control of different call control entities. An example of this is an Automatic Call Director (ACD) that might be under the control of one group and the IP-PBX that might belong to a different group. In an enterprise, the need for trunks between entities is usually based on one of the following implementation challenges:

■ **Timing:** When one solution such as an IVR has been upgraded and changed, other solutions, such as call control might not have been changed. This requires a trunking solution between these entities to compensate for the differences.

- **Acquisitions:** Many times occur when a single enterprise has acquired another enterprise, and the most effective way to quickly transition that enterprise is to trunk the two call control entities together.

- **Security:** Within an enterprise often various levels of security exist that might require different levels of call control. Each individual device might have a different level of security in the two different areas, but they still have the need to communicate. In this case, you might have a trunking solution between the high-security devices and the lower-security devices.

- **Different Features:** Finally, the largest difference that occurs within an enterprise is the features required by various groups. These diverse features necessitate differing call control environments and, as such, a trunking solution between them is required.

Trunking solutions are always required in an enterprise. As a result, a number of trends in these trunking solutions are important to understand. One trend that occurs in an enterprise is the trend toward trunking different UC solutions with SIP trunks. SIP trunks provide a widely acceptable and standardized method to get at least basic connectivity between a wide range of different call control solutions including both voice and video. The trend toward utilizing SIP within the enterprise as the default method to trunk different call control mechanisms is replacing both TDM trunks and H.323 trunks between these devices.

A second major trend for trunking in enterprise is the more extensive use of video. Video solutions range from desktop video, to low-cost room-based video, to high-end Telepresence solutions. These video solutions have developed at different stages with the earliest H.320-based ISDN solutions still used in many cases today. Because of this wide variety of video solutions, there is a requirement for a method to interconnect these together. This is a major trend in enterprise SIP trunking as a method for interconnecting disparate video communications technologies. One of the major challenges that exists today is that these technologies do not natively use SIP; therefore, a great deal of interworking with older technologies occurs, such as H.320 and H.323 that is required.

Finally, the third major trend for enterprise trunking solutions is the nonvoice/video traffic between different areas of call control that need to be interconnected. These areas include traffic such as instant messaging traffic and presence indicators. When this traffic is based on the SIP protocol, it is easy to extend the borders of trunking between applications to include these nonvoice, nonvideo applications. It is important that these communications do not get siloed or require special translations to enable them to interconnect, which is why these other methods transition to SIP.

In summary, you need to be aware of the important trends for trunking in an enterprise:

- Transition from traditional methods, such as TDM or H.323, to SIP for voice communications

- Adoption of SIP as a method to interconnect various video endpoints within an enterprise

- Expansion of SIP to interconnect nonvoice/video traffic such as instant messaging and presence indicators

Feature Trends in SIP Trunking Between Enterprises

As multiple companies adopt IP telephony, a natural trend toward federation occurs. Federation is the capability to enable rich communications between companies without the use of an SP that offers anything beyond basic IP connectivity.

The types of companies that want to form federations vary. At one end of the scale are two companies that are close for a long period of time. A good example is the outsourced legal counsel of an organization. These companies are often close for a long period of time and would benefit from integration of their UC infrastructures, but because they want to maintain independence, wholesale adoption of the other party's UC infrastructure is not possible.

At the other end of the spectrum are companies that come together for a short period of time to collaborate for a specific service or function.

The level of collaboration between the federated entities would greatly benefit from rich communications, but the standard method for collaboration with people outside of an organization is to use the PSTN for a phone call to collaborate via audio and use the Internet connection to collaborate via a shared web experience such as WEBEX from Cisco. However, this communication often takes place outside the control of the IT department, utilizing the general Internet connectivity of the enterprise.

A current method that companies utilize that enables individuals, such as outsourced contactors, to collaborate more effectively with company employees is to enable the contractor to have an account on the company systems. This generally consists of a USERID, phone, and access to email, internal websites, and some type of file access. This naturally leads to individuals having a phone number associated with them as contractors for the company (that is, Company A) and a phone number for the company at which they are employees (that is, Company B). One idea that is possible with this arrangement is to have an IP phone associated with the IP-PBX that belongs to *both* Company A and Company B. This idea of having a single extension that is homed to the IP-PBX at Company B to a user in Company A is possible; however, it does pose challenges. These include the inability for most IP Phones to respond to multiple call agents, the lack of a widely used method to authenticate an IP Phone against an IP-PBX, and the use of NATs or firewalls that would prevent incoming signals that would be required for registrations and to allow the phone to ring. However, this method would have distinct benefits over other methods of collaboration because it can be monitored and controlled by the IT department using the same methods in place for intercompany communications.

Because the capability to have an IP endpoint controlled by an IP-PBX at multiple companies is problematic, one option that companies have examined and are beginning to adopt is the use of SIP trunking between enterprise PBXs. This service enables companies to take advantage of the current IP-PBX features, such as conferencing, billing, and recording of calls, but if federated could provide connectivity beyond the basic walls of the enterprise.

As such, there is a trend occurring in which companies will adopt a SIP trunking solution between each other to take advantage of many of the benefits of SIP trunking without giving up the independence of their IP-PBX. This intra-enterprise SIP trunking carries with it many complications in addition to benefits. The most basic complication is the issue of IP address reachability. The basic premise of a trunking solution is that a shared IP address exists between the two entities. However, many UC communications solutions use private IP addressing schemes. As such, enabling these to interconnect requires the use of a shared IP addressing space such as the Internet or a signaling aware network address translation (NAT).

Utilizing the Internet as the method to interconnect does not ensure any quality of service (QoS) guarantees, and as such there is no capability to ensure that the service can occur at the required level of quality. One workaround for this is the use of a shared MPLS network, as shown in Figure 2-4. In this arrangement, two companies share the same MPLS provider. This allows a reasonable expectation of a high quality of connection between the two companies' MPLS networks. The interconnection of the MPLS network would traverse only a single SP network, and that SP would have a service level agreement (SLA) with each of the enterprise customers. This generally leads to a reasonable high level of expectation of a good QoS.

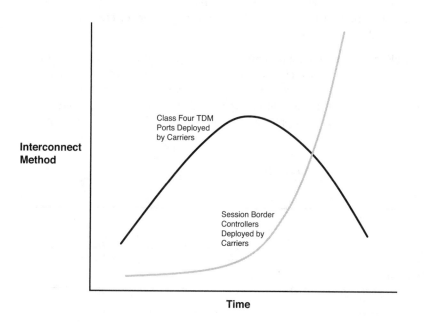

Figure 2-4 *Interenterprise Connectivity Methods*

When utilizing this shared trunking service between federated enterprises, the use of nonvoice services is a natural extension. The only widely used current method of video conferencing between enterprises is ISDN video endpoints and H.320 services. These ISDN video endpoints share the same E.164 universal addressing as regular PSTN phones and have a level of interoperability that enables video calls between unaffiliated networks. The downside of these types of networks is that they have been purposely built by SPs. Specifically routing ISDN video calls, which are identified at signaling time over specific circuits to ensure connectivity, leads to much higher costs, as compared with IP routing. This higher cost has lead to a much lower adoption rate.

The use of a border element at each enterprise and simultaneous connections to an MPLS network for each enterprise in combination with a routable IP address at the edge of each network is a growing trend for interenterprise connectivity via SIP trunks.

Feature Trends in SIP Trunk for PSTN Access

SIP Trunks for PSTN access is one of the fastest growing services currently offered by SPs. The basic service is purely as an ISDN replacement that offers no service beyond the same functionality of a TDM ISDN connection. The essential features provided in this basic offering are shown in Table 2-2.

These are the least common denominators of SIP trunking features. Just getting all the SPs throughout the world to determine how those basic services are offered has taken years and, as of 2009, is still not consistently offered.

The macro trends in the area of advanced SIP trunks for PSTN access are based on the other trends described in this chapter. The long-term direction of SIP trunking services is to be enhanced to deal with the increased number of endpoints, and the diversity to this trend is that the SP needs to deal with a larger number of problems as the interconnect methods for different types of premise equipment can result in additional maintenance costs.

Table 2-2   *Essential Features of a Basic SIP Trunk Offering*

Signaling Method	SIP
Signaling Transport Mechanism	IP
Physical Layer 3 Connectivity Method	Over the top, DSL, T1/Frame Relay, cable modem, Metro Ethernet, 3G, other
Compression Method	G.711, G.729
Features	Call setup and teardown, Hold, Resume; ability to send DTMF tones; support for setting a CALLERID and CALLING NAME

A second major developing trend is the transition to offer a more complete replacement to an ISDN circuit. ISDN circuits have built-in redundancy and alarming mechanisms not native to SIP trunks. SPs find that customers demand these features with this alternative connectivity method. They also are discovering that lower prices are no longer a motivator to replace traditional TDM circuits. Specific examples of this are SPs offering Layer 7 Keepalive ping messages to simulate what was previously done in Q.921. In SIP, the method to do this is using an *Options Ping* sent from the SP to the customer and from the customer to the SP to determine that the device is up and functioning.

A second example is the use of multiple IP addresses as a way to simulate the multiple D-channels used for signaling in large-scale ISDN networks. The transition from TDM to IP trunking involved many steps, such as those shown in Figure 2-5.

Finally the quality of IP trunking needs to meet and exceed the quality of TDM trunking. This is most evident in the area of FAX, in which long duration and complex fax scenarios have a higher success rate on traditional TDM-based interconnect services than IP trunking services.

Table 2-3 summarizes trends in SIP trunk offerings.

The long-term trend to IP trunking as a replacement to TDM trunking is strong and is expected to replace TDM as a method for interconnecting enterprise customers to the PSTN within the next 5 to 10 years.

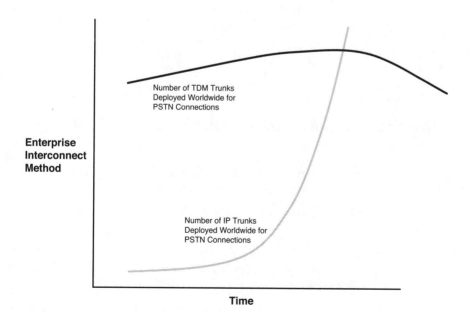

Figure 2-5 *Transition from TDM to IP Trunking*

Table 2-3   *Trends in SIP Trunk Offerings*

Trend	Why Is This Trend Occurring ?	What New Service Offering Results from This Trend?
There is a trend toward more diversity in endpoints that can connect to SIP trunking service.	This trend expands the customer base as end users look toward a variety of IP-PBX vendors.	SIP trunking services required to connect to a specific device, instead of allowing any device to connect.
Customers are becoming more sensitive to the ability to quickly respond to outages.	Customers have the same expectation from SIP trunks as from TDM trunks.	*Options Ping* and SLAs based on SIP are available.
Better FAX connectivity options.	Customers have an expectation of FAX quality that is not met. TDM trunks are perceived to have a higher quality.	T.38 FAX and SLAs around FAX success rates will be offered to alleviate the expectation that SIP trunking is not as high quality as TDM trunking.
Better redundancy in signaling methods.	ISDN has a natural redundancy in connectivity methods by offering multiple signaling channels (for instance, D-channels) for each bearer channel. The natural tendency in SIP was to offer as few signaling channels as possible.	Multiple signaling channels for a single SIP trunk with common billing.

Feature Trends in Advanced SIP Trunking Features from Service Providers

The long-term advanced SIP trunking trends that exist are a specific reaction to the enhanced technology offering in endpoints and applications.

These features are also developed based on new and better equipment provided to SPs.

One advanced SIP trunk feature dependent on equipment providers is the capability for SIP trunking providers to offer quality monitoring for all calls. This can be accomplished today through the use of either *inline* or *port spanning* technologies. However, both of these options have built in weaknesses.

Port spanning is the act of duplicating all Ethernet traffic destined for one physical port to a second physical port. This replicates the traffic from SIP trunking devices to a secondary device. This device scores the quality of the calls. The issue with this method is the inherent security threat created by replicating the packets. As such, this method is not expected to be a long-term method of quality scoring offered by the SP.

The second method for offering call quality scoring is via an inline device that is specifically dedicated to call quality scoring. Such boxes do exist, but an issue with these is that adding this box for call quality scoring can impact the quality of the voice connection and lower the reliability because a failure in the box will disconnect the call, and the box will add some amount of latency to the connection.

Because of the inherent weaknesses in these two methods, the best and most widely used method to determine the quality of a call is to have the network itself involved in the measurement of the quality. Specifically, the advanced trend in call quality scoring is to use the network layer to gather and report statistics about the quality of the voice connections. One methodology to determine latency and packet loss in a network, which are important components of quality, is the use of the IP Service Level Availability (IP SLA) Probe used in Cisco IOS. Other, more advanced versions of network-based call quality scoring use a virtual or physical DSP to provide call quality scoring. This information would then naturally lead to enforced SLAs based on call quality monitoring.

A second advanced feature of SIP trunking services that is developing is the sharing of presence information. Currently, federation of presence is normally done between two different entities using an Internet protocol and a tunnel that shares information. This information is normally dependent upon the presence application that exists within the organization. For example, it is easy for two companies that both utilized Microsoft OCS services to federate and share presence information between them. It is also possible for a service provider to act as the central depository for presence information from multiple companies. As such, companies utilizing this SP would share presence information. These federated presence information services often use portions of the SIP protocol; however, the SIP trunking services offered are distinct from the presence services offered.

Due to this trend, an additional developing service trend is for the SP to utilize a standards-based mechanism for exchanging presence information over a SIP trunk, and as such, the same trunk that is used to interconnect for PSTN access service and Video Interconnection service can be used for sharing presence information among companies.

The benefit of using the same connection for advanced SIP trunking services, such as presence federation and call quality scoring, is the ability to utilize the same policy across any media or service that share that pipe.

Another advanced SIP trunking trend is SP offering more supplementary services across a SIP trunk. Examples of these supplementary services include

- Support for shared or overflow conferencing services in which some conferencing resources are used within the enterprise and some conferencing resources are used in the SP.

- Support for multicast music on hold support.

- Support for SNR where a call is placed to ring at two devices at once.

- Support for encryption of the media between the endpoints; known as Secure Real Time Protocol (Secure RTP).

The advancement of supplementary services over a SIP trunk is most difficult because it requires a close tie between the systems and methods used for these features by the service provider and the system and methods used by the enterprise.

The final example of an advanced SIP trunking service trend is media shuffling. This is a service in which the SP allows the signaling to traverse a separate and distinct path than the media. For many SPs this basic functionality already exists, but the enhancements are that the media shuffling will, in the future, take the most direct path from the endpoint of the customer to the endpoint that needs to be connected at the SP without any centralization of hairpinning of the media.

Today's services often have a solution with media shuffling available to the enterprise. The media can come from any location at the enterprise premise to a central location of the SP; however, a true media shuffling solution, in which the media is optimized for both the SP and the enterprise is a trend that has yet to fully develop but will offer improved call quality across all services.

Feature Trends for Call Centers Services from SIP Trunk Providers

SIP trunking for call centers is a unique challenge for SPs. Call centers were one of the first groups to embrace the utilization of SIP trunking because they used such a high number of TDM trunks.

This direct replacement for basic large-scale trunks has been the major, first application provided by many SPs; however, there are unique services required for call centers that are beginning to be developed.

One trend starting in the SP offering of SIP trunking services to call centers is the capability to support many different methods to move calls in and out of call centers. Historically, trunks sold to call centers utilized either a "*8" transfer method, SS7 signaling for call transfer, or Two B channel transfers (TBCT).

Each of these TDM-based call transfer mechanisms has strengths and weaknesses, as shown in Table 2-4.

As customers adopt SIP trunks for call centers, the first method that was used was a replication of the existing services. However, a trend toward a more SIP-specific method for transferring calls between call centers is developing. This trend is toward the use of *Refer* and variant of this signaling method to move calls with a high degree of confidence and with the capability to carry information from one call center to another.

A second major trend is the support for teleworkers. As home-based teleworkers adopt the use of SIP trunking for their voice communications, the first option provided to them was to extend the WAN coverage of the enterprise to the teleworker's house. This required that a tunnel be created from the remote worker to the enterprise and that the enterprise use a centralized SIP trunk.

Table 2-4 *Strengths and Weaknesses of TDM-Based Call Transfer Mechanisms*

Transfer Method	How Does It Work?	Applicability to SIP Trunking	Downside of Methodology
"*8"	When a transfer needs to be initiated, an audio signal is sent from the end IP-PBX to the network in the audio path. The network is listening at all times to the audio of a call. When a "*8" is detected in the network, the subsequent digits are collected and used as the location to place transfer the call to. This is the most common method used for call center transfers today.	"*8" transfers can occur across SIP Trunks. IP-PBX connected to SIP trunks can play the same audio tone, and this will continue to be detected in the network. Cisco voice gateways and Enterprise Session Border Controllers implement the playout of "*8" via a TcL script.	The use of a "*8" transfer can be heard by the caller, is not guaranteed to work, and require that DTMF digits be sent within the audio stream. These requirements limit the flexibility of this transfer method.
SS7 Network Transfer	In SS7 Network Transfer, the IP-PBX must signal to the SS7 network that the call should be transferred from one bearer channel to another.	There is no direct mapping to have a SIP message generate a SS7 Transfer Message. The closest solution would be the use of SIP-I that encapsulates the ISUP Message that would signal the transfer. (ISUP is a type of SS7 messaging variant.)	The originator of an SS7 transfer point must send SS7 messages, and this requires an expensive Signaling Termination Point (STP) and point code. There is no direct mapping of the signaling used for this in SS7 to SIP.
TBCT	A TBCT is used on PRI lines on TDM trunks. In this type of transfer, a transfer is initiated on one channel, and the call is connected until the second channel acknowledges receipt of the call and is connected.	Cisco SIP solutions for call centers, such as Cisco Voice Portal in combination with Cisco Voice Gateways and initiation of a TBCT on a TDM trunk; however, there is no standard method to initiate on a SIP Trunk.	The capability for a TDM trunk or IP Trunk to accept the signaling for a TBCT transfer and complete the transfer is not well supported.

This method does provide immediate connectivity; however, it does not allow the media to flow in the most efficient manner from the teleworkers house to the local SBC or voice gateway. As such, a trend is developing to allow for SIP trunking from remote teleworkers, where the SP connects directly to the site of the teleworker and provides an optimal media signaling path.

A third trend that is occurring is the use of more bandwidth resilient codecs for remote teleworkers. Codecs such as internet Low Bandwidth Codec (iLBC) compensate for packet loss by having an effective packet concealment algorithm. This enables for a consumer-level Internet service that does not have guaranteed bandwidth, yet still accomplishes close to toll quality voice connections.

Finally, a trend toward a new service from SPs offering SIP trunks is a recording service. Recording calls for call centers is an important task that was usually carried out in house before the call was sent out the TDM connection to the SP. With the adoption of SIP trunking, this feature can easily be moved into the cloud of the SP using shared methods to reduce the cost of recording conversations. Using the call center service provided on the SIP trunk enables enterprise customers to still be in charge of their recording requirements, but they are not required to deal with the large-scale infrastructure to complete the recording.

In summary, three major trends affecting how call centers will use SIP trunking in the future include

- Utilization of advanced signaling to move calls between call centers.

- Adoption of SIP trunking services with specific features to enable for termination and optimized media for remote teleworkers.

- Cloud-based recording services offered on SIP trunks that enable the customer to remove the burden of maintaining equipment, but still have the features required for compliance and to get the job done effectively.

SIP trunk trends in the call center have a long way to go, but this is one area in which the SP and enterprise customers are working together to offer services that are in great demand.

Summary

IP telephony has traditionally been about connecting new IP endpoints, such as IP-PBXs from businesses, or IP phones from consumers, to the traditional TDM-based PSTN. The latest trend is for the SP to offer IP-based PSTN connectivity services or trunks. This allows traditional IP-PBX customers, in both large and small businesses, to purchase IP trunking services as opposed to traditional TDM trunking services. This chapter provides an overview of the industry trends in both IP endpoint and IP trunk technologies.

Chapter 3

Transitioning to SIP Trunks

This chapter covers the following topics:

- Phase I: Assessing the current state of trunking

- Phase II: Determining the priority of the project

- Phase III: Gathering information from the local service providers

- Phase IV: Conducting a pilot implementation of SIP trunks for PSTN access

- Phase V: Transitioning a live department to SIP trunks

- Phase VI: Transitioning to SIP trunking for call center locations

- Phase VII: Transitioning to SIP trunking at headquarters locations

- Phase VIII: Transitioning to SIP trunking of branch locations

- Phase IX: Transitioning any remaining trunk to SIP trunking

- Phase X: Posting project assessment

This chapter explains the stages that an enterprise might want to plan or execute when transitioning its current Unified Communications (UC) systems from utilizing time division multiplexing (TDM) or H.323 trunks to a system that uses Session Initiation Protocol (SIP) trunks. The transition method can generally be applied to two distinct use cases for trunks that need to undergo transitions:

- **Trunks used for interapplication connectivity:** These are generally TDM trunks used between different Internet Protocol Public Branch Exchange (IP-PBX) solutions or UC applications within an enterprise. Typical examples of these trunks are connections from an IP-PBX to a voicemail system or connections from the IP-PBX to an Interactive Voice Response (IVR) system.

- **Trunks used for Public Switched Telephone Network (PSTN) access:** The method that is most widely deployed today to connect a UC system to the PSTN is the use of

TDM trunks. These trunks can be in the form of digital T1/E1, analog Foreign Exchange Office (FXO) ports, or other types of TDM connections. This is the transition methodology companies need to consider as they move to adopt SIP trunks as a replacement for TDM trunks.

When transitioning from TDM to SIP trunking, a company needs to consider the current state of both the TDM and SIP trunking that exists within the enterprise. We discuss two trunking solutions that are alternatives to SIP trunks:

■ **H.323 trunking:** Transitioning H.323 trunks to SIP trunks is normally completed to provide enhanced features not available with H.323 and to ensure that the UC signaling protocols used throughout an organization are consistent. The issues with transitioning H.323 trunks to SIP trunks can be considered throughout this chapter; however, most of the focus is on the transition of TDM trunking.

■ **TDM trunking:** TDM trunking from an application to the PSTN is the method that is most widely used by enterprises, commercial, and Small and Medium Businesses (SMB) today and is the focus of most of the discussions in this chapter on the transition to SIP trunks. As of the publication date in early 2010 in the United States, more than 90 percent of all PSTN access from companies is accomplished via TDM trunks provided by a service provider (SP).

When transitioning from TDM to SIP trunks, it is best to break the overall process into steps. During each step, different information needs to be gathered, different groups need to be included, and different challenges need to be overcome. Depending on the needs and circumstances, each company follows a different set of steps. The variability of this process can be in both the order and methods for accomplishing each step. However, all companies need to address certain issues, which are discussed in the following sections.

The phases of transition follow:

Step 1.   Assess the current state of trunking.

Step 2.   Determine the priority of a trunk transition project.

Step 3.   Gather information from SPs: The SIP trunk request for proposal process.

Step 4.   Conduct a pilot implementation of SIP trunks for PSTN access.

Step 5.   Transition a live department to SIP trunks for PSTN access.

Step 6.   Transition to SIP trunking at call centers.

Step 7.   Transition to SIP trunking at headquarters locations.

Step 8.   Transition to SIP trunking at branch locations.

Step 9.   Transition any other remaining trunking to SIP trunking.

Step 10.   Complete a post project assessment.

As noted, not all companies need to complete all these steps, and the steps might occur in a different order, but following a distinct process for transition with distinct phases can result in a transition that occurs faster and with fewer issues when compared to an unplanned transition from TDM to SIP trunks.

Phase I: Assess the Current State of Trunking

Before transitioning into a new method of interconnecting applications or interconnecting to the PSTN, the company needs to do a complete analysis of the PSTN connections and the connections between applications that currently exist.

Companies often have many different points of interconnection to the PSTN or points of interconnection between applications that have developed over years and are not always recorded in a consistent manner. There might be cases in which two applications are actually connected via the PSTN, and a company is often paying for both incoming PSTN trunks into an application and outgoing trunks from another application that are connected.

A complete audit of the TDM PSTN access to determine the physical location, size, and cost of trunking is an essential first step to determine the state of trunking at the company.

This assessment should be conducted from both a technology infrastructure and SP billing point of view.

From a technology infrastructure point of view, gathering a complete list of equipment and applications that utilize trunking needs to be undertaken. For most large and well-used applications, such as PBX interconnection to the PSTN, this list is easy to determine; however, several applications, such as postal meters, alarm monitoring systems, or paging systems might utilize trunking that is not obvious but is essential for gathering an accurate assessment of trunking requirements.

The assessment from a billing point of view is important to ensure that no trunks are paid for by the company that are not needed, understood, or controlled by the central information technology (IT) organization. Simply completing the steps to determine a complete and an accurate list of equipment, application, and costs involved in trunking between application and to the SPs for PSTN access can be an important step and can uncover areas of savings that can be further examined. These might include the following:

- A trade-in of credit for unused or underused trunking hardware

- Redundant or unused SP trunking charges that can be consolidated or minimized

- Features, such as call waiting, being purchased but are not required

- Inbound Direct Inward Dial (DID) numbers being purchased but are not utilized

One method you can use to ensure that all installed trunking is considered and recorded is to start with the accounting department. Specifically, utilize the bills paid to the various SPs as the first step to gathering an accurate count of all trunking that occurs. Some trunks might have been ordered outside of the IT infrastructure and their consolidation under a centralized bill can result in major cost savings.

In summary, an important first step to determine the current state of trunking infrastructure at a company includes

■ Listing and reconciling all applications that utilize PSTN connectivity. One important caveat in this is the percentage of fax calls that exists. Fax has unique challenges when transitioning to SIP trunks, and the percentage of fax traffic can be an important factor in selecting the right SIP trunk provider.

■ Listing all TDM trunking services and features on these trunks (for instance, call waiting, voicemail, and so on) purchased by the company. You can accomplish this by examining the charges levied by the SPs.

■ Determining if there are any nonstandard applications, such as postage machines or alarm systems, that utilize PSTN connectivity.

When a final audit is completed, you should have a full assessment of the company's current trunking costs and equipment infrastructure. The larger the current trunking infrastructure, the greater the benefits will be when transitioned to SIP trunks.

Phase II: Determining the Priority of the Project

Generally two major reasons exist that you need to consider when transitioning to SIP trunks at an enterprise: cost and features. There are also several secondary reasons that lead enterprises to consider utilizing SIP trunks. These include the lack of availability of TDM trunking services from providers or the lack of availability of data center or remote office space to implement TDM trunks.

After you determine the primary reason for the consideration of SIP trunks, the next step is to determine how this program can fit within the context of the larger IT transitions and programs that occur. When considering a SIP trunking implementation as a method of *cost-savings*, you need to understand what the payback period is and that the estimates used to determine this payback period are realistic. A successful implementation of SIP trunks can be used as a cost-savings method to help pay for the implementation of other components of a UC solution. This is an important point to stress when considering the implementation of SIP trunks, and a ROI calculation is provided in Chapter 4, "Cost Analysis."

The other major reason for implementation of SIP trunks is to access new features that could not be accessed with TDM trunks. An example of a feature that is more widely deployed on SIP trunks than previous trunking methods is video calls. You can implement high-definition video calling on H.323 trunks and TDM trunks; however, the most advanced features, such as Cisco Telepresence, are currently implemented utilizing SIP trunks. Other new features implemented using SIP trunks that should be included when considering the priority of the project include the following:

■ High-fidelity calls utilizing wideband codecs

■ Calls with subject lines that appear in addition to caller ID and caller name

- Multimedia calls that include voice, video, chat, and file exchange

- Presence indicators across and within companies

After proceeding with the adoption of SIP trunks is deemed a priority for the IT organization, the technological steps toward implementation can begin.

Phase III: Gather Information from the Local SPs

An important early step in the transition to SIP trunks for PSTN access is to determine what services are available in your area and to your company and to plan the overall transition to SIP trunking. This is best done by understanding the most formal process, the Request for Proposal (RFP), and to determine which of the steps of this formal process are essential to gather a complete and accurate understanding of the SP offerings.

A complete RFP is provided in Chapter 9, "Questions to Ask of a Service Provider Offering and an SBC Vendor;" however, a formal RFP is not required in all cases in which a company considers utilizing or transitioning to SIP trunks. For example, internal applications that might have previously used TDM or H.323 trunks can often easily be transitioned to SIP trunks without the help or hindrance of an external entity such as an SP.

However, the outline and formality of an RFP is important to help frame the questions and understand the answers provided by SPs that look to offer SIP trunking services. Some of the important things to note are

- All the questions in an RFP might not be answered by the SP.

- Use of an arbitrary scoring system of an RFP is not the best method to determine which SP to use.

- Trials deployment can and should occur without or before completion of a formal RFP.

An RFP and overall plan is an important and essential part of any large scale transition from TDM to SIP trunk for PSTN access at a company. However, the responses from an RFP alone are not enough to determine the architecture and plan required for a transition from TDM to SIP trunking.

Phase IV: Conducting a Pilot Implementation of SIP Trunks for PSTN Access

One of the key attractions to SIP trunking solutions is that they can easily scale up and down. One of the benefits that this offers is an easy method of conducting trials with various providers to better understand their services.

When considering adopting SIP trunks for PSTN access from an SP, conducting a trial implementation is an important method to help determine how successful any large scale project will be; help to define the process and create a plan for transitioning sites and locations; and help work out any issues that might not have been foreseen in the initial planning and RFP stage.

When conducting a SIP trunk trial, you can use several methods. One of the easiest and most effective methods to conduct a trial is to acquire new phone numbers and add an additional dialing pattern to existing UC implementation to enable them to utilize the SIP trunks. This is normally implemented for a small group of users, such as the IT department or an alpha user community, which can deal with any issues that might result.

One idea is to make sure that a company's vendors, including the SP that provides the SIP trunk, communicate with the IT department using the new SIP trunking numbers that have been created. This helps to ensure that the solution is used in a mission critical manner.

A pilot implementation needs to include both an inbound and an outbound SIP trunk trial. Another important component of the pilot should be piloting the porting of phone numbers from a TDM trunk to a SIP trunk to better understand the issues that might occur. The porting of DID numbers from a traditional telephony service to a SIP trunk service is often one of the most problematic parts of a transition, and completing a trial run by porting numbers that are not mission critical is an important first step.

Some of the best practices for a pilot implementation of SIP trunks follow

- Ensure the pilot is large enough to realistically gather feedback. For example, a pilot implementation that is of at least ten users and two or more sites can gather more accurate information than a small pilot.

- Ensure that the duration of the pilot is long enough to accurately gather realistic feedback from the pilot participants. Most pilot implementations are typically more than one month in duration.

- Ensure that you have well-defined method to provide feedback on the quality and issues with a SIP trunk from the end-user community. Note both the reproducible issues, such as the inability to call to specific numbers, and the transient issues, such as low quality audio on a specific phone call. Both reproducible and transient issues are important to understand the quality of a specific SP.

- Implement an outgoing calling method via the use of a special dial pattern. For example, have end users dial an **8** in front of PSTN numbers, instead of the traditional **9** when making outbound calls using the trial SIP trunk. This ensures end users of both a backup method of calling via TDM if the SIP trunk fails and an easy way to compare the call quality and experience of calls made from a SIP trunk versus those made from a TDM trunk.

- Add incoming calling numbers before porting existing numbers. Adding an incoming number and having these ring at existing or new phones helps to isolate any issues with the pilot from issues with the production system.

- Port DID numbers of support staff as a method to ensure that the porting process occurs smoothly and is well understood and documented. Porting DID numbers of all the participants in the pilot should eventually be undertaken, but this can be a long process and should be planned to not affect mission-critical work if porting of numbers is delayed.

- Test various types of calls, by calling various locations and systems, including

  - **International locations:** Ask what cadence of ring-back tone is heard and what type of caller ID is displayed. Different international mobile and international land lines should be called to effectively test the provided SIP trunk service. Compare issues to when calling via a TDM trunk to the same number.

  - **Cellular phones:** Ask the called party if a distinct difference exists between calls from TDM lines and SIP trunks and what caller ID is displayed.

  - **Other phones on the same carriers SIP trunking service:** Ask if the caller ID is correct and be aware of the call setup time and overall call quality.

  - **IVR systems:** Test the connection via the SIP Trunk to IVRs that will be used by the end users such as airlines flight status check number (1-800-UNITED1) or a movie information hotline (1-415-777-FILM).

  - **Fax calls:** Both long (such as 50 pages) and short (such as 2 pages) duration fax calls should be made to ensure that the SP performs as expected.

  - **Nonvoice Band calls:** If you have a plan for nonvoice band calls (that is, low speed modem, Baudot connections, and so on) to be supported on the SIP trunk, these types of calls should be made in the trial.

In summary, the goals of a pilot implementation of SIP trunks should be to understand the SP offering and to ensure that the level of expertise that the IT department has for SIP trunking and the transition from TDM to SIP trunking is adequate to ensure a successful large scale implementation of SIP trunking throughout the company.

Phase V: Transitioning a Live Department to SIP Trunks

The first live transition to SIP trunks from solutions that were previously live on TDM trunks can be complex and stressful for an organization. You need to select an area that is appropriate for the first live deployments. A successful first transition of SIP trunks is contingent upon many things, such as the quick and accurate porting of phone numbers and the quality of the calls over the new infrastructure and leads to further deployments.

With large companies, after a pilot is completed, the order of transition of different users groups that is often undertaken is shown in Figure 3-1. Each company has different considerations for which area is appropriate for the first large-scale transition to SIP trunks. Some of the considerations of which area to transition first include the complexity of the transition and the cost-savings that will be seen with the transition.

After the first live deployment, companies generally evaluate the rest of the transition to SIP trunking to determine if any material changes from the initial estimates completed in the RFP occur. A partial live implementation does not need to be active for an extended period before a company considers the transition of other live departments.

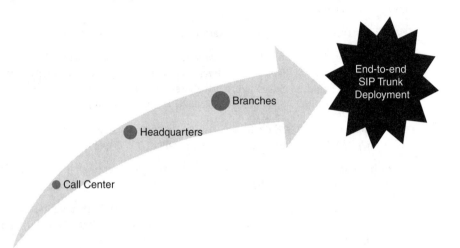

Figure 3-1   *Areas for Transitions to SIP Trunks*

In summary, the first live deployment is an essential step in the successful deployment of SIP trunking throughout a company.

Phase VI: Transition to SIP Trunking for Call Center Locations

Call centers are always important for an organization; however, they can be either the primary role of the company (that is, the company is in business offering call center services) or a support role (that is, the call center supports the company's other primary function). Outbound promotion call centers that play a supporting role for a company, such as outbound call centers for sales leads generation, are often a good, low risk early target for transition to SIP trunking. Outbound call center solutions often have prerecorded announcements played before live operators are engaged, and because of the high number of calls that need to occur, often a high trunking cost is associated with these types of locations.

Furthermore, outbound calling is easier to transition than inbound call centers because there does not need to be any changes in the carrier network to indicate new routing of calls. The company initiates all calls and as such the risk for misrouting is low.

Inbound call centers often have some type of toll free number (such as 1800 or 1888) that is routed to a physical location by mapping to a standard (for example, E.164) phone number. Because inbound call centers have a history of utilizing the SP to route calls to multiple locations, the additional of a SIP trunking solution to also route calls is easily accomplished. Carriers often offer a different SIP Trunk service for call centers than for standard DID calls. The difference normally stems from the distinct calling pattern and features of call centers (that is, one number with thousands of incoming calls of varying duration). Inbound call centers do not normally make outbound calls (except for transfers); however, they do need the capability to burst above predefined call limits. (For example, if 200 trunks were purchase, inbound call centers normally want the capability to accept the 201st call if possible.) Transitioning inbound call centers from TDM to SIP trunks, can result in:

- Additional flexibility in deployments because the call center can be outsourced by changing where the SIP messages route.

- A high degree of cost-savings because incoming call centers often generate a large number of minutes and can be responsible for a high percentage of a company's TDM carrier charges.

- Improved resiliency because call center overflows and outages can be handled quickly and easily by rerouting the SIP messages.

Companies are also focused on merging their incoming and outgoing call centers, and as such, a consolidated SIP trunking architecture for both can result in additional cost-saving.

In summary, transitioning call center traffic is often an effective early transition option for companies looking to deploy SIP trunks. Outbound call centers are a good candidate for early transition to SIP trunking because of the low complexity of the solution. The risk of misrouted calls is low, and few issues with nonvoice calls occur. Transitioning inbound call centers from TDM to SIP trunks, even with the issues of possible misrouted calls and the additional complexities in possibly having to handle fax or other nonvoice (such as Baudot connections) calls, can result in some of the largest cost-saving when transitioning to SIP trunks for PSTN access.

Phase VII: Transition to SIP Trunking at Headquarters Locations

The capacity requirements at large headquarters locations and the amount of equipment required to support this capacity is one of the primary drivers for transitioning to SIP trunking at large headquarters (HQ) locations. A typical large HQ location in the United States can require the capacity of 5,000 simultaneous active calls at a single location to support between 25,000 and 50,000 end users.

The cost benefits of SIP trunking at these large locations is compelling because the number of active trunks required per user, to ensure that no users' attempt to make a call, results in all trunks being busy (that is, call blocking), goes down dramatically with higher amounts of trunking consolidation.

When combined with the following benefits, the transition of the HQ to SIP trunking results in a great deal of saving and should occur early in the transition to SIP trunking for an enterprise:

- Lower number of trunks required per user because of the consolidation

- The lower cost per minute of calls and cost per trunk

- The capability to connect to the SP via an IP link

When transitioning the HQ location, the types of calls that should be considered are local, long distance (LD), and international long distance. Most companies, to ensure that the caller id on outbound calls is not changed, use the same SIP trunk provider for both local and LD calls. The decision for which SIP trunk provider should be selected for international LD calls depends on whether these calls make up a substantial portion of the SP charges.

Transitioning of outbound and inbound calls at HQ locations requires the porting of a large quantity of DID numbers and can be complex. The time to transition a large number of widely advertised phone numbers from TDM trunks to SIP trunks can be the most complex part of this transition.

In summary, you can realize many cost benefits when transitioning to SIP trunks at a large HQ location, and this transition should occur early in the overall transition to SIP trunks for a company. The cost benefits come from several factors, including the consolidation of the number of trunks; however, the complexity in the porting of a large number of DID at a HQ location should not be underestimated.

Phase VIII: Transition to SIP Trunking of Branch Locations

Large enterprise companies that have a large number of branches traditionally had to pay for TDM circuits at each of these branch locations. This can result in large charges from SPs and complex equipment requirements at the branch.

This has resulted in the demand for transitioning branch locations from TDM to SIP trunking. There are at least two methods for transitioning branch locations to a SIP trunking. These are distributed and centralized SIP trunking, and information about these different architectures are discussed in Chapter 7, "Design and Implementation Considerations."

Regardless of the method that you select, the transition of a branch infrastructure is a large and complex undertaking that requires a detailed analysis of the following:

- **Branch IP addressing schemes:** Is a high-quality IP network in place that will not have any topology issues (such as overlapping IP addresses, NAT, and so on)?

- **Branch phone numbers porting possibilities:** Is the branch in a location that enables the porting of the phone number to a different location and different SP?

- **Available branch bandwidth:** Does the branch have enough high-quality IP bandwidth to transition to SIP trunks? The amount of bandwidth required changes based on the architecture utilized.

- **Branch equipment specifics:** Does the branch have specialized equipment, such as teletext machines for the deaf and postal meters, or is colocation at a shared premise?

The overall goal of porting the branch infrastructure to SIP trunks needs to maintain or improve the end user quality of experience by providing new features while reducing costs by lowering TDM trunking expenses.

In summary, the complexity of transitioning a large branch infrastructure from TDM to SIP trunks is the most complex of any of the transitions but can result in the greatest reduction in TDM trunking costs. The complexity results from the various different locations, regulations, and equipment that might be used in an extensive branch network. Due to this complexity, transition of a large branch infrastructure from TDM to SIP trunks is often one of the final steps a large enterprise takes on when completing a project to transition from TDM to SIP trunks.

Phase IX: Transition Any Remaining Trunk to SIP Trunking

One of the last stages in the transition is to ensure that any remaining TDM trunking infrastructure that still exists in the company after the primary transitions are completed is analyzed to determine if it can be retired. This final stage in the transition often involves utilizing more novel solutions such as call forwarding locations where SIP trunks cannot be purchased to other locations.

The final state of an organization might be that some amount of TDM trunking exists for emergency calling if power failures occur or as a method to connect equipment in harsh or hardened environments where power is a concern. However, after the majority of TDM trunking costs are removed from a company by the adoption of SIP trunking, TDM trunking should be seen as a valuable tool for the last-mile connectivity of UC application in remote locations.

In summary, a company should not expect to have 100 percent of its trunking transitioned from TDM to IP trunking. Instead the goal should be to minimize cost, increase features, and provide a flexible and reliable communications architecture. Within these constraints, a small amount of TDM trunk will most likely still exist in all companies regardless of size.

Phase X: Post Project Assessment

At the end of any full-scale, live deployment of SIP trunks, an important learning tool that should be utilized is the post project assessment. Generally a post project assessment includes

- Reviewing original project goals

- Determining objective measures, such as dates of cutovers, costs incurred, and number of cases opened
- Interviewing key stakeholders

In the post project assessment of a project to implement SIP trunks, important components to measure include the following:

- **The speed of the implementation:** How quickly was the implementation done? Was it completed on schedule? Were there any major delays?
- **Hardware cost:** Were these in line with expectations and budgets?
- **Soft installation costs:** Was the cost of new firewall code, updated WAN router software, and so on as expected?
- **New ongoing fixed costs:** What new bandwidth was required to be purchased on an ongoing basis because of the adoption of SIP trunking?
- **New ongoing variable costs:** What is the cost per local minute, cost per trunk and cost for long distance of voice calls using the SIP trunk?

Another important component of a post project assessment is interviews with the end users. In the interview of the end users, determine if the quality of the experience of the new solution with SIP trunks is as well accepted as the quality of their experience with TDM trunks. Note if an increase in the number of calls to the help center occurred or an increase in the number of cases have been opened with respect to call quality. Furthermore, during the interview process you need to determine if there are any issues or anomalies to areas that traditionally have few issues, such as the accuracy of call detail records, the display of an appropriate caller ID and caller name to the called party, and an accurate display of incoming caller ID or caller name.

During the post project assessment, gather information about the settings and specifications used. Successful configurations files of various items, such as WAN routers, security devices such as firewalls, and the Cisco Unified Border Elements (CUBE) used at the customer site should be recorded.

The process undertaken for the porting of the DID numbers from their TDM trunks to SIP trunks should also be well documented as part of the post project assessment. The process might vary in each geographic location, but having the steps recorded as part of the post project assessment can help to ensure any future projects do not have to re-create this step.

After you gather all the information, complete a rigorous assessment of the success of the SIP trunking project from both the financial and technological standpoints. The ROI calculator in Chapter 6, "SIP Trunking Models," contains a tool to analyze this.

Summary

Transition to SIP trunking requires the following steps, as shown in Figure 3-2:

Step 1.   Determination the current status of trunking and project priority.

Step 2.   Complete SIP trunking RFP/start pilot.

Step 3.   Complete a post project assessment to determine if the pilot transition was successful.

Step 4.   Make any appropriate changes to the plan based on lessons learned from pilot program/RFP and post project assessment.

Step 5.   Expand and complete LIVE deployments.

Figure 3-2   *Steps Required in the Transition to SIP Trunks*

The exact steps and issues encountered when transitioning a company from TDM to SIP trunking will be as different as each company's TDM trunking environment is today. The transition will occur differently for different applications and location, and the timeline for each can vary dramatically.

This chapter discussed the steps required for this transition and considerations that need to be understood when this transition occurs. Each company's transition to adoption of SIP trunks is unique; however, after the major steps to determine what needs to be transitioned, what type of equipment and connections currently exists, and what the end goal is, the architectural choices of which method of trunking, and a complete RFP, which is examined in subsequent chapters can be considered and explored.

Chapter 4

Cost Analysis

This chapter covers the following topics:

■ Capital costs

■ Monthly recurring costs

■ Cost of usage

■ Cost of security

■ Cost of expertise/knowledge

■ Other areas of costs and savings

This chapter focuses on the cost structure of deploying the Session Initiation Protocol (SIP) trunks. This is also one of the major criteria to select the SIP trunk service provider. Different service providers offer different cost models. You should consider some common criteria during your cost analysis.

SIP is the protocol for creating, modifying, and terminating sessions (voice, IM, conference call, and so on) with one or more participants. It is widely used as the signaling protocol for Voice over IP (VoIP) calling and is widely thought of as the standard. So when we talk about SIP trunks, it is similar to a phone line used for making and receiving phone calls.

SIP trunking enables the convergence of voice and data on one circuit. In some cases, you might want to keep your voice network and data network separate (more on this in Chapter 7, "Design and Implementation Considerations"). However, the same physical wire might be used to connect to your service provider. Cost structure also depends on your deployment architecture (that is, centralized, distributed, or hybrid).

Following are some leading reasons why people are switching to SIP trunking:

■ Increases the availability of the service from multiple services providers. You are no longer dependent on your local PRI providers.

- Increase the redundancy of the services; for example, if you have contact centers in different locations and want to move one of them to another location. It is easier to do migration, load balancing, capacity increment, and so on.

- Allows rich media such as wideband audio, video, presence, telepresence, and so on.

- Reduces or eliminates the costs associated with the purchase of T1 and analog trunk cards.

- Reduces toll charges for long-distance, international, and local access calls.

- Reduces or eliminates the costs of the ongoing support and maintenance costs of those trunk cards.

- Reduces the recurring monthly costs of separate voice and data circuits (some dedicated to voice, some to data).

- Eliminates the over-subscription of voice; for example, a traditional PRI circuit has 23 useable voice channels that might be more than a small business requires. SIP trunking is available on a per channel/port basis.

- Affordable Direct Inward Dials (DID) that enable each employee to have his own phone line.

- Supports multiple forms of communication including video and instant messaging enabling for greater levels of user presence.

- Enables for single-channel orders, which increase the flexibility and ease of adding, subtracting, or changing a line.

- Enables remote users to have a local telephone number.

- Protects your investment. With the proliferation of Unified Communications (UC) everything moves toward Internet Protocol (IP). Deploying SIP trunking is just one step toward that direction.

- You don't need to deal with the telephone company, its extraordinarily long lead times, poor customer service, and lack of flexibility and responsiveness.

These are some of the criteria why customers are moving toward SIP trunking. But this might not always be the case. Different customers might have other reasons to use SIP trunks. Let's look at the costs in more detail.

Primarily, two kinds of cost involvement are in a SIP trunking solution: capital costs and recurring costs. We look into each cost structure for our solution.

Capital Costs

You might need to make a one-time capital investment just to acquire the service. In a broad sense, this is all about your equipment cost and the installation of that equipment and services.

Cost of Installation

The cost of installing a SIP trunk can vary depending on the following factors:

- Installation of physical connectivity

- Installation of Customer Premise Equipment (CPE)

- Installation and configuration of Session Border Controller (SBC) at customer side

- Configuration of a softswitch and SBC at service provider side

- Testing and certification

If you are considering deploying SIP trucks, most likely you have solid IP communication established. The existing physical connection for your data network can keep costs down because you might run your SIP trunks over the same connection. But, if you need to increase the bandwidth capacity of, for example, Gigabit Ethernet, you might need to install a new CPE. This kind of physical connectivity might cost between $3500 and $5000 (one time). So, before you deploy a SIP trunk, check your required bandwidth to support new calls. In this case, you might need to check the number of simultaneous calls and the codec for those calls. Just to give you an idea, a G.729-based call takes approximately 32 kbps IP bandwidth, whereas a G.711 call takes approximately 80 kbps.

In most of the deployments, you need Cisco Unified Border Element (CUBE) as your SBC. In the Time Division Multiplexing (TDM) world, things are mature, and most of the cases are plug-n-play. You can find plenty of examples to configure your T1/DS3 ports in Cisco voice gateway. But you need to configure different kinds of parameters to make a successful SIP trunk deployment. You might try to configure your own CUBE by yourself; or you might ask your service provider to configure for you. Service providers usually configure their side. If they are asked to configure your side, they might ask for some money. So, when you order SIP trunk, check who will configure and test your side of the network.

There is no need for additional hardware from your service provider, although your service provider might charge for provisioning a softswitch and SBC.

And finally, the service provider needs some time to test the SIP trunk and certify the deployment. You might end up with significant testing efforts (depending on the complexity of your network and solution) before it goes into live operation. So, you need to negotiate with your service provider to clarify the setup costs. If you sign up for a service for a few years, some tier-2 and tier-3 SIP providers do not charge for the installation.

Cost of Equipment

To deploy traditional Public Switched Telephone Network (PSTN) trunks, you need gateways. You can have multiple T1s/E1s or T3/DS3 based on your requirements, but in most cases, a small gateway with single T1/E1 (or few T1s/E1s) is sufficient for branch offices. Most branches in the United States do not need a full T1 in which they can have 23 concurrent calls.

To deploy a SIP trunk, you need CUBE and a session border controller that works as a demarcation point between your network and service provider network. The following sections discuss the costs associated with Border Element.

Border Element Chassis Cost

You need to buy a border element chassis based on your requirements. In the current business deployment scenarios, you can buy Cisco Integrated Service Routers (ISR), which can perform as a data router, SBC, and a PSTN gateway.

Cisco supports Border Element functionality in all ISR platforms (Cisco 2800 series and Cisco 3800 series), ISR Generation-2 (ISR-G2) platforms (Cisco 2900 series and Cisco 3900 series), Cisco AS5000XM series, and 7200 series routers. If you are already using any of these routers and gateways, you might use these as a Border Element. One thing to know is that the total number of concurrent calls is important for those platforms. If you are already using those as voice gateway, you need to check with Cisco to find out the right platform that can support your expected performance.

You might need to keep your gateway to connect to PSTN for backup and limited usages. You might want to keep some FXO ports to connect your fax machine and to support during backup.

Port Cost

Traditional analog or T1/E1 lines require extra hardware (for example, FXO port, PRI port, and so on) in the gateway chassis that can cost you from $600 to $3500 per card. In the case of SIP trunking, you don't need that card. If you can do everything over an Ethernet interface, there is substantial savings in using a SIP trunk.

You also might need to buy a software license to run SIP features. We discuss that in the next section.

Digital Signal Processor (DSP) Cost

In theory, you can find a lot of references on SIP trunks. You don't need any DSP in an SBC. This might not be true for all the vendors because different vendors support different features in their SBCs.

The cost of the DSP is one of the major components in your PSTN gateway. Traditionally, DSPs are expensive. If you can design your network with a single negotiated codec (such as G.711 or G.729) end-to-end, you might avoid using DSPs. However, if you need the codec translation and conferencing feature in the same router, you need DSPs. Moreover, Cisco IOS Software might use DSPs to improve your voice quality even though it is IP end-to-end. So, when you calculate your cost for DSPs, check the features with your vendors to determine whether they need DSPs. If you can avoid the codec complexity, you can avoid the cost of DSPs.

Software License Cost

Although you don't need extra hardware to run SIP trunking, you might need a software license to enable all the SIP features. In general, the price of a software license is determined by the number of ports or concurrent calls. You might have enough bandwidth to run hundreds of simultaneous calls, but your software might enable only the number of calls your license buys.

Licenses can be incremented by a single port. So, if you need to add more concurrent calls during peak hours, you can expand accordingly. When you sign up with service providers, you might not need to pay for a software license separately but it can be built into your package. If the enterprise owns SBC, you might need to buy a separate software license depending on your traffic.

A primary benefit of SIP trunks over PRIs is that SIP trunks can be purchased in increments of 1, whereas PRIs need to be purchased in increments of 23 channels.

Monthly Recurring Costs

You should expect some monthly recurring costs for any telecom services, unless it is at a per usage basis. When you want to pay as you use, the cost of the service can be significantly higher. A common practice in the telecom industry is that it charges a certain amount of money to keep your service running, irrespective of your usage. The two types of recurring costs for SIP trunks are the port/line charge and the bandwidth charge.

Port/Line Charge

In general, in the United States, analog lines cost approximately $16 per month. A PRI costs between $450 to $650 depending upon the carrier. Table 4-1 shows the typical line charge.

A SIP trunk costs between zero (you pay for only calls you make) to $25 per channel or port. In the industry, some large carriers charge even $50/port or concurrent calls. And, there is a high possibility that they include some free voice minutes with that port.

Therefore, you might recognize substantial savings in monthly charges.

Table 4-1 *Port/Line Charges*

Service	Amount
Analog (FXO port)	$16–$25/month
PRI (T1)	$450–$650/month
SIP Trunk (per channel)	0–$50

Bandwidth Charge

The bandwidth for voice communication is not significant when you compare it with your data bandwidth requirement. When you deploy SIP trunks, you need to increase network bandwidth everywhere.

Following are the two areas where you might need to spend money to increase your bandwidth:

- **Bandwidth between headquarters and the branch:** When you bring all your branch voice calls to headquarters to terminate through SBCs, you need to increase your bandwidth at each branch location. Your branches might connect to headquarters through MPLS/VPN, so you need to ask your MPLS service provider to increase the bandwidth as needed to handle the concurrent calls.

  You might have an interbranch calling facility already in place over the MPLS network. If this is the case, you just need to add extra bandwidth for other calls that are made to locations outside the organization.

- **Bandwidth between headquarters and the service provider:** You also need to increase the bandwidth at your central SBC location, which is connected externally to the service provider. This location can handle hundreds of concurrent calls. However, you might not see a significant increase in bandwidth (compared to your existing data bandwidth to support a large organization).

Therefore, depending on the number of SIP trunks purchased and the amount of excess Internet connectivity, a business should consider purchasing more Internet access. However, it's important to know that when a SIP trunk is not used, the bandwidth otherwise allocated to a SIP trunk is freed up for use in less-intensive applications, such as email and general web use. This dynamic allocation of bandwidth is yet another feature of SIP trunks versus more traditional technologies, such as analog or PRI circuits.

Although you can increase your bandwidth, the cost might not be significantly higher. Although bandwidth increase is not substantial for large deployments, it is still high on the Small and Medium Business (SMB), especially because a G.711 or wideband call on a SIP trunk takes 80 Kbps whereas a TDM takes only one T1 channel of 64 Kbps.

Service Level Agreement Charge

Quality is a big issue in the case of VoIP. In the case of TDM circuit (such as T1 PRI), a call takes the full channel of 64 kbps, which is always guaranteed for that specific call. But, in the case of VoIP, the service provider might need to sign up a service level agreement (SLA) with the customer to ensure the following parameters:

- **Link quality:** Measures the downtime of the system and the link. Some service providers offer you 99.999 percent uptime.

- **Equipment quality:** If your SBC and IP-PBX is managed by the service provider, it might give you a certain guarantee to keep running your mission critical systems.

- **Signaling quality:** Measures call signaling and setup performance. When users pick up the phone to make a call, they expect that call to be quickly and reliably established on the first attempt. Signaling quality metrics, such as post-dial delay and registration delay, assist in troubleshooting the call setup infrastructure.

- **Delivery quality:** Measures transport performance. Problems such as long latencies, lost packets, and signal strength all contribute to overall call satisfaction.

- **Call quality:** Measures a user's overall call experience. Call quality metrics, such as the Mean Opinion Score (MOS), reported on a scale of 1 (bad) to 5 (excellent), make it easy to assess call quality on a call-by-call basis.

This is not a complete list of SLAs. You might need to get a detailed service plan and quality assurance from the service provider, which might cost you extra money to achieve that SLA.

Cost of Usage

Cost of usage is the area that makes the difference. SIP trunking enables you to eliminate PRIs, T1s/E1s, and local charges, replacing them with a single pipe to the service provider, which terminates directly at the IP-PBX on your premise. Different analyses show that you should save from 25 percent to 50 percent on your voice call charges through SIP trunks. Fundamentally, it's the VoIP cost savings of as much as 50 percent over TDM charges. However, some service providers lower their TDM charges for a large volume of calls.

There are different offering models. The pricing structures vary widely by providers. Let's check those closely.

Pay as You Use

Some service providers offer a pay as you use plan. The going rate for regular lines is from 2.2 cents (local) to 3.9 cents (long distance) per minute. SIP providers charge in the range of free (local) to 2.9 cents per minute.

The major advantage of this model is that you don't make any volume commitment. If you want to keep multiple service providers and use them based on their rates (different destinations, time of day, and so on), you can do it without any fixed overhead. But, the major disadvantage is that you might not get good rates from the service providers.

Bundled Offer

Some SIP providers sell SIP trunking at $20 per month per trunk, which comes with one phone number. They can reduce the rate to as low as $10 per month with a 3-year plan. Additional phone numbers are sold in packs of 10, 20, or 100, ranging from $7.50 per month to $50 per month. So, if a company wants to enable five concurrent calling lines to be spread across 15 people, you can take five trunks and a pack of 10 additional numbers.

Some service providers offer per-minute plans and a 1500-minute plan for $39.95 per month. When you buy bulk, the price might go down to $10 per month bundled with 2500 minutes per month, and you pay between 5 and 10 cents per minute based on your volume.

You will not get a volume discount for a distributed solution. This is one of the major reasons to go for centralized or hybrid deployment solutions. In some cases, a metered approach fits better with a customer's accounting system, but you might get a better deal with a bundled offer.

We analyzed a large national retailer that is expected to save 25 percent on its monthly telecommunications and networking costs by using SIP trunks. That retailer has 1130 stores nationally, with approximately 12 local lines per store, resulting in approximately $736,000 in monthly costs for all its stores with traditional TDM technology. By switching to SIP trunks and related upgrades, the retailer cut in half the number of trunks it needed to operate.

Burstable Shared Trunks

Some service providers enable you to share the trunks among multiple locations. This is a much better way to manage trunking resources because it uses idle trunk capacity in one location to accommodate an increase in traffic from another location. For example, assume you have offices in three different locations and you need T1 (23 channels) capacity to support the peak hour calls for each location. However, when it is the peak hour in location-1, you might have unused channels in location-2 and location-3. So, location-1 can use the capacity of other locations when needed. If you combine the channel capacity for all the locations together, it will always be less than the sum of all the capacity at individual locations. This ensures you purchase fewer concurrent calls at each location and share resources to provide time-of-day benefits and peak usage management.

It leverages a better trunk utilization that is not feasible with standard TDM lines with physically defined connections.

Figure 4-1 explains the operation model of the burstable shared trunk concept.

Three sites have a limited number of concurrent call capacity (for example 10 port/location). Under this configuration, each site can have ten simultaneous calls including both incoming and outgoing calls.

If Location-C receives more than ten calls in a certain period of time, the system refuses those calls even though unused trunks might be in other locations. If your service provider enables you to share the extra trunks from other locations, the extra calls will go through, saving you a lot of money. This is not possible in TDM network.

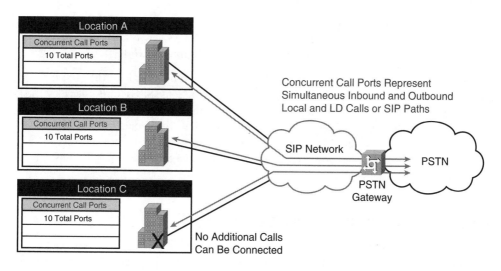

Figure 4-1 *Burstable Shared SIP Trunk*

Cost of Spike Calls

Some businesses might require additional trunk capacity for certain periods of time (for instance, before Christmas, New Year's Eve, Mother's Day, or a special sales campaign). It is difficult and costly to increase the capacity of a location for a few weeks and then dismantle it again.

Increasing capacity in SIP trunks is just increasing the bandwidth for that location and changing the configuration in the network. You can manage your seasonal spikes in call volumes with most of the service providers. They might not charge you anything extra for this service; rather, you can negotiate a better price when you buy more from a single vendor.

Cost of Security

When you take any service over the IP network, you need to take some security measures. This is one of the main differentiators between TDM trunks and SIP trunks. For a TDM trunk, an intruder needs access to your physical wire to do any harm to your network or play with your privacy. But for a SIP trunk, your network is accessible from anywhere on the Internet. With that in mind, your network is subject to the following threats:

- Denial of service (DoS) threats, call hijacking, or spoofing the call control system

- Losing privacy to eavesdropping, man-in-the-middle attacks, or media tampering

- SPAM attacks with unsolicited or malicious messages such as SPIT or phishing

- Fake identity threats that result in toll fraud, impersonation, and illegal modem calls

Your service provider provides some degree of protection. However, in reality, most intruders try to access a network through the Internet or SP network. Do not depend solely on the service provider to ensure the security of your network.

To ensure security, you might want to deploy firewalls in the middle of the SIP call flow. You can do this before the SBC, after the SBC, or both. Some SBCs (or Border Elements) support native firewalls. You might think your data firewall will perform well enough for your voice/video network; however, this might not occur when you receive SIP INVITEs from anyone in the cloud. You might need to upgrade your firewall (or features) to secure your UC. Whether you use a native firewall within SBC or a separate firewall box, you need to budget for this.

Cost of Expertise/Knowledge

A SIP trunk is a new trunking solution. Service providers have just started offering SIP trunks for enterprises, and deploying a successful SIP trunk is not as easy as deploying TDM trunks. People have worked with TDM trunks for many years; and it is a mature technology. You can find enough experts to install and troubleshoot your TDM trunks, but for SIP trunks, you might not easily find SIP trunk experts. Over time, though, it will be an easier task for professionals.

Because few people are trained in this domain, you might need to hire a consultant to help you design and run your network. This will likely cost more than installing a TDM trunk.

In the SMB market, Cisco is trying to alleviate the cost associated with this expertise by doing SIP Trunk interoperability testing with the larger service providers and documenting this in various tools and application notes to overcome the learning-curve hurdle.

Other Areas of Costs and Savings

We have already discussed the major areas of cost to deploy the SIP trunk. In this section, we discuss where you might need to keep some budget money, and we talk about ways to save money.

You might need to maintain some backup links to keep your communication up and running during the failure of WAN or SIP trunks. Based on the size of the users, you can put some FXO or T1 ports connected to PSTN to support during failover. Some companies use separate analog lines to connect their modem or FAX machine. Although these cost a small amount of money, it is better to account for them.

A big benefit of the new agreement comes with disaster recovery because IP trunks enable automated switching around locations damaged in a storm or other disasters. Before SIP trunks, reconfiguration for a disaster would have been done manually, resulting in lost time.

Although a SIP trunk takes away complexity, it also enables easier scalability. If you need to expand your operation, you need to order a new interface card for T1s/T3s; you need to get local loop (a trunk roll is involved); and you have to wait for provisioning the entire thing. To accomplish the expansion, you need to plan and execute ahead of time. You also need to engage people from different departments and vendors. These all cost money. With a SIP trunk, it's a matter of provisioning enough bandwidth on your broadband pipe and simply adding new numbers. It can be up in a couple of days, without a truck roll.

Summary

SIP trunks are the future of UC. Things are moving much faster than we can anticipate. It is inevitable that you will migrate your network from TDM to IP. You will migrate not only to save money, but also to enable other new rich features in the area of UC. You will embrace new things everyday. You can't set up something and sit idle for a long time. We have already seen the migration of digital PBX to IP-PBX. Now, it is time to see the migration of TDM trunk to SIP trunk. In the long run, it can enable you to enjoy a richer communication. In the short term, it is clear that you can save 25 percent to 50 percent of your operating cost by migrating to SIP trunks.

Further Reading

The following documents and references provide additional information on the topics covered in this chapter.

SIPTrunks.org: Using its tool you can instantly compare SIP trunking pricing from multiple SIP trunk providers. http://siptrunks.org.

SIP Trunking Quotes: It offers SIP Trunking quotes from different reliable providers in the United States. Services available include local and long distance SIP voice, business VoIP, hosted IP-PBX, T1, IP Centrex, and more. http://siptrunkingquotes.com.

VoIP Review: You can find reviews of different kind of residential and business SIP trunk providers. http://www.voipreview.org.

Chapter 5

Components of SIP Trunks

This chapter covers the following topics:

- Service provider network components

- Enterprise network components

The term *Session Initiation Protocol (SIP) trunk* can mean many things, but generally a few important components make up any system that includes SIP trunks. This chapter describes the essential components that make up a SIP trunk solution, from both a service provider (SP) and an enterprise perspective.

SIP trunks facilitate the communication of voice and video (and other real-time communications) over the Internet Protocol (IP) network within and between the realms of communications such as companies. SIP trunks are widely utilized to replace the traditional Time Division Multiplexing (TDM) trunks to access the Public Switched Telephone Network (PSTN) from an Enterprise TDM or Internet Protocol Public Branch Exchange (IP-PBX). SIP trunks provide the platform for companies to communicate with other companies over IP networks. They also enable end-to-end IP communication to ensure rich media experience for end users.

SIP trunking consists of several important components from the IP-PBX to the SP. This chapter describes the major components used to deploy SIP trunks within and outside of enterprises. This chapter also describes the differences in components for SIP trunks into large enterprises, medium-sized enterprises, and small-medium businesses. Although basic SIP technology knowledge is assumed for this book, a brief overview of basic SIP technology concepts such as SIP proxies, redirect servers, and back-to-back user agents are also given.

SP Network Components

SPs that offer a SIP trunking service for PSTN access have specific requirements to offer a service that they can make a profit on and a service that customers find compelling enough to purchase. Because the ultimate goal of a SP is to generate profit, its network design decisions are different then the decision factors of enterprise customers. The details of their network components are described in the subsequent sections.

SP Network—Edge Session Border Controllers

One of the most important components of a SIP trunking solution for SPs is the SPs' edge Session Border Controller (SBC). The edge SBC can be defined as the SBC that the SP uses to connect to end customers that it offers services to. One of the primary functions of the edge SBC is the capability to terminate the different IP addresses that each customer's network has and interwork them with the IP address space of the SP. A second important feature of the edge SBC is securing the SP networks. The inherent requirement of an edge SBC is to ensure that any of the SP components behind the SBC are protected from any attacks that might occur. This security is inclusive of what would normally be provided by an edge firewall but extends deeper into the application-specific security issues. This implies that the edge SBC or the edge SBC in combination of a firewall and intrusion protection system ensures that no attacks from traffic generated at the enterprise can infect or impact the SP. In addition, the edge SBC ensures that no harmful traffic from the SP can infect or impact the enterprise and that one enterprise's traffic cannot affect another.

Attacks that the edge SBC is designed to prevent are in both the realm of signaling and media attacks. Signaling attacks occur when an INVITE or other SIP signaling messages are sent from a "rogue" device in the enterprise or SP network. These rogue signaling attacks use techniques similar to IP attacks to determine information about a network and vulnerabilities. An example of an attack would be a rogue device sending INVITEs to sequential phone number ranges to determine what numbers are valid and what numbers are not.

Media-based attacks include sending random Real-Time Transport Protocol (RTP) traffic or flows to impact active calls. This random RTP traffic would "guess" at open RTP ports and sequence numbers and inject media to these open ports. Edge SBCs are usually large in scale and designed to support thousands of customers for a SP; however, large customers of a SP can have a dedicated edge SBC. The capability to hide IP addresses from the multiple customers that utilize the same SBC is an essential capability of the edge SBC and is often accomplished through the use of multiple Virtual Routing and Forwarding (VRF) routing tables. Another important component of an edge SBC is the capability to support a myriad of different signaling methods that might be encountered by the SP. For the SP to serve the largest audience possible, it needs to interconnect with the widest variety of edge enterprise devices that support SIP trunks. The capability to translate the SIP messaging into a signal that is understood by the SP is accomplished by either the edge SBC or the Customer Premise Equipment (CPE) device that is traditionally provided by the SP.

Due to the essential nature of the edge SBC in the SP network, it must be highly resilient and capable of achieving a five nines level of availability (for example, 99.999 percent uptime). This is usually accomplished by a combination of a redundant box-to-box hardware, deployed in either ACTIVE/ACTIVE or ACTIVE/STANDBY pairs to support increased availability; and in-box redundancy in the form of redundant hardware that would provide protection from individual component failure, such as a failure of a central processing unit, forwarding plane, or power supply. Finally, a redundant software solution for the edge SBC that can support the rerouting of calls, in the event of any individual device failure, is essential for ensuring the required availability.

Many SPs have a legal requirement to record phone calls and calling information and provide this to the appropriate authorities. Compliance with this capability is often a requirement that must be fulfilled to allow the SP to offer services. This functionality is usually referred to as lawful intercept and is often accomplished on the edge SBC through the use of media or signaling packet duplication to dedicated devices.

Finally, the edge SBC is often the first place at an SP site that alarm information about a specific customer is captured. This is typically the case when an SP does not provide or monitor any CPE deployed for the service. In this case, the edge SBC must generate alarms in response to issues that affect individual customers.

The general architecture and important interconnects of a SP edge SBC are shown in Figure 5-1.

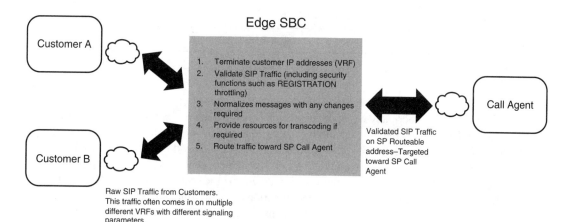

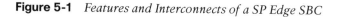

Figure 5-1 *Features and Interconnects of a SP Edge SBC*

SP Network—Call Agent

The central call agent in a SP network is the component that maintains the list of IP address or Fully Qualified Domain Names (FQDN) and the list of Direct Inward Dial (DID) numbers that those FQDN or IP Addresses correspond to. All call agents must have some type of table, as shown in Table 5-1, to determine the destination of SIP messages that it received.

The mapping database is by no means the complete set of functionality that the call agent needs to accomplish the task of routing SIP messages. It also needs an extensive set of routing functionality and to maintain the state of the calls that are in progress at any given time. The most complex requirement of the call agent is this maintenance of individual call states. One of the reasons that this is difficult is because maintaining state in a highly scalable system is inherently complex. Because many different calls occur simultaneously, the call agent requires a software design that locks the most scarce resource to ensure that contention does not occur. This scarce resource can be any number of things such as the bandwidth to particular locations, or it might be the number of PSTN offnet media gateway ports available. Regardless of the item that is the constraint with the particular SP, a system designed to handle and process new calls while maintaining an accurate count of any constrained resources is an essential requirement of a SP call agent.

Table 5-1   *Mapping of IP Addresses to FQDN*

Fully Qualified Domain Name	Phone Number
CustomerA.customer.com	+1-408-555-1212
CustomerB.customer.com	+011-44-555....
CustomerC.SecondRange.edc	99..
1.1.1.1	408-555-1212

The SP call agent normally has access to the customer database that holds essential information that a SP has determined about each customer. Some of this information is not essential for ensuring that the call is complete, such as billing addresses, but other information, such as the maximum number of calls that the customer has paid to accept, might be an important parameter required to determine the accurate routing and disposition of a call. Some call agents might also function as the routing node for emergency services such as 911 calls. In these cases, supplementary information such as the physical location stored in the customer database might be required to ensure that the call is routed to the correct Public Service Answering Point (PSAP).

Generally, the SP call agent is the entity that generates the fully defined SIP messages that eventually make it to the enterprise IP-PBX, and it is the entity that interprets response to these messages. The capabilities and design of the call agent that is deployed is the major differential amount SP is offering to similar SIP Trunking services.

The features available in the call agent are usually what determine the final feature set that the SP offers; however, some supplementary services can be accomplished by external servers.

Architecturally, a call agent is most often a back-to-back user agent (B2BUA) in SIP terminology, and the general architecture and important interconnects of a SP call agent are shown in Figure 5-2.

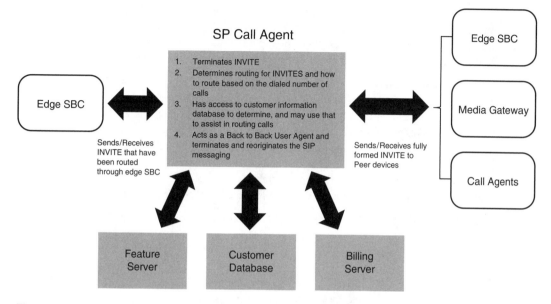

Figure 5-2   *Features and Interconnects of a SP Call Agent*

SP Network—Billing Server

All SPs are in business to service customers. Most SPs are in business to collect remuneration for these services, and a few SPs are in business to make a profit. These things require that accurate records of what has occurred be kept. This is no different when providing SIP trunks. A SP network that is set up to offer SIP trunks must have a billing server that can accurately determine when calls have been made and in a post processing or real-time method, determine the charge that will be assessed for these calls to the end customer.

Generally, the billing mechanisms that are required for TDM-based PSTN services must be replicated if SPs are offering SIP trunks for PSTN access. This includes the requirement to accurately maintain records of all transactions that have occurred on the SIP trunk for legal intercept reasons. If the SP is offering enhanced services, beyond those of just PSTN offnet, the billing service needs to interact with the service that is controlling these functions to maintain an accurate record and eventually generate an accurate bill for these transactions.

Generally billing servers fall into two major groups:

- **Real-time billing servers:** Those that can affect the call signaling path of every call.

- **Post-paid billing servers:** These generally gather billing information at the end of the call and update customer records in large batches after the call is completed.

Because they are involved in the call setup for every call, real-time billing servers have a much greater impact on caller experience. If they are slow or inaccurate, real-time billing servers can result in long call setup times or the disallowance of calls in real time that should be allowed. This can have a major effect in real time on customer experiences with SIP trunks. Errors or slow processing of post-paid billing servers have a less immediate impact on customers as they only impact bills that are sent on a periodic basis.

For services beyond basic SIP trunks for PSTN access, the SP must have a method for billing these alternative transactions that is normally beyond just per-minute billing. One idea that has not caught on is billing based on the number of packets that have been sent during a call. This enables customers and SP to introduce unique new features such as video calls or application sharing over SIP trunking while maintaining a steady billing mechanism. Unfortunately, the billing mechanism directly impacts the types of new features that are offered. Unless a SP can accurately bill for a new service and the service generates more revenue than the cost to maintain it, there is little innovation that occurs at SPs.

The features and interconnection of a SP Billing Server are shown in Figure 5-3.

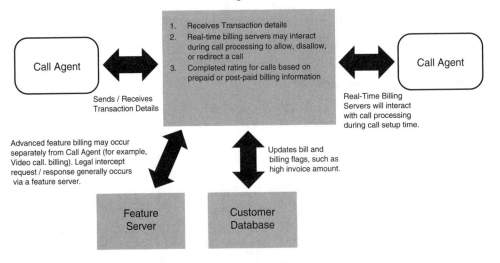

Figure 5-3 *Features and Interconnects of a SP Billing Server*

SP Network—IP Network Infrastructure

One area that is often assumed and overlooked when examining components of a SIP trunking solution is the basic underlying IP Infrastructure. This infrastructure is often just shown as a "cloud" in architecture diagrams with the assumption that all devices can connect equally and with high quality in this network. This might be the easiest way to display the solution architecturally, but this is often not the case.

A high-quality IP network is an essential underlying component of a SIP trunk solution offered by SPs. If this SIP trunk solution is for PSTN access, the level of quality of the IP network should equal or exceed the level of quality and reliability of the PSTN network that is seen as a 99.999 percent (often called "five nines") network. Because other features are often seen as enhancements to "basic" SIP trunks for PSTN access, the "five nines" level of reliability is most often seen as a floor, not a ceiling, and other SIP trunking services are assumed to increase the reliability of the overall solution.

Two of the major benefits of SIP trunking rely on that the underlying infrastructure is an IP network. These are

- Flexibility in services

- Enhanced reliability

First, flexibility in services is the capability to transmit many different types of traffic over the same physical medium. For example, the traffic can be narrow-band traditional audio, wide-band/high-fidelity audio, or video. The packetization of these different types of content over an IP network ensures that a single network can be used for many services.

Second, an IP network's inherent capability to route around areas disconnected or congested can provide reliability that is beyond what can be accomplished in traditional TDM trunking networks that relied on point-to-point connections. Another important component to note is that not all IP networks are created equal. For a SP to offer a high-quality SIP trunk solution, it must have a high-quality IP network. A high-quality network from a SIP trunking perspective optimizes the following important components:

- Latency

- Packet loss

- Jitter

These three items, which have a devastating effect in any VoIP environment, are especially problematic in SIP trunking networks. A network with a high level of latency has long delays in speech from originator to terminator, and this results in people talking over each other. This can also result in many signaling timeouts as confirmation packets for certain events are expected to be received in certain time frames. Packet loss has a negative effect on any network, and in the IP network of a SP offering SIP trunks, the effect of excessive packet loss is that the voice quality is below acceptable levels and that call setup times can be long because of lost call setup packets. Finally, jitter, which is variability in delay, has a negative effect on the adaptive jitter buffers of endpoints in SIP trunking solutions. Generally, endpoints adapt to a specific amount of delay by creating a packet buffer that is long enough to store packets for the expected largest delay (such as a 30 ms dejitter buffer, or holding area for voice calls).

However, if there is a sudden, large increase in delay in the work (that is, to 300 ms for example), the adaptive jitter buffer has to expand to accommodate this (as such, delaying all packets 300 ms before playing out). If there is a sudden decrease in delay, the adaptive jitter buffer has to contract to accommodate this (for example, back to 30 ms). This expansion and contraction of the dejitter buffer because of changes in delay of a network, known as jitter, has a negative effect on overall voice quality.

The impacts of these network impairments are even larger when SIP trunks are used for video, which has less tolerance of bad-quality IP networks than voice networks.

Another basic aspect of a high-quality IP network is security. Security implies that the basic network should not be full of bots, worms, or other infected devices that try to attack valid network traffic. A secure network also implies that there are not rogue elements snooping on packets and that the traffic that flows across the network is from known sources and is valid. Generally, the Internet, which has thousands of infected entities doing port scans and IP ping attacks, is not a secure network. However, a SP MPLS network should be considered a more secure network. A basic assumption for most customers is that a SP-provided MPLS network should be less vulnerable to a hacker snooping packets or sending inappropriate ping messages, then the customers own network. This requirement for a secure IP network infrastructure is inherent for any SP that wants to offer a high-quality SIP trunking solution.

In summary, a SP should ensure that it has a high-quality, reliable, and secure basic IP network infrastructure with low packet loss, jitter, and delay to deliver a high-quality SIP trunk solution. SIP trunks that act as replacements for TDM trunks have an expected "five nines" reliability, and SIP trunks used for enhanced services, such as video, have even more susceptibility to impairments than basic voice-only networks.

SP Network—Customer Premise Equipment

As SPs look to offer SIP trunks as a replacement service for TDM trunks, an important component can be lost. This component is the mandatory requirement for a physical connection at the customer premise. The ability for an SP to offer a SIP trunk service without any equipment physically at the customer premise has both a positive effect and a negative effect. The positive effect is that the SP can deploy a service with less capital. As a result, this can lead to improved profitability; however, the negative effect is that without a physical presence at the customer, the capability to troubleshoot and determine quality on the customer premise, which existed in TDM networks, is lost without some type of CPE.

Generally, CPE refers to physical hardware that is mandated, managed, and owned by the SP and enables it to monitor and control the experience down to the customer premise. The expectation is that any issue that occurs beyond the boundary of the CPE is an issue that the customer is responsible for, and any issue that occurs at the CPE or at any device owned by the SP is an issue the SP is responsible for.

The type, complexity, and features of CPE that are provided when SP offers a SIP trunk service vary widely based on the SP and the type of features offered on the SIP trunk. A common deployment for SIP Trunk services is when SP offers SIP trunks for PSTN access over its own physical infrastructure. In this case, the typical components of a CPE are

- Physical connection to the SP, generally Layer 1-based, such as T1 or DS3, but could be Wireless (for example, 3G) or other connectivity methods

- Ethernet (either FE or GigE) connection to the enterprise LAN

- Control and monitoring software on the devices that ensure that the SP can troubleshoot issues

The software in the CPE is often in the form of a B2BUA. In this case, the CPE device would physically terminate the SIP messages and regenerate a new SIP message toward the SP for messages from the enterprise to the SP. For messages from the SP to the enterprise, the CPE would terminate the message from the SP and regenerate a new message to the enterprise. Generally, the role of the CPE is to take SIP messages (or in some cases H.323 messages) from the IP-PBX on the customer premise, terminate them, extract the relevant information for routing (for example, calling number, called number, codec, privacy indicators, and so on), and reconstruct a new SIP message that would come from the CPE directed to the SP. This ensures that the SP core network needs only to route and respond to messages presented in a manner that is understood, from a device that is controlled by the SP. Similarly, because messages in a B2BUA can be "tweaked" to conform with the customer equipment that it is sending messages to, the SP can ensure that there is compatibility with a wide range of customer equipment.

Another form that the software in the CPE can take exclusively is a Network Address Translator (NAT) and security device. In this case, the SIP messages are not terminated by the CPE equipment; they are instead validated to ensure that they conform to a predetermined set of standards. These include things such as length of message, contents of Session Descriptor Protocol (SDP), and so on. After the validation, the messages are passed through a SIP Firewall and Application Layer Gateway (SIP ALG). This is a component of a firewall that utilizes NAT, that takes the addresses of the outside network exposed to the SP, and translates them into IP addresses valid for the internal network of the enterprise and vice versa. The other function of the firewall is to open a hole in the firewall to let RTP traffic flow between the enterprise and SP based on the information within the signaling packets. This NAT and SIP ALG function is usually coupled with some type of specialized troubleshooting or network testing software. The troubleshooting software included in the CPE can often simulate VoIP packets and calls and act as an independent termination point for call signaling to aid in troubleshooting. This helps to complete the role of a CPE as an aid in the troubleshooting functionality of the SP. The IP Multimedia Subsystem (IMS) is an architectural framework for delivering many services over an IP network, including SIP Trunking. In the IMS architecture, the CPE equipment is known as a Border Gateway (BGW).

The features and roles of SP CPE are shown in Figure 5-4.

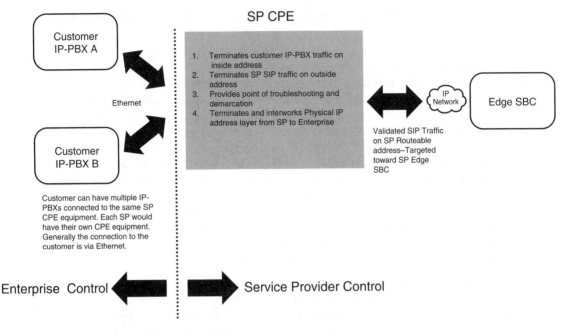

SP CPE

Customer IP-PBX A

Ethernet

Customer IP-PBX B

1. Terminates customer IP-PBX traffic on inside address
2. Terminates SP SIP traffic on outside address
3. Provides point of troubleshooting and demarcation
4. Terminates and interworks Physical IP address layer from SP to Enterprise

IP Network

Edge SBC

Validated SIP Traffic on SP Routeable address–Targeted toward SP Edge SBC

Customer can have multiple IP-PBXs connected to the same SP CPE equipment. Each SP would have their own CPE equipment. Generally the connection to the customer is via Ethernet.

Enterprise Control

Service Provider Control

Figure 5-4 *Features and Roles of SP CPE*

SP Network—Media Gateways (Voice and Video)

As SPs look to offer service on SIP trunks, the first and most obvious service is a TDM trunk replacement service for PSTN access. To accomplish this, the SP has to include connectivity to the PSTN through a media gateway. Media gateways have existed for years with the role of transitioning TDM traffic into IP. Initially, this was for transit across an IP network, where the end traffic would ultimately be converted back to TDM via another media gateway. However, when used as a component of a SIP trunk solution, to provide interconnect to the PSTN, a media gateway serves the role of converting TDM traffic to IP that stays IP until it is converted into an analog signal at the customer premise.

A media gateway has many functions, but the primary purpose of a media gateway to an SP offering SIP trunks for PSTN access is as an origination/termination device. Effectively, the solution is taking what was once a dedicated resource that each individual enterprise owned, specically a TDM to IP gateway, and instead, using a shared resource owned by the SP. This is an important point to understand in the development of SIP trunks for PSTN access. Effectively, deploying SIP Trunking at an enterprise is the outsourcing and transfer in ownership, control, and location of the TDM gateway from the enterprise to the SP.

This transfer in ownership and location of the media gateway away from the enterprise and into the SP resulted in a transfer of the use of the asset from being dedicated to a particular company to an asset shared among many customers. Because the asset is now shared, the capability to optimize for the particular requirements of a specific customer becomes much more difficult.

Table 5-2 outlines some of the changes that have occurred with the location, network design, and configurations as customers have transitioned from TDM gateways owned by enterprises as a method to connect IP-PBX to the PSTN to the use of SIP Trunks for PSTN access by SPs.

Table 5-2   *Comparison of Media Gateway Architectures*

	TDM Gateway Owned by Enterprise to Connection IP PBX to PSTN	SIP Trunk Service Used by Enterprise to Connection IP PBX to PSTN
Bandwidth requirements	IP Bandwidth only had to be measured within the enterprise.	Bandwidth of the trunk between the SP and the enterprise needs to be measured and can be the primary limiting factor in the number of calls supported.
Echo cancellation	Echo cancellation parameters could be tuned to specifics of particular companies' network on their dedicated media gateways.	Echo cancellation parameters need to be optimized to support the widest variety of media endpoints.
Signaling requirements	All SIP signaling would be terminated at the enterprise, and only TDM signaling would interconnect with SP.	SIP-based signaling traverses the border between the enterprise and the SP.
DTMF interworking	All DTMF interworking would occur onsite and in control of the enterprise.	DTMF parameters and interworking features are dependent on the DTMF interconnect types offered by the SP.
Echo Return Loss (ERL) and Gain/Loss db levels	All levels could be controlled at the enterprise and optimized for the specific enterprise.	ERL and Gain/Loss db levels need to be set to accommodate the widest number of customers.
Codec selection	The selection of codec used within the enterprise is not influenced by the codec used by the SP.	The codec used by the SP affects the choice of the codec used by the enterprise because some codecs might require additional hardware and others do not.
Delay	The IP delay budget could be entirely used within the enterprise.	Additional consideration should be given when determining a delay budget for the delay for the media to transition the SP network and its media gateway delay.

Another type of media gateway used by a few SPs is a video-enabled media gateway. This device can transfer video that comes across SIP trunk networks to video that can be utilized in other networks, such as 3G-based cellular networks. These media gateways can be an expensive component of SP networks; as such, they are normally billed, managed, and maintained separately from the TDM gateways.

In summary, in a SP network, the media gateway fulfills all its traditional roles of translating SIP signaling and RTP media to TDM signaling and analog media. However, it accomplishes this task as a shared resource among many customers.

The features and interconnects of a SP media gateway are shown in Figure 5-5.

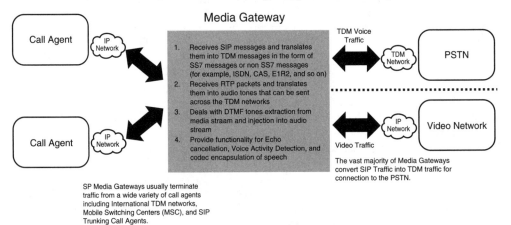

Figure 5-5   *Features and Interconnects of a SP Media Gateway*

SP Network—Legally Required Supplementary Services Systems/Legal Intercept and Emergency Services

As SPs look to offer PSTN replacement services via SIP trunks, they might be mandated and required to offer some of the same services that currently exist on TDM trunks. The major mandated supplementary services are

- Legal intercept of voice calls

- Emergency calling

As previously discussed, in the United States, as in many countries, SPs are required to maintain records of calls, including such information as calling and called party, time of day, and duration of call. This requirement is the same regardless of whether the technology to make those calls is done with TDM trunks or SIP trunks. As such, SPs are required to ensure that they have in place some architecture that enables them to comply with this requirement.

The SP that currently has TDM infrastructure and can provide these mandated supplementary services via the TDM infrastructure often reuses this infrastructure to provide the same services to their SIP trunking service. In this method, all calls, regardless of whether they can stay within the SP IP cloud completely, are sent to the PSTN for billing and Legal Intercept. This enables the SP to reuse the systems in place to legally intercept and report to authorities any information about a call; however, it hinders the capability of the SP from innovating on services because all calls need to terminate on the TDM network.

A second method that can be used to accomplish the goal of fulfilling the legally required supplementary services is to acquire a purpose build IP-based Legal Intercept Server. This supplementary feature service would provide the ability to terminate the request for a Legal Intercept or "tap" from the authorities, configure the call agent with any special requirement to enable the tap to start, and convey the captured information to the authorities. This type of dedicated supplementary service server is used only in a small percentage of calls but has an important purpose that is mandated by law.

A third method that has failed in many countries is an attempt to get a waiver for SIP trunks to identify them as a distinct feature that should not be required to comply with the existing laws. This argument has not been successful in most cases and any SP who will be a long-term provider of a SIP Trunk service needs to have a method to implement required supplementary services. Table 5-3 outlines the different method discussed for implementing legally required supplementary services.

The second legally required service that is often mandated is emergency calling. In the United States and most western countries, there is a single, countrywide number to call to summon help. The routing problem that occurs with this type of solution is that the routing of this call, which is normally based on the number that is the CALLED, needs to change to be based on the CALLING number. This is because there is a single emergency services number, such as 911, that is used throughout a large geographic region, but the call is routed to different locations based on where the call is originated.

Table 5-3 *Method to Implement Legal Intercept*

Method	Advantage	Disadvantage
Use PSTN resources	No change in implementation required.	Hinders ability to offer new services. All calls must go through PSTN.
Use new IP-based Legal Intercept Server	Allows for new services and optimized calls.	Requires new infrastructure to be implemented that can have significant additional costs.
Request a waiver	No new work to enable SIP trunk service.	Unlikely to be granted.

When using SIP trunks for PSTN access, routing the call to the correct PSAP requires that the physical location of the CALLER be known and the CALLED number is converted in what has historically been referred to as a "SELECTIVE ROUTER" to the phone number of the correct PSAP to call. With SIP trunking, as with TDM trunking, this same lookup needs to occur. However, there is a chance, because of the transient nature of IP addresses, that the physical location recorded is no longer correct. As such, a more complex system that is defined in the E-911 service requirements for SIP trunk providers is required to be implemented in the United States. Other countries have similar requirements.

In summary, in many regions of the world, there are two required supplementary services of SIP trunks for PSTN access that SPs need to consider in their design. These are legal intercept services and emergency calling services. Both of these services have well-defined solutions that can be implemented to ensure that a SIP trunk service can be deployed and complies with appropriate regulations. If an SP designs a system without consideration for these services, it could not be a service that is considered viable for customers in the long term.

SP Network—Enhanced Services

To differentiate their offerings, SPs try to offer services on their SIP trunks that are beyond basic PSTN replacement. These advanced services often require some type of enhanced service servers and infrastructure. These devices can either be logical entities that are co-resident on the same physical hardware as the call agent or other servers of the SP, or they might be distinct and separate both physical and logical devices. Generally, as SPs scale their services, enhanced services are deployed on dedicated hardware to enable the SP to optimize the deployment of servers to match their customer profiles.

The specific roles that enhanced services servers provide to SPs that deploy a SIP trunk service vary widely depending on the service offered. Typically, the service is offered such that the SP call agent can provide the basic functionality, but the SP can sell an additional service that might be provisioned on the enhanced services servers. Some examples of services include

- **Fixed Mobile Convergence (FMC) services:** SP offers this on top of the SIP trunk that enables for the intelligent routing of calls to both cellular and fixed locations.

- **Network-provided voicemail services:** A service that SP offers that provides a hosted voicemail service. In this case, when a call exceeds the maximum number of ring attempts, instead of being forwarded to a local voicemail solution, it is forwarded across the SIP trunk to a network-based voicemail solution.

- **Video calling services:** Enables an SP to intelligently route calls to endpoints such as those that support the capabilities of video calls are routed to special equipment. This service is often done to support either high-end video, such as Telepresence video calls over SIP trunks, or in combination to FMC services to connect fixed-line SIP video calls to cellular network video calls.

These are just a few of the many possible enhanced functions or services that SPs can offer on their SIP trunks. Regardless of the specific service offered, the enhanced services server needs to interact with the call agent to ensure that the service is correctly invoked and to interact with the billing server to ensure that an accurate and complete detail of the enhanced service that was invoked is maintained. Depending on the complexity of the feature invoked, the enhanced services server might need to invoke other features that involve interaction with the network layer, (such as setting QoS policy), interaction with the security layer, (such as opening specific pinholes in firewalls to allow additional traffic), or interaction with the customer database to ensure correct routing policies are followed.

The features and interconnects of a SP enhanced services server are shown in Figure 5-6.

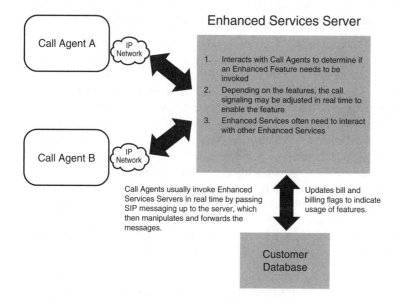

Figure 5-6 *Features and Interconnects of a SP Enhanced Services Server*

SP Network—Peering Session Border Controllers

SPs focused on deploying trunking services know that the number of endpoints accessible with the trunks directly impacts the potential market acceptance of the trunking offering. Generally, when competing with TDM trunks that offer connectivity to 100 percent of valid, phone numbers, there is no alternative for a SP that offers SIP trunks for

PSTN access but to also offer connectivity to 100 percent of phone numbers. Of the features of the PSTN, wide accessibility with a universal routing plan (for example, E.164 phone numbers) is the most important feature. Without this, the phone network would have splintered into a set of incompatible networks that would have required end users to maintain different devices on each network. This, for example, is the case and problem with most two-way radio network and is a major reason that they are not more widely deployed. The only other network with the same level of interconnectivity as the PSTN, and as such with the same level of success, is the Internet. On the Internet, any address entered should result in a path to the endpoint. This same expectation exists in the area of SIP trunking.

One way that an SP can ensure that it is connected to the largest number of endpoints at the lowest cost is by exchanging traffic with other SPs via a peering SBC.

A peering SBC, unlike an edge SBC, is focused on connections to a smaller number of "peer" SPs. The trust relationship with these SPs is different than the trust relationship between SPs and customers. Because the peered SPs can be both a customer, who provides the SP revenue in exchange for terminating minutes and vendors who charge the SP for terminating minutes, the trust relationship is more complex than traditional customer/vendor relationships that exist with connections to end customers via the edge SBCs. Because of this complex trust relationship, there needs to be security in place, but it is also much more likely that the two SPs will use a fully routable Internet-based IP address space for the connection, whereas with an edge SBCs, this is much less likely. One aspect of security that is often different than with customers is *contractual security*. This is security derived from the legal contract that exists between the peered SPs. These contracts can require the SP who is at fault for malicious activity, whether under its control or not, to be liable to the other SP, if any damages result. Though these contracts might not practically provide any additional security, they do exist.

SPs that offer SIP trunks generally peer directly with other SPs (for example, two large SPs such as Verizon and British Telecom) or via a peering service, such as XConnect that offers connectivity to a large number of peers who have connectivity to a larger number of PSTN locations at low cost. When an SP needs to complete a call to a phone number that it does not own, it needs to send the call on a route to get to the terminating provider. However, due to the complex series of agreements in the area of peering networks, there is no definitive logic that dictates specifically how each call will be logically routed (routed via TDM versus IP, and so on).

One aspect that is distinct between Internet peering and SIP trunk peering is that with SIP trunk peering all traffic between SPs is measured and compensated for on a per-call basis. With Internet traffic exchange peering, traffic is usually exchanged at no cost between SPs without detailed examination of the specific destination of each traffic flow.

Peering SBCs are usually deployed at shared central locations, such as large shared data center facilities. These shared facilities enable for the peering of traffic across a similar medium. This is usually done via an Ethernet connection between two providers. Each provider generally has its own peering SBC, and as such, the number of SBCs that a particular call traverses from start to finish can be very large.

Another important role of peering SBCs is to ensure that traffic that is both originated and terminated by IP endpoints—when they belong to the same SP—is *not* converted into TDM traffic unless required. (That is, if a call is tagged for Legal Intercept, conversion to TDM may be required.) This direct routing of calls over the IP link between customers of an SP is not always the method used to connect customers but is the ideal scenario. As SPs peer their SBCs and generate and terminate IP traffic, there is no reason that the traffic between two IP PBXs connected to two different SIP trunking networks from different but peered SPs should not stay IP end to end. Figure 5-7 shows how these connections occur most often today with a transition and interconnect over the PSTN network as they are converted to TDM traffic. However, the future deployment as connections over an end-to-end IP network is becoming more prevalent.

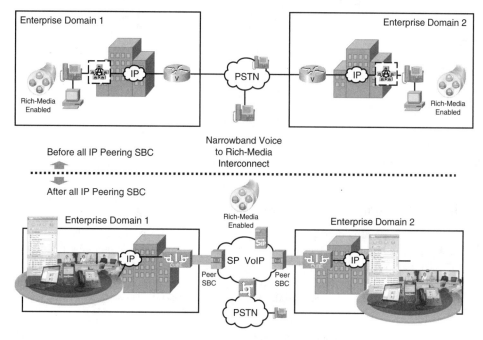

Figure 5-7   *Before and After an all IP Connection End to End*

Within the next ten years, the end-to-end IP connection will become the dominant means for interconnecting real-time IP traffic as described. The intermediate steps of conversion to TDM traffic occurs less frequently and provides no benefit in an all IP network. When traffic between SPs is maintained as all IP, the overall interconnect cost is lower, and the variety of traffic that can be exchanged, such a wideband audio and video, are more extensive than with TDM-based interconnects.

In summary, a peering SBC provides the essential role today of enabling the SP to inter-connect to each other, ensuring that all PSTN destinations are connected when offering a

SIP trunk for PSTN access service. In the future, this will play an essential role as more and more traffic becomes IP end to end between customers.

The features and interconnects of a SP peering SBC are shown in Figure 5-8.

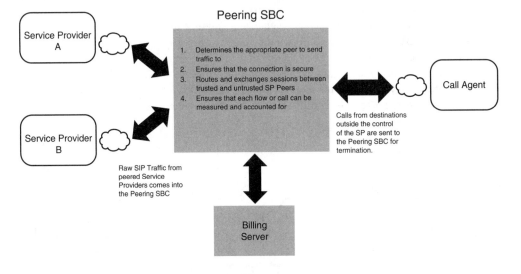

Figure 5-8   *Features and Interconnects of a SP Peering SBC*

SP Network—Monitoring Equipment

An often-overlooked component that exists throughout all SPs networks is the monitoring equipment. In the TDM trunking world, monitoring equipment is quite mature, having been developed for more than 75 years to provide an extensive alarming system that helps SP deliver a quality service. However, in the new world of IP networks connected with advanced services over SIP trunks, there is much less standardization with respect to monitoring equipment.

One standard that does generally exist is Simple Network Management Protocol (SNMP), which is a standard method to relay information from a host to a monitoring device. Most equipment that an SP owns and deploys supports SIP trunks for PSTN access support and SNMP-based monitoring. However, because of the complexity of the implementation and the amount of network traffic that can be generated, SNMP might not be a long-term network management solution for SIP trunks. Several new candidates, in the form of XML-based messaging systems, are possible replacements for SNMP-based network monitoring solutions.

Regardless of the method used for the transport of the status, the specific items that need to be monitored are similar. Some of the typical items monitored by the SP of a SIP trunk service, regardless of what specific piece of equipment is used, are shown here:

- **CPU utilization:** What is the average and peak CPU utilization of the various devices involved in the SIP trunking solution?

- **Connectivity:** What is the status of the interfaces? Are they UP or DOWN? How much traffic flows across them?

- **Failure, traps, and warnings:** Are there any failure, trap, or warning messages sent from any of the components of the SIP trunking solution?

- **Active calls:** How many active sessions exist on the component being monitored? This is an important measurement to ensure that the ultimate goal of providing an active SIP trunk services is accomplished.

One of the areas that is most problematic with SIP trunk services that is not a major problem with TDM trunk service is the capability to determine if a trunk is "UP." Because of the lack of connectedness of SIP trunks when compared with TDM trunks, there is no definitive way, as there was when monitoring TDM trunks, to determine a trunks active status (for example, if it is "UP"). In the TDM world, a Layer 2 keepalive, such as an SS7 File in Service Unit (FISU) or a Q.921 Layer 2 keepalive would send periodic messages to determine if a trunk was active could accept new calls. If these messages were either received with errors or not received, the trunk would be marked as DOWN and action taken to resolve the issue. In a SIP trunk solution, because there is no permanent connection when a call is not active, an alternative method to determine the status of a trunk needed to be developed. The solution that is most widely deployed is the OPTIONS PING method. In this case, a SIP OPTIONS request is sent outside of an active call dialog (often called Out of Dialog [OOD] OPTIONS PING) to determine if the entity on the other side is responding. If the SIP target of the OPTIONS message is not responding, an alarm condition is met, and a response would be required. Utilization of the OPTIONS PING message is a distinct method of monitoring a SIP trunk solution outside of the standard IP-based services monitored for ping, power, and path.

In summary, device and solution monitoring in a SIP trunk solution, as with most solutions, is essential, and SP networks need to ensure they have in place methods and procedures to monitor all the components of the network.

Enterprise Network Components

Enterprise networks have many of the same components as SP networks with respect to SIP trunks. The biggest difference is in the size and complexity of deployments, though many large-scale enterprise architectures for SIP trunks look like small-scale SP solutions. SP networks are optimized to have as little maintenance required for as profitable a service as possible. Whereas enterprise networks are more about offering enhanced services and value to the end customer that can distinguish one enterprise from another. In this section, the focus is on features and requirements that are different and distinct from the components of a SP SIP trunking solution.

Enterprise Networks—SP Interconnecting Session Border Controllers

Enterprise networks have many of the same issues to resolve as SP networks, and as such, many of the same solutions are appropriate. An SBC solves enterprise problems with respect to:

- **Session management:** Ensures that sessions from multiple devices can share the same resources.

- **Interworking:** Ensures that non-homogenous Unified Communications (UC) applications utilize the same SP SIP trunk and connect to one another.

- **Demarcation:** An SBC can act as the edge of an enterprise network to assist in problem resolution.

- **Security:** An SBC has the requirement to protect an enterprise network from attacks that come from outside of the network.

These functions are not all unique to an enterprise; however, there are a few distinct features that an enterprise SBC requires that an SP SBC does not.

One of these requirements for an enterprise SBC that is unique from an SP SBC is tight integration with the current enterprise UC architecture. This is an important component because most enterprises have a goal of providing a consistent user experience to their end users or customers. This is often accomplished by sharing a common UC infrastructure. The integration can be in the form of common tools and management configuration methods that extend from the UC call agents to the enterprise SBC to the capability for the UC to share resources such as transcoding resources with the SBC. In the case of Cisco products, the Cisco Unified Communications Manager (CUCM) can for example, share transcoding resources, with the Cisco Unified Border Element (CUBE). And the CUBE shares a common CLI for configuration with other Cisco voice infrastructure components such as TDM gateways and conferencing bridges.

In small and medium business (SMB) networks, the functionality of the enterprise SBC is often included in the call agent. For example, the Cisco Unified Communications Manager Express product, which includes call control capability for up to 350 phones, includes the software functionality of the CUBE within the same devices. This combination of multiple functions is common in SMB-based solutions and is different from large scale enterprise solutions that normally have distinct SBC devices.

In summary, the enterprise SBC has most of the features and requirements in common with an SP edge SBC; however, the integration with the existing UC infrastructure is a requirement that goes beyond that of an SP edge SBC.

Enterprise Network: IP Network Infrastructure

The IP infrastructure requirements of an enterprise are almost identical to that of an SP, but there is one major difference. An SP generally needs to connect to thousands of end customers that might share a common overlapping IP address space. This interconnect is often in the form of VRF interworking.

An enterprise generally needs to connect only with a few SPs that most likely do not have overlapping IP address spaces. Generally, the problem of the interconnecting of overlapping addresses spaces and connecting them via VRF interworking is one that is primarily seen only by SPs and not a primary issue for enterprise IP network infrastructure deployments. However, there are some exception cases when VRF interworking is required for enterprise IP networks that are used as a foundation for SIP Trunks.

The major issues of latency, delay, and jitter affect an enterprise and SMB network in the same way that they affect an SP. As such, the same effort should be used to ensure that a secure and robust IP networking infrastructure is provided as the foundation to ensure that any SIP trunk solutions can be successfully deployed.

Enterprise Network—Enterprise Session Management

A new trend that is developing in large enterprise UC deployments and is transitioning down to smaller deployments is the use of a Session Management layer to have a single point of control and interconnect for SIP trunks. The requirements of an enterprise session manager are similar to that of a call agent in an SP network; however, there are many distinct features that set them apart. Generally, an enterprise session manager is a B2BUA that acts as a central control point for the signaling aspects of SIP trunks and can provide some additional value-added capabilities. Cisco has offered the CUCM (Session Manager Edition) since late 2009 to fulfill this particular role.

Session managers are similar to SBCs; however, they generally interact only with the signaling layer and not the media layer and can be used to invoke supplementary services independent of the final UC application. This area of session management is a growing area in the field of SIP trunks and is important because it provides a level of abstraction where each individual UC component can point to the session manager and the session manager can take advantage of the additional features of the session border controller as required. Figure 5-9 describes how a session manager is deployed in an enterprise UC network. Generally, Enterprise Session Management is only required for a large or medium network and is not a component that is deployed in SMB networks.

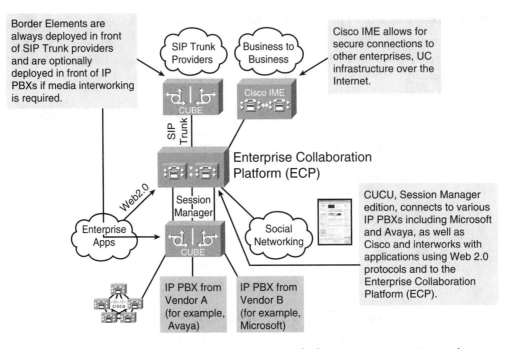

Border Elements are always deployed in front of SIP Trunk providers and are optionally deployed in front of IP PBXs if media interworking is required.

SIP Trunk Providers

Business to Business

Cisco IME allows for secure connections to other enterprises, UC infrastructure over the Internet.

CUBE

Cisco IME

SIP Trunk

Enterprise Collaboration Platform (ECP)

Session Manager

Web2.0

Enterprise Apps

CUBE

Social Networking

CUCU, Session Manager edition, connects to various IP PBXs including Microsoft and Avaya, as well as Cisco and interworks with applications using Web 2.0 protocols and to the Enterprise Collaboration Platform (ECP).

IP PBX from Vendor A (for example, Avaya)

IP PBX from Vendor B (for example, Microsoft)

Figure 5-9 *The Role of Session Management in a Unified Communications Network*

Enterprise Networks—Application Interconnection Session Border Controller

As enterprises grow larger, they typically have more than one UC application that can take advantage of SIP trunks. These applications can in some cases peer directly to one another; however, as the number of applications starts to increase, the number of peered connections also increases dramatically. One method to avoid this is the use of an application interconnection SBC or enterprise session manager (discussed previously) within an enterprise.

This application interconnection SBC has a function similar to a peering SBC in an SP. However, most of the requirements, when deployed in an enterprise, focus on interconnecting the disparate signaling aspects of the various UC applications, and there is less of a concern around security between the applications because all the applications are under the control of the same information technology infrastructure. Generally, an application interconnection SBC connects internal applications such as an Interactive Voice Response (IVR) or voicemail system to the internal call agent that controls endpoints that create media steams.

The roll of an application interconnection SBC is generally being taken over by the enterprise session manager. This is because a session manager can be optimized to deal with only the signaling issues that occur between the different UC components and can provide the additional feature of the ability to invoke supplementary services.

Enterprise Networks—Intercompany Media Engine

A new technology that has recently been developed by Cisco is the Cisco Inter-Company Media Engine (IME). This technology allows for enterprises to connect to each other directly across the Internet with the use of the PSTN or a SP SIP Trunk as a backup connection and the use of the PSTN as a validation method for ensuring the correct routing. This technology takes advantage of new development techniques including peer-to-peer networking and advanced cryptography to ensure that as customers can deploy advanced UC applications within their enterprises, there is an secure and reliable method to extend these applications to other enterprise customers who have deployed similar technology across the Internet. The Cisco IME is shown in Figure 5-9. As of press time, the Cisco IME is still in the early deployment stage.

Summary

The components that make up a SIP trunk solution deployed by SP, enterprise, or SMB customers were outlined. This chapter provided some details of the functions and interconnect behavior of the various components. Some of the differences in the behavior when a component, such as a SBC, is deployed at a SP versus when the same device is used in an enterprise or SMB environment were discussed.

Though all the components are not required for every deployment, when shown together, they illustrate the majority of the required interconnects of a solution.

Figure 5-10 includes all the components described in this chapter for both enterprise and SP networks.

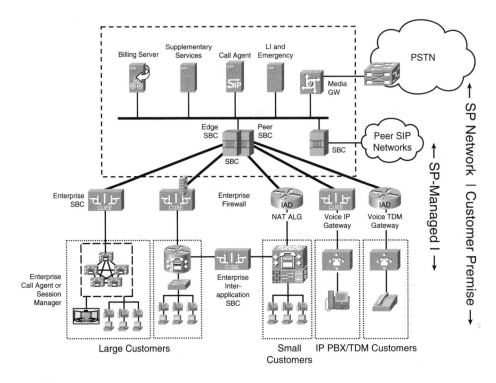

Figure 5-10 *Components of SIP Trunking Solutions*

Chapter 6

SIP Trunking Models

This chapter covers the following topics:

- Understanding the traditional PSTN gateway connection model

- Choosing a SIP trunking model

- Centralized model

- Distributed model

- Hybrid model

- Considering trade-offs with centralized and distributed models

- Understanding the centralized model with direct media model

This chapter explains the network topology alternatives for connecting a Session Initiation Protocol (SIP) trunk from a service provider (SP) into an enterprise network for Public Switched Telephone Network (PSTN) access. The sections of the chapter discuss the different methods of connecting, guide you through choosing which model is the best fit for your network, and describe the implications each model has on your network architecture and implementation. The two fundamental models used for SIP trunking follow

- **Centralized model:** Calls from all sites in the network are routed to a central site through your Internet Protocol (IP) WAN and use a single, shared SIP trunk at a campus or headquarters site.

- **Distributed model:** Calls from each local site to the PSTN use a local SIP trunk at that site.

Several variations of these fundamental models are often a better fit for any particular network. However, it is important first to understand the characteristics of the fundamental models and what these mean to your network before explaining the variations or deciding among them. In the sections following the initial discussion of the fundamental models, we explore the variations in more detail.

Understanding the Traditional PSTN Gateway Connection Model

Before diving into details of SIP trunking, it is instructive to review how traditional Time Division Multiplexing (TDM) PSTN trunking was done and why.

Traditional TDM PSTN access from the enterprise network is accomplished with a voice gateway located at each site connected to the local PSTN central office. The PSTN trunk connectivity can be analog or digital, depending on the size of the site, the number of channels of voice required, and the service available from the local provider. Calls to and from the PSTN are routed through the gateway and converted between TDM and IP by the voice gateway. Figure 6-1 shows a traditional PSTN trunk network connection topology.

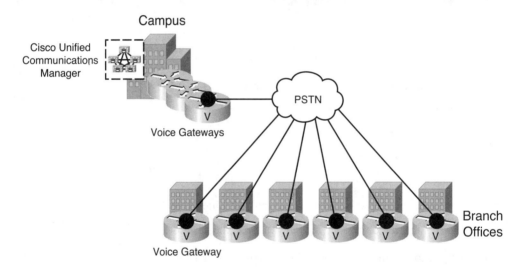

Figure 6-1   *Traditional PSTN Trunk Connectivity*

Salient characteristics of traditional TDM connectivity from an enterprise network to the PSTN include

- Each site has a voice gateway and trunks to the PSTN.

- Local calls are almost always routed using the local site's PSTN voice gateway. Long distance calls might also be routed using this same gateway but are sometimes aggregated and routed via a central PSTN gateway at a campus site.

- Direct Inward Dial (DID) numbers at the site are tied to the physical location of the PSTN delivery into the site and use the local voice gateway.

- Toll-free service or incoming calls to the business's main number (that is, non-DID calls) are often routed to a central voice gateway at a campus location and then to the branch office via the enterprise's IP network.

- Emergency calls from the site are routed using the local PSTN voice gateway to the local authorities.

- Small sites use low-density analog or Basic Rate Interface (BRI) trunks. These often become noncost-effective above 8 channels to 12 channels, at which point digital T1 or E1 connectivity becomes cheaper even if the full 24 or 30 channels are not needed by the site. This situation results in sometimes significant PSTN oversubscription in the network as a whole.

Choosing a SIP Trunking Model

Adding SIP trunk PSTN access to your network might imply changes to both call routing and the placement of SIP trunk access points in the network. SIP trunk calls have fewer geographic dependencies than TDM trunks. When determining where to connect a SIP trunk in your network, consider the following:

- The types of calls carried by the SIP trunk.

- Whether the cost of the service offering is based on a single or multiple physical entry point.

- Whether the service offering provides international call access.

- What organization in your network controls the physical termination of SP traffic into your network.

The following sections describe these considerations in detail. In addition to working through the considerations and designs discussed in this chapter for a single SP, you might want to consider connecting to multiple SPs either for capacity, cost, or redundancy reasons. If you connect to multiple SP SIP trunks, the considerations that follow apply to each one of those in the same manner, and you might even choose different models for each. For example you might select SP X with a centralized model to serve your contact center sites or endpoints, whereas you select SP Y with a hybrid model for your normal business call needs.

Types of Calls Carried by the SIP Trunk

SIP trunk providers often make a distinction between long-distance and local calls. The concept of local calls is becoming nebulous in the current era of SIP trunks where a geographic tie between a phone number and call routing is tenuous at best. If local calls are included in the SIP trunk offering from the provider, are the calls local only to the site where the trunk physically terminates into your network, or also for local calls to geographically distant sites, or a subset of sites in your network? Each geographic region has a different definition of local and long-distance calls, and you should consider these requirements for each site and discuss the definition of these call types with your SIP trunk provider.

Single or Multiple Physical Entry Points

If the provider offers a single physical connection, the best choice might be to place this connection at your head office (campus) or data center. If the offering includes multiple physical entry points (within the cost bounds of the service you are willing to consider implementing), having connectivity from multiple sites might make more sense. This type of offering is frequently the case if the provider already offers your Multiprotocol Label Switching (MPLS) data services to remote sites, and there is already physical connectivity into each of your sites from the provider's network.

International Call Access

If your network spans multiple countries, you might require a different SIP trunk entry point per country, and these entry points might be from different SPs, within each region or country (for example, one in the United States and at least one in Europe). This determination can be important for regulatory requirements, emergency call routing, and network efficiency.

Physical Termination of Traffic into Your Network

If you are a smaller business and have a small integrated information technology (IT) organization, getting voice (SIP trunk) and data access on the same physical connection from the provider might make the most sense.

On the other hand, if your organization is larger and has distinct voice, security, and data IT operations staff, the voice organization might want to control the SIP trunk service whereas the data organization might not want this connection to risk its already existing and secured data infrastructure. This situation might be an argument for bringing in a separate physical connection that carries only the SIP trunk traffic and terminates on dedicated routers and border controllers supervised entirely by the voice team.

Centralized Model

As part of the TDM to IP transformation of PSTN trunking, many customers have a strong desire to consolidate all trunking into a central point in the network to gain operational cost benefits. SIP trunking is seen as a way to achieve this goal because it has few geographic and size (how many channels can be delivered on the provider connection) limitations.

The centralized model of SIP trunking predicates that a single SIP trunk, of the appropriate capacity for all calls to and from all sites in the enterprise, is delivered on a single physical connection. By virtue of serving the entire enterprise, this SIP trunk typically terminates in a large campus or data center site and carries hundreds or thousands of simultaneous channels.

Figure 6-2 depicts the network topology of an enterprise with one campus location and several remote sites with a single, or aggregated, SIP trunk.

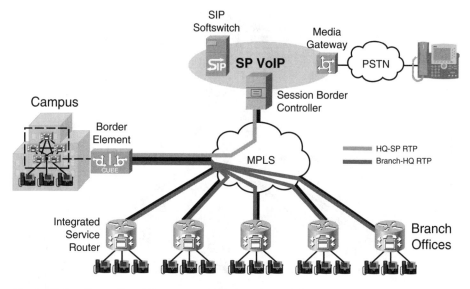

Figure 6-2   *Centralized/Aggregated SIP Trunk Model*

Calls to or from the site that terminates the SIP trunk are routed much as they were for TDM PSTN trunking. Remote offices, however, no longer have any direct PSTN connectivity, and all calls to and from the PSTN from remote offices are now routed (often referred to as *hairpinning*) through the central site to reach the SIP trunk entry point. This is usually a different call routing path from how TDM PSTN calls from the remote sites would have been routed and, therefore, constitutes different volumes of Voice over IP (VoIP) traffic across your enterprise IP network.

The centralized model is also referred to as the aggregated model because it aggregates all calls from all sites and funnels them into a single SP entry point.

Centralized SIP trunking is conceptually simple, and customers often gravitate to this early in their analysis of SIP trunking services. However, it looks better on paper than it does in a real network deployment. The trade-offs and points of analysis are discussed in more detail later in this chapter in the "Considering Trade-Offs with the Centralized and Distributed Models," section that compares the centralized and distributed models.

Distributed Model

The distributed model of SIP trunking predicates that each site has its own SIP trunk termination of the appropriate capacity for calls to and from that site.

Figure 6-3 depicts the network topology of an enterprise with one campus location and several remote sites with a dedicated SIP trunk terminating into each site, a model that constitutes distributed trunking.

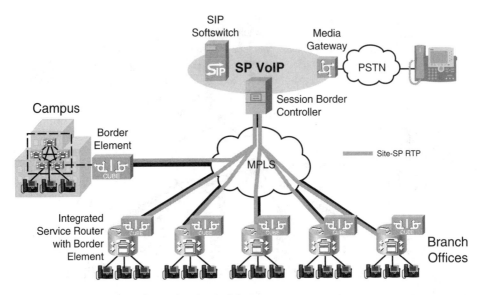

Figure 6-3   *Distributed SIP Trunk Model*

The distributed model is similar to a traditional TDM PSTN trunking model where each site has its own dedicated voice gateway. Because the placement of entry points into the network are the same as for TDM PSTN access, your dial plan and the routing of voice paths on your network typically do not change as you migrate from TDM access to SIP access for PSTN calls. However, your Cisco Unified Communications Manager (CUCM) or IP-PBX might need to be adjusted to do source-based routing (Calling Search Spaces if you use CUCM) in addition to routing calls based on the dialed destination number.

Distributed SIP trunking is often attractive because it means virtually no changes to your network design and bandwidth provisioning as you migrate from TDM to IP trunking. It is essentially a one-to-one upgrade, and you can convert each site, or a group of sites, with little to no effect on the rest of the network or existing dial plan routing. The impact of a SIP trunk outage is also minimal to the network as only calls to and from that site are affected, unlike in the centralized model where a large number of sites in the network are impacted by a single SIP trunk failure.

Hybrid Model

Centralized trunking implies a single SIP trunk for your entire network, regardless of country and continental boundaries and delays of routing remote site voice streams through a potentially geographically distant central site. Distributed trunking implies every site has a SIP trunk, no matter how small. The five-to-ten-person office that makes one call at most in the busy hour hardly warrants a dedicated SIP trunk. The extremes of both the centralized and distributed trunking models are usually impractical for the average medium business or enterprise network.

The hybrid model depicted in Figure 6-4 is a middle ground that accrues most of the benefits of both models.

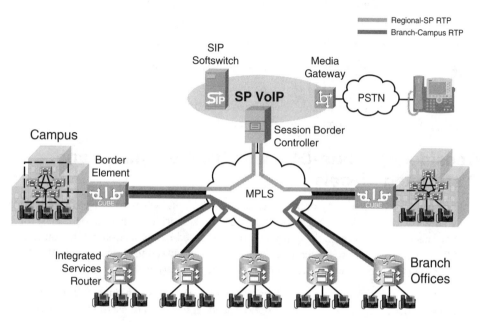

Figure 6-4 *Hybrid SIP Trunk Model*

A number of sites in your network have a SIP trunk termination, but not all do. The desired number of multiple SIP trunk entry points might be small, in which case you would likely connect your major sites, or the largest site within each geographic region.

Smaller sites, in particular geographies or regions, aggregate into a larger site with a SIP trunk in their area. Aggregating the calls from a site implies sufficient IP bandwidth must be available. If a number of remote sites have restricted IP bandwidth, you should consider connecting a SIP trunk into those sites to lower the number of calls and bandwidth crossing your WAN to the head-office site. This determination is similar to the way traditional PSTN connectivity is determined.

The hybrid model provides most of the operational and cost benefits of centralized trunking, while also providing contained latency for sites that do not have a dedicated SIP trunk, and high availability alternatives for all sites.

Which sites in your network warrant a SIP trunk connection is a decision based on one or more of the following considerations:

■ Country and continental boundaries.

■ SP service areas and DID number availability.

- Distance (and therefore latency) of routing remote site calls via an intermediate site, especially for local calls to or from the remote site.

- How many campus or data centers you have and your existing high availability design between these for other enterprise services.

- Cost or tariffing on the SIP trunk services you are considering.

- Whether the SIP trunk provider is also your data network (for example, MPLS) provider.

- To what extent you are able or willing to upgrade your network provisioning and dial-plan routing to accommodate SIP trunking.

Considering Trade-Offs with the Centralized and Distributed Models

You need to consider many points when deciding how and where to bring SIP trunks into your network and whether a predominantly centralized or distributed model is best for your needs. Work through the considerations discussed in this section before you engage SPs for proposals on their offerings. Use the points discussed to formulate questions to your own network design IT team and to evaluate SP offerings for SIP trunks.

SIP trunk service has not reached the maturity of TDM trunk offerings, and the variations in costs, features, connectivity options, and regulations are far from settled. A thorough evaluation of SIP trunk offerings is therefore recommended.

DID Number Portability

There are well-understood rules in TDM PSTN trunking regarding number portability. Do not assume these rules apply to SIP trunking, even if the service is from the same provider. Your existing DID numbers have geographic attributes and are likely owned by several SPs in different geographic areas. The DID numbers owned by the SP that you evaluate for SIP trunk service will most likely port these. However, the DID numbers owned by other providers will most likely not be portable.

This means one of two actions on your part:

- Implement distributed SIP trunking to retain the DID numbers that cannot be ported to a centralized SIP trunk architecture. Or if your business case rests heavily on costs savings resulting from centralized trunking, simply leave these sites with nonportable DID numbers on TDM trunking until a later date.

- Implement centralized SIP trunking and change your DID numbers where they cannot be ported.

DID numbers from different countries can most likely not be ported. For example, if you have several offices in both California and Mexico and consider a single centralized SIP trunk out of one your California offices, it is likely that your Mexico offices' DID numbers will not deliver via that central SIP trunk. You need to put in at least two SIP trunks, one in California and one in Mexico. The other sites within these regions can most likely be aggregated, and numbers might be portable within each region.

Tip   Evaluate what DID numbers you have in different regions and offices and determine which SPs own these today. Further, determine which DID numbers will adversely impact your business if they change and which ones can change without much impact. Armed with this analysis you can more easily evaluate different SIP trunk SPs' answers to DID portability questions.

For example, if you are in the high technology business, your outbound marketing division might be located in a city where SP X serves the DID numbers to the people in this organization. Further, your engineering division might be in a different city in which DID numbers are served by SP Y. If you start investigating SIP trunking, it is important that SP X preserves and ports the DID numbers for your marketing division, but it might be much less important that SP X can port the DID numbers of your engineering division (currently owned by SP Y). Changing the engineering DID numbers might have little impact to your business and be worth the trade-off to get SIP trunk service from SP X for your entire organization.

Regional or Geographic Boundaries

SIP trunks are often touted to have no geographic dependency as it is all IP traffic and therefore can be routed anywhere regardless of geographic boundaries. This is technically true, but nevertheless geographic implications of routing voice calls are independent of TDM or IP traffic.

One implication is that of DID number portability discussed in the previous section. DID numbers can likely not be ported across international boundaries.

Outgoing calls from your enterprise might have similar considerations. For example, consider a German-owned bank with offices in both Germany and France. The campus site with the central SIP trunk is in Germany. When an employee in the branch in a French town calls a local customer in the same town, routing that call via the centralized SIP trunk in Germany makes an international call out of what is essentially a local call. Because of hand-offs between SPs, this is considered an international call and using a centralized SIP trunk for this call path is most likely not cost-effective. If both towns were in the same country, the exact same call path (that is, the distance between the locations) would more likely be cost-effective.

Tip   Evaluate the cost-effectiveness of local calls against your planned SIP trunking model. Ensure that you bring SIP trunks into the optimal number of sites into your network.

Regulatory Considerations

When crossing geographic boundaries, you also need to keep in mind regulatory considerations. Consider again the German bank example given in the previous section. Although the call routing described might not be cost-effective, the call path from a French branch office to a local customer via a German SIP trunk is still possible to do and the call will complete successfully.

There are regions in the world where such a call would constitute an illegal call, violating country regulations regardless of whether you can technically route and complete the call along that path.

When considering aggregated SIP trunking and your business spans country or regional boundaries, ensure that you are familiar with the regulations in the areas where you operate to determine what a legal call path is. Areas of careful evaluation include India and the Middle-Eastern countries but might also be applicable in other parts of the world, or in some cases between regions of the same country.

Tip   Become familiar with regulations that govern which call paths are considered legal. If you prefer not to invest in this analysis, plan to have a largely distributed SIP trunk model where you have a SIP trunk in at least each region where your business operates. If you do not aggregate calls at all—that is, if you implement a fully distributed SIP trunk model—this consideration becomes a nonissue.

Containing Oversubscription

One of the key attractions of a centralized SIP trunk is that you can consolidate the inherent oversubscription many TDM PSTN connections have because the only physical connectivity choice is a T1/E1 trunk even though the site might require, say, only 12 simultaneous calls.

When you consider this benefit to underpin your cost evaluation to justify a central SIP trunk model, ensure that you truly understand your traffic patterns. Today, if that local remote site that ostensibly requires only 12 calls but has a full T1, occasionally bursts to 20 calls, there is no impact on your network and no customers or employees complain. However, if you provision a central SIP trunk for only 12 calls and the 13th call of the burst is rejected because of Call Admission Control (CAC) on the SIP trunk, those employees are now impacted and will either complain or fail to conduct the business they have to complete.

Containing oversubscription also does not necessarily imply that you have to choose centralized SIP trunking. Because SIP trunks are IP-based, you can have a SIP trunk in each branch office, but it does not have to be equivalent to the T1/E1 trunk currently there. If a remote office requires only 12 calls, get a SIP trunk with 12 calls into that office. How cost-effective this is again depends on what granularity of service you can get from your provider.

Tip TDM PSTN trunk oversubscription can be solved by SIP trunking in multiple ways, and both the centralized or distributed trunking models can provide this benefit.

Quality of Service (QoS) Considerations

Following are two considerations related to voice quality or QoS:

- **Bandwidth provisioning:** How is the WAN bandwidth provisioned for each site impacted by the SIP trunk model?

- **Latency:** How is the delay or latency of calls impacted by the SIP trunk model and call paths through the network?

The following sections describe both considerations in greater detail.

Bandwidth Provisioning

Another bandwidth-related consideration is the call path VoIP calls take on your network after you implement SIP trunking. A call from a remote office to another site with a central SIP trunk impacts the bandwidth provisioning and QoS queue settings for both sites. First, the PSTN off-net call from the remote site now traverses your WAN where it did not for TDM PSTN trunking, so the remote office's WAN connection requires more bandwidth than before. Second, the remote site's PSTN call traverses the WAN connection of the central site with the SIP trunk twice: first, on the VoIP connection from the remote site to the central site, and second, from the central site to the SP. The physical connection for both legs of the call is most likely the same pipe so that doubles the bandwidth required for all calls hairpinning from a remote site to a central SIP trunk.

The distributed SIP trunking model follows the same call paths as the TDM trunking model and therefore does not put any extra VoIP calls onto the WAN backbone.

Tip If you are considering centralized or aggregated SIP trunking, the bandwidth provisioning of all sites in your network must to be reviewed and likely changed.

Latency Implications

In the distributed model, the call path is direct between the remote site and the SP, and latency is similar to what it was for TDM trunking. For centralized or aggregated trunking, the call path from a remote site hairpins through a central site that can be geographically distant. When evaluating aggregated SIP trunking, be sure to consider the increased latency imposed on calls from remote sites and whether the resulting voice quality would be sufficient for your business needs.

> **Tip**   If you are considering centralized or aggregated SIP trunking, the increase in latency of calls from all sites that do not have direct SIP trunk access needs to be reviewed.

Operational and Equipment Implications

A single, central SIP trunk is often attractive because that means equipment to terminate the trunk is required in one (or perhaps two for redundancy) site. The capital costs and management aspects of a gateway at each site goes away and is consolidated to a single or small number of sites in the network.

However, each remote site still requires a router and a WAN connection, and it probably already has a PSTN voice gateway. That same Cisco router that is already present in the site and is the data router or the voice gateway, or both, can be upgraded to be your SIP trunk terminating Border Element (that is, add Session Border Controller [SBC] capabilities to the router). So new equipment might not be necessary; you might simply need a software upgrade and configuration change to the equipment you already have and already know how to manage.

> **Tip**   Equipment can be consolidated by using a centralized trunk model. However, if a distributed model fits your network better, this might not necessarily mean more equipment. Cisco routing equipment already present in your remote sites can be upgraded to do SIP trunking.

Cost

In most parts of the world, TDM PSTN trunking is a regulated service in which the costs for installation and recurring monthly costs are well understood or regulated or both. SIP trunking on the other hand is an unregulated service, and these costs can vary widely between providers and geographic regions.

Although per-minute call costs might perhaps be cheaper on SIP trunks, you must look at all the costs associated with validating, installing, and running the trunks in production compared to TDM trunking. SIP trunking is not as mature as TDM trunking, and feature operation and features offered on different SIP trunk services vary. This requires you to run through a fairly extensive test and verification procedure and trials before installing a SIP trunk for your production voice calls.

> **Tip**   Evaluate all costs related to SIP trunking, not just per-minute call rates. Factor in a validation test cycle before running SIP trunks in production.

High Availability

A distributed SIP trunk design provides inherent high availability and redundancy because every site has its own access and can use one of numerous neighboring sites' access if its own is unavailable. Additionally, each site's SIP trunk carries only a small volume of traffic; if you lose one of these SIP trunks, the impact on your business is relatively contained.

A centralized SIP trunk design introduces a number of availability considerations. Because many remote sites' traffic is aggregated onto a single physical connection, there can be a considerable business impact if the SIP trunk becomes unavailable. A central SIP trunk is also often sized for hundreds or thousands of simultaneous connections, making the loss of this number of calls at once a severe impact to ongoing business in your network.

If a TDM trunk went down, it was usually a T1's or E1's worth of lost calls while neighboring T1/E1 connections continued to operate. If a 2000-session SIP trunk goes down though, it takes the equivalent of 84 T1s or 67 E1s down. It is therefore imperative to design redundancy and availability measures into SIP trunk access, especially for centralized or aggregated designs. The failover call routing mechanism also affects your SP because DID calls must be deflected to a different geographical site's SIP trunk entry point when the primary SIP trunk access is unavailable.

Cisco Survivable Remote Site Telephony (SRST) is widely used for branch office IP phone survivability and continues to play this role in networks using SIP trunks for PSTN access. If the SIP trunk is centralized and therefore out of reach during failover (because it enters the network at a site distant from the SRST site), SRST alone cannot provide PSTN call routing for the site isolated by the network or device failure. For continued PSTN access, the SRST site either requires backup TDM trunks, legal sanctioning of using employees' mobile phones for PSTN access during failover, or a distributed SIP trunk directly to the site. Mobile phone fallback might or might not be a legal form of providing business emergency call access depending on the geography where the site operates—check your local regulations for more information on this situation. High availability SIP trunk network design techniques are discussed in more detail in the next chapter.

Tip   Design a SIP trunk with high availability along with the SP that you select for SIP trunk service. The more simultaneous channels a SIP trunk carries, the more imperative it becomes that you have solid failover alternatives.

Emergency Call Routing

Most Tier 1 SIP trunk providers also provide emergency call routing, but you should investigate if this service is available, and if so, how it operates for calls from each site.

One alternative is to leave emergency call routing on the TDM PSTN trunks that are already in each branch office and to use SIP trunking initially only for nonemergency calls until SIP trunk offerings become more mature and all offer comparable basic services.

If you decide to route emergency calls over your SIP trunk to the provider, the distributed model best accomplishes this. Calls from the site enter the PSTN locally, and routing to the local authorities is not a challenge. Also, in a distributed trunking model, the Border Element is collocated at the site that originated the emergency call, and location information is intrinsically correct when delivered to the provider, and in turn by the provider to the authorities.

In the centralized SIP trunking model, ensuring correct location information is more challenging. If an emergency call originates from a remote site in the state of Utah, but enters the PSTN through a centralized SIP trunk in New York, the SP has two challenges:

- The call must be routed to the correct authorities in Utah, which might be under different regulations and jurisdictions than New York.

- The location information available to the SP is that of your Border Element in New York where the call was delivered to the provider's network. How can the information that this is actually a call from Utah be available to the SP?

Tip   Carefully consider emergency call routing and location information delivery for SIP trunks, especially in the centralized model. Discuss emergency call routing with your SP, and if the answer is unsatisfactory, keep emergency calls on TDM trunks for the time being.

Dial Plan and Call Routing Considerations

If you choose the distributed model, your dial plan and call routing implementation most likely needs to change much less than for centralized trunking to accommodate the migration from TDM PSTN to SIP PSTN access. Although it could change if you decide, perhaps based on cost benefits, to route only certain types of calls (for example, long distance calls or contact center calls) or calls to and from only certain sites over the SIP trunk.

Different business drivers motivate SIP trunk use for different types of calls, and there isn't a single answer about which calls you should use your SIP trunk for first. The typical possibilities for evaluation include the following list, and you can choose one or several of these for your implementation:

- Contact center calls (inbound, outbound, or both).

- Normal business calls but only for specific locations (for example, initially perhaps only for your campus sites and later for remote sites). Or perhaps cost benefits are accrued only if you use it for all sites.

- Call direction, for example, all inbound calls use the SIP trunk but not outbound calls. Or perhaps all incoming and outgoing calls from the campus site but only inbound calls for remote sites.

- Call type, for example, long-distance calls use the SIP trunk, but local calls remain on TDM trunks. Or perhaps all normal business calls from all sites use the SIP trunk, but fax and emergency calls remain on TDM trunks until a later phase of rollout.

Tip   Whichever call patterns you decide to use your SIP trunk for are likely to precipitate both call routing and dial-plan adjustments that affect both your network and your call agent configurations. Consider these carefully and coordinate these changes, or phases of changes, with installing a SIP trunk to various sites in your network.

IP Addressing

Centralized SIP trunking typically uses two publicly routable enterprise IP addresses to which the SP's session border controller points. Sometimes up to ten IP addresses can be available for a single logical SIP trunk. Few providers today use Domain Name System (DNS) for IP address resolution and redundancy or alternative destinations. If your SIP trunk provider is also your MPLS data network provider, the SIP trunk address space is more flexible and likely falls within your already allocated MPLS site address space.

A distributed SIP trunking model is often most beneficial if your existing MPLS data provider offers this. In this case an IP address per remote site and security considerations are not hurdles to the installation of a multiple SIP trunks, and you can easily derive the many benefits of distributed trunking.

If your SIP trunk is not from your data provider, there might be more incentive to do centralized trunking. For example, if the offering comes with only two IP addresses, you can at most connect two sites to this offering. In this case, the two IP addresses are almost invariably used for redundancy purposes (as opposed to it representing two separate logical SIP trunk offerings), and both IP terminations could come into the same site of your network or could go to two different sites. It often makes sense to connect these to two different data centers or campus sites geographically separate from each other for maximum disaster recovery benefits. Some SPs use these two IP addresses in a strict primary/secondary arrangement; others offer load balancing over both.

Tip   Discuss IP addressing of the SIP trunk offering with your provider because this scheme varies among the offerings, has design implications on your network, and can affect redundancy and failover design options.

Understanding the Centralized Model with Direct Media Model

Another variation to centralized and distributed SIP trunking worthy of discussion is a model where the signaling follows a centralized design, but the media flows directly from the remote sites to the SP network. This is often referred to as the direct media model and is illustrated in Figure 6-5.

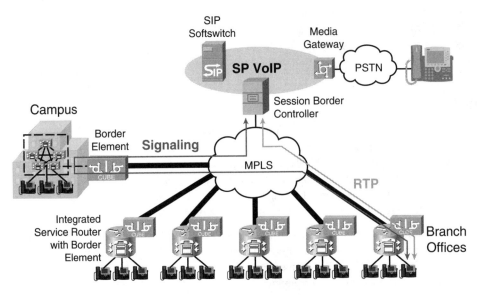

Figure 6-5   *Aggregated Signaling, Direct Media Model*

This model provides many of the benefits of the centralized model in the sense that dial-plan management, call routing decisions, and SIP trunk management (such as CAC) is done and viewed centrally. Yet it offers the media path and bandwidth optimization of the distributed model.

Deploying this model in your network requires the following additional considerations:

■   A Border Element is required in each site because the central signaling Border Element cannot provide media stream functions such as topology hiding and transcoding if it does not manage the media.

■   The signaling Border Element can communicate with the media Border Element via a media resource control protocol such as H.248 or similar protocol.

The direct media model has the following advantages:

■   The media path is optimized.

■   Signaling is centralized for optimal control and management.

The direct media model has the following challenges:

■   Remote sites using SRST for phone backup might not use the local media border element for SIP trunk access without having the signaling border element in contact.

■   Presents the same DID number porting and other challenges characteristic of the centralized trunking model.

Summary

SIP trunks are becoming an increasingly viable option for small businesses and larger enterprises wanting to deploy new IP-based services to their users when communicating with customers and vendors external to the enterprise network.

This chapter discussed the different architectural models for SIP trunking that can be deployed between the enterprise and the SP networks and the network changes this might precipitate on the design of your network. The considerations and trade-offs when choosing the most appropriate model for your business were explored in depth. The characteristics of the centralized and distributed SIP trunking models were discussed in detail, and a few practical variations of these were touched on. The questions you should ask of your IT team and of your SP to determine the most beneficial deployment should now be clear.

Starting with the next chapter, the network design of connecting SIP trunks into the enterprise are explored in considerably more detail.

For quick reference, the main points discussed in this chapter regarding the centralized, distributed, and hybrid SIP trunks models are summarized in the following sections.

Centralized SIP trunking has the following implementation characteristics:

■   A Border Element placed at a central location.

■   A single SIP trunk IP address to SP.

■   All remote site calls hairpin through the campus site where SIP trunk terminates.

The centralized model has the following advantages:

■   Operational and management savings

■   Equipment savings due to less equipment needed in fewer sites

■   Central call routing and dial-plan management

■   Simplified provisioning of PSTN access

■   Consolidation of oversubscription

■   Potential per-minute call rate savings because of a larger volume of calls from a single point

The centralized model has the following challenges:

- Bandwidth, QoS, and CAC concerns as RTP for remote site to PSTN calls traverse WAN twice.

- Nonoptimal media routing.

- Number porting of DID numbers to the aggregated SIP trunks.

- High availability in the campus (single point of failure).

- Survivability (backup branch call routing).

- Correct routing of calls to emergency services; emergency calls might need to continue to use TDM trunks.

- Legal, regulatory, and geographical considerations.

- Failover must be provided at each site with SRST and TDM PSTN ports.

Distributed SIP trunking has the following implementation characteristics:

- A Border Element placed at each site.

- A SIP trunk IP address per site to SP.

- Calls flow directly from the remote site to the SP.

The distributed model has the following advantages:

- The call media path is optimized.

- DID numbers remain local to the area where they were issued and do not have to be ported.

- The remote site Border Element can also act as the local MTP and the SRST router; the same router can also maintain TDM PSTN trunks if required.

- Emergency call location information is tied to the local site (Border Element) and is hence more accurate.

- A one-to-one mapping between TDM PSTN interfaces and SIP trunks simplifies the migration.

- CAC is handled the same way as for TDM PSTN trunking.

- High availability is inherent as the SIP trunk remains active during SRST failover, and each site has its own trunk making the sites independent of each other for PSTN call routing.

- Bandwidth requirements between branch sites and the campus sites do not change.

The distributed model has the following challenges:

- Manageability of a SIP trunk at each site.

■ Multiple SP SIP trunks entering different sites in the network—there may be feature or call operation differences between the SIP trunks; each provider's offering must be validated individually.

■ No equipment consolidation.

Hybrid SIP trunking has the following implementation characteristics:

■ A Border Element at each regional location.

■ A SIP Trunk IP address per regional site to the SP.

■ Remote site calls hairpin through the regional site where SIP trunk terminates.

The hybrid model has the following advantages:

■ All the advantages of the centralized model for sites with a SIP trunk; all the advantages of the distributed model for sites not directly connected.

■ More redundancy and disaster recovery options compared to centralized model.

■ Easier DID migration than the fully centralized option.

■ Flexibility to route calls through various trunk options.

The hybrid model has the following challenges:

■ All the challenges of the centralized model for sites with a SIP trunk.

■ The challenges of the distributed model for sites not directly connected.

Chapter 7

Design and Implementation Considerations

This chapter covers the following topics:

- Geographic and regulatory considerations

- IP connectivity options

- Dial plans and call routing

- Supplementary services

- Network demarcation

- Security considerations

- Session management, call traffic capacity, bandwidth control, and QoS

- Scalability and high availability

- SIP trunk monitoring

This chapter focuses on network design and implementation considerations after a decision has been reached to connect to a service provider via Session Initiation Protocol (SIP) trunking and the choice has been made regarding the appropriate network model (centralized, distributed, or hybrid) as discussed in Chapter 6, "SIP Trunking Models."

Considerations about the network design and implementation of SIP trunking include

- Geographic and regulatory considerations

- Internet Protocol (IP) connectivity options

- Dial plans and call routing

- Supplementary services

- Network demarcation

- Security considerations

- Session management, call traffic capacity, bandwidth control, and Quality of Service (QoS)

- Scalability and high availability

- SIP trunk monitoring

Another key area of consideration includes interworking and interoperability, which is discussed further in Chapter 8, "Interworking."

Sample configurations of specific implementation examples to select service providers in the market are provided in Chapter 10, "Deployment Scenarios."

Geographic and Regulatory Considerations

If your network spans multiple geographic boundaries, continents, or countries, keep in mind both regulatory and distance considerations:

- **Regulatory:** Not all countries regard Voice over IP (VoIP) calls in the same way, and although virtually no country regulates what can be deployed inside an enterprise network, several countries regulate to varying degrees what calls can be handed off between an enterprise and a public (service provider) network. Ensure that you become familiar with country-specific regulations when deploying SIP trunking, especially if the endpoint (the site where the call originates) and the SIP trunk (where the call enters a public network) are in different regulatory jurisdictions.

- **Distance:** A second consideration is sheer distance, with the hairpinned media paths resulting from the centralized SIP trunk model discussed in the Chapter 6. If the remote office originating the call is in California and the central SIP trunk is in New York whereas the PSTN destination of the call is again in California, the media path for this call traverses the North American continent twice, adding latency to the end-to-end call.

  Adding latency to signaling paths is much less of a concern (it might add marginally to post-dial delay but does not impact voice quality on the active call), but latency of the media path directly affects voice quality and should be taken into consideration when designing and connecting a SIP trunk into an enterprise network.

IP Connectivity Options

Several different types of service providers offer SIP trunks. Enterprises can find offers from service providers to transport just their data services or just their voice services, or both. When the data and voice services are delivered by different providers, each traffic type is typically delivered over a separate physical medium. Also, when the SIP trunk carries high traffic, for example 1000 sessions or more, a separate physical medium for the SIP trunk is often used.

Consider two aspects of IP connectivity when connecting to a SIP trunk:

- Physical medium of delivery
- IP addressing

Physical Delivery and Connectivity

A dedicated physical connection for a SIP trunk is not uncommon for larger enterprises. The physical delivery for these types of terminations is often optical fiber (OC-3 or higher) and through a series of multiplexing, switching, and routing equipment eventually terminates as a gigabit Ethernet connection onto the enterprise's Session Border Controller (SBC). This connection model is shown in the left panel of Figure 7-1.

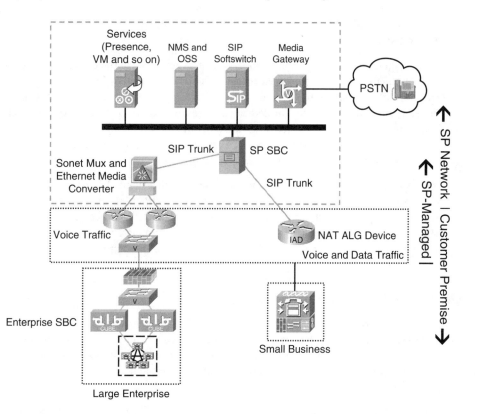

Figure 7-1   *Physical Delivery of a SIP Trunk*

For smaller businesses this dedicated delivery model is not cost-effective and these organizations predominantly get their voice and data services from the same provider over the same physical connection. The connection in this case might be Digital Subscriber Loop (DSL), cable, Integrated Service Digital Network (ISDN), T1/E1, 3G wireless, or any other medium capable of carrying QoS-enabled IP traffic. This connection might connect directly to the customer's routing equipment, or the provider might drop off a Customer Premise Equipment (CPE) access device (for example, a DSL, cable modem, or a low-end router), which connects with Ethernet to the customer's routing or switching equipment. This connection model is shown in the "Small Business" model in Figure 7-1 using an Integrated Access Device (IAD).

It is important to note that only service providers that have complete control over the QoS of the physical connection can offer business-class voice services over a SIP trunk. VoIP services that ride on non-QoS enabled networks owned by a separate Internet provider cannot provide guarantees of quality levels because they do not control the sequencing of packets on the physical medium of delivery into your premises.

Physical connection options include Ethernet, DSL, cable, wireless (3G cellular), and traditional T1/E1.

IP Addressing

The configuration of a SIP trunk requires coordination between the enterprise to configure its border element and the service provider's border element before starting to exchange SIP traffic. The provider allocates either explicit IP addresses or access via Domain Name System (DNS). For dedicated voice-only connections, most providers allocate two addresses per SIP trunk, whereas some offer more. If only two addresses are provided, these can often be used (per agreement with the service provider) in either a primary-secondary failover or a load-balancing algorithm.

For integrated data and SIP trunk services, there is often a single IP address. Several service providers that offer both data and voice over a single IP interface also offer Multiprotocol Label Switching (MPLS) services and require that voice be sent with an MPLS label. This setup enables the service provider to terminate voice traffic, whereas data traffic marked with a different label can be tunneled through the network.

Dial Plans and Call Routing

Adding a SIP trunk service to your network most likely means there are service changes (accessible numbers and their associated cost), and you should optimize call routing in your network for the most cost-efficient calling patterns. This optimization, in turn, can affect current call admission control (CAC) and bandwidth-allocation policies implemented in your network.

Some specific items that might affect your dial-plan and call-routing configuration include

- If you currently have a separate dedicated Time Division Multiplexing (TDM) Public Switched Telephone Network (PSTN) voice gateway per Cisco Unified Communications Manager (CUCM) cluster or IP Private Branch Exchange (PBX), then you have a single enterprisewide SIP trunk shared between them.

- If the SIP trunk offers only long-distance (or certain types of inter-regional) calls, then your TDM PSTN gateways offers both local and long-distance calls.

- Whether the SIP trunk is going to be used by all the users in your network (all sites) or only by users colocated at the site where the SIP trunk terminates.

- Whether routing of emergency or fax, modem, Point of Service (POS), or Telecommunications Device for the Deaf (TDD) calls need to be rethought because they might not initially make use of the SIP trunk service.

Certain service providers require that a "+" be added to the front of a phone number sent on a SIP trunk. Specifically, the From field in a SIP message must be valid, as in From: +14085551212. When interconnecting through CUCM, this configuration can be accomplished by using translation rules on a Cisco Unified Border Element (CUBE) between CUCM and the SIP trunk service provider.

Certain SIP trunk providers require users to complete a registration before they can use the service. This security practice is a good one for service providers to ensure that calls originate from only well-known endpoints. CUCM does not natively support registration on SIP trunks, but this support can also be accomplished by using a CUBE. The CUBE registers to the service provider with the phone numbers of the enterprise on behalf of CUCM.

Two additional considerations regarding call routing include

- Direct Inward Dial (DID) number reachability

- Emergency call routing

Porting Phone Numbers to SIP Trunks

When an enterprise starts using a SIP trunk for *incoming* calls, the phone number must be ported to this service. When external end users call the number, rather than ringing at the traditional TDM gateway owned by the enterprise, it rings in the service provider's core network, and the call is routed to the enterprise with the SIP trunk.

Because of the complexity of porting phone numbers, most SIP deployments find it easier to start services with *outbound* calls or with *inbound* contact center toll-free service calls (non-DID). It is important for the enterprise to understand the timelines and transition plans offered by the service provider for porting DID numbers. Enterprises' business users cannot afford to be unreachable on their primary PSTN phone numbers while this porting activity occurs.

Emergency Calls

Emergency calling is an important consideration to account for when integrating SIP trunk access into the enterprise. Traditionally emergency calling is based on the emergency responder knowing the physical location of the TDM connection from which the call is coming. With a SIP trunk, that relationship between the physical location and the calling number no longer exists.

Options for handling emergency calling include

- Continuing to route emergency calls through your TDM PSTN gateways

- Having a small number of TDM trunks dedicated to this function at the physical location of the service provider

- Adopting a SIP-based emergency calling solution

All SIP trunk providers should provide clear explanations of their solution for providing emergency calling when an IP connection is evaluated. Some aspects to emergency calling have not been solved technologically or with the currently offered services. In the United States, the Federal Communications Commission (FCC) continues to work with the industry to define E911 operation, and a geolocation SIP header is in an Internet Engineering Task Force (IETF) draft status.

Investigate these issues in all countries and areas of the world where your network is considering a SIP trunk for PSTN access because the capabilities and regulations vary significantly.

Supplementary Services

Cisco Unified Communications deployments offer a rich set of supplementary services. With the use of SIP trunks, how these services operate might change, and you need to evaluate how they can be maintained when a SIP trunk brings external calls into your enterprise.

Following are different areas of supplementary services to evaluate:

- Voice calls

- Voice mail

- Transcoding

- Mobility

Voice Calls

Telephony features such as call hold/resume, call transfer, call waiting, three-way conferencing, distinctive alerting, calling line identification (CLID), calling name, and call toggle can be provided by CUCM Express and CUCM for IP phones and by a voice gateway for analog phones. IP Centrex or Class 5 type features (for example, call forwarding, call screening, call park, call return, and so on) can be provided by central SIP servers resident in the service provider's network. An analog phone in the enterprise can trigger these features with access codes (typically starting with an asterisk) provided by the service provider. Cisco Unified Voice Gateways send the access codes in the SIP INVITE message over the SIP trunk to the service provider to trigger these features.

Voice Mail

You can provide voice mail within the enterprise network in a distributed design using Cisco Unity Express or with a centralized design using Cisco Unity or Cisco Unity Connection. You can also choose to get voice mail services from the service provider using a hosted solution (a cloud-based service).

Message Waiting Indicator (MWI) is a visual light on IP phones; it is indicated by a stutter dial tone on analog phones. MWI for enterprise-provided voice mail systems is not impacted by SIP trunking, but if a service provider hosted solution is chosen, MWI indications are provided via SIP indications (as per RFC-3842) from the service provider system and are relayed to the enterprise endpoints. Be sure to test these scenarios for SIP trunking if this is your deployment model.

Dual-tone multi-frequency (DTMF) interworking is often needed for voice mail as well. Even if all the communicating systems use SIP, there are various ways of relaying DTMF in SIP. DTMF interworking is discussed in more detail in Chapter 9, "Questions to Ask of a Service Provider Offering and an SBC Vendor."

Transcoding

When offnet access was provided by TDM access to the PSTN, codec choices were entirely within the control of the enterprise. Codecs were configured on IP endpoints, enterprise applications, and TDM PSTN gateways. Codec choices did not affect offnet calls in any way.

With SIP trunking entering your network, this is no longer the case. Codec choices are now end-to-end on the IP segments and enterprise endpoint negotiated codecs with external endpoints and application controlled by other networks. Codecs offered by external endpoint might be against the bandwidth (call admission control) policies of your enterprise network, or your older endpoints might be incapable of supporting some of the newer codec choices, resulting in failed calls or inappropriate bandwidth use on your network.

Sometimes SIP trunking is a cost-effective choice only when G.729 is the codec chosen (for bandwidth delivery reasons), especially for high volume contact centers operations.

For all these reasons, it might be necessary to do transcoding at the border of your enterprise network to change the codec to the appropriate one before these calls enter your network. Local Digital Signal Processing (DSP) can provide transcoding for a call that uses a high-bandwidth codec such as G.711 on one side and a low-bandwidth codec such as G.729 or Internet Low-Bitrate Codec (iLBC) on the other side. Transcoding is discussed in more detail in Chapter 9.

Mobility

Mobility of users in the enterprise is often aided by various call forwarding features. Calls between internal numbers can end up being forwarded externally due to a call forwarding mobility feature.

Another call flow to consider is an external call that arrived via the SIP trunk into your enterprise, which, in turn, is forwarded from the internal endpoint to a second external destination via the same site's SIP trunk, or if you have distributed SIP trunking deployed, perhaps a different site's SIP trunk. This call flow consumes the bandwidth equivalent to two individual calls.

Single-number reach call flows, where a single phone number is set up to ring a user's desk phone and an alternate mobile device such as a cell phone (which is often physically resident on an external network), should also be considered and tested. These call types have unique requirements for transfer, forwarding, voice mail.

Network Demarcation

Demarcation has to do with defining and protecting the borders between networks owned or managed by different entities while maintaining interconnectivity and interoperation of traffic and features between the two networks.

TDM PSTN gateways offered an implicit enterprise network demarcation point. Until recently VoIP has been deployed only in private enterprise and small business networks for on-net calls—calls that remain within the organization's own network. Off-net calls that went from the enterprise to (or from) the PSTN were converted between IP and TDM at the PSTN interconnect point (even though many service provider backbone networks have also been VoIP for many years).

With SIP trunking the provider-to-enterprise interconnect is now also migrating to using VoIP technology. This means you no longer need TDM PSTN gateways, but it also means you lose all the demarcation features TDM gateways implicitly provided to your network. These demarcation features include

- Compliance with service provider's User-to-Network Interface (UNI)
- Codec choice
- Fault isolation
- Statistics and voice quality reporting
- Billing and call accounting
- QoS marking
- Topology hiding (security)

These demarcation features are critical to the maintenance, security, and management of your network. An SBC, such as the CUBE, can be placed at the edge of your network to terminate the SIP trunk entry point and fulfill the needed demarcation role in an all-IP network connection. For smaller businesses CUCM Express might be deployed, which includes SIP trunk capability and border element demarcation features.

All the areas of demarcation are discussed in the remainder of this section, except topology hiding, which is further discussed in the "Security Consideration" section in this chapter.

Service Provider UNI Compliance

SIP trunk service providers offer an explicit UNI specification of what message types, formats, and fields are valid on their service offering. For the enterprise to comply with this UNI, it is often easier to place a border element at the edge of the network to *normalize* all the variants from different enterprise applications and endpoints than to try to configure each individual application or endpoint to comply with the UNI. It is especially true if the enterprise connects to multiple different SIP trunk providers, per-haps for least-cost routing or for redundancy purposes.

For the service provider, it is often easier to drop off a validated border element CPE device to ensure that the enterprise or small business network complies with its UNI—rather than certify each possible vendor and release combination of the possible applications and endpoints, the enterprise or small business might want to connect to their service.

Different deployment scenarios result from this need for network demarcation. Often enterprises want to manage their own border element so that they can control the config-uration of this device and adjust it for new applications, application upgrades, or call flows. Alternatively, the service provider might provide a border element as a CPE device as part of the SIP trunk service to ensure UNI compliance regardless of the enterprise equipment. In some cases, especially for larger enterprises, both exist, and there is a pair of border elements at the enterprise edge, one side owned by the service provider (CPE), the other by the enterprise. This is separate from the SBC that always exists at the service provider edge and is a shared device among many SIP trunk customers.

The SIPConnect forum has been established by a consortium of members as an industry organization to focus on specifying and defining the SP UNI as a standard to ease some of interconnecting and interoperability issues currently still experienced.

Codec Choice

Codec choice was briefly discussed previously in this chapter in the "Transcoding" sec-tion. Transcoding is one of the demarcation features you might want to deploy in your network to normalize codec use at the border of your network to the choices you have engineered your network for, independent of the codec choices on the SIP trunk or those chosen by the offnet destination of the call. Newer wideband codecs, such as G.722, can be used in your network but might not yet be available on SIP trunks services. The choice of SIP delayed offer or early offer also has some influence over what codecs can be chosen for any particular call.

To control the use of codecs on your network to comply either with bandwidth engineering (call admission control) or with other enterprise policies, you have the following choices:

■ Allow calls with inappropriate or incompatible codecs to fail.

■ Involve a transcoder to resolve calls with incompatible codecs and to change incoming codecs to those you prefer to use on your network.

■ Configure features to control codec negotiation and filtering in SIP call setups as the call passes through the border element.

Fault Isolation

In traditional TDM PSTN access, the PSTN gateway terminated the TDM connection from the provider's network and originated a VoIP connection inside your enterprise network. If voice quality or connectivity problems existed, this demarcation point was an easy place to conduct testing and isolate whether the problem existed within your enterprise network or whether it was the service provider's problem. TDM loop testing is common, enabling the service provider to test the TDM loop to the edge of your network to determine if the problem exists on that part of the connection.

Bringing a SIP trunk into the enterprise removes this demarcation point and, therefore, also the problem isolation techniques that existed for TDM interconnection. If voice-quality problems occur, it can be difficult to isolate whether they are caused by something in the service provider's network or by an element in your enterprise network.

Using a CUBE as an IP demarcation point restores this troubleshooting capability, enabling testing within the enterprise network up to the CUBE and testing from the service provider's side to the CUBE to determine where a fault might exist. The IP *loop* can be tested in the same conceptual manner (RTP loopback capability and Service Assurance Agent [SAA] responder support) as the TDM loop to allow the service provider to determine if the service is causing a problem or whether the problem exists in the enterprise.

Statistics

Metrics, such as delay, jitter, and voice quality scoring, help enterprises and providers monitor and control the voice quality on their networks. These metrics can typically be derived only at the endpoint (DSP) of a VoIP call and not in the middle of it. (No DSP is involved in the middle of the call.) For calls on SIP trunks, it is necessary to calculate, or estimate, some of these metrics at the border element to reflect the quality of the call on the enterprise side of the network, separate from the metrics of the call leg on the service provider side of the network.

You can use different features to derive a reading of the metrics at the network border. One is to use transcoding on the CUBE, which terminates the VoIP call leg on a DSP and re-originates it on the other side—because a DSP termination is involved, actual statistics on both call legs are available from the DSP.

Another method is snooping on the Real-Time Control Protocol (RTCP) statistics as they travel through the border and to report on some of these statistics. However, many VoIP endpoints do not support RTCP.

The IP Service Level Agreement (IP SLA) Real-Time Transport Protocol (RTP)-based VoIP operation feature provides another method to provide statistics. This Cisco IOS feature uses test calls to a DSP to determine values for voice quality metrics over different network segments. The CUBE can be either the originator or the destination of the IP SLA probes to provide readings for voice quality statistics up to your network border.

There is also the Cisco IOS Voice Performance Statistics on Cisco Gateways feature (using the command **voice csr statistics**) that collects call statistics such as active calls, failed calls, packet loss, latency, and jitter.

Billing

Typically, service providers bill without any information from the enterprise. Call detail records (CDR) from the CUBE can provide a consolidated aggregate view of calls sent and received on the SIP trunk and can be used to validate the service provider's billing.

Drawing billing records from your border element also provides a consolidated view of SIP trunk traffic use if you share a SIP trunk among multiple CUCM clusters or IP-PBXs.

Cisco IOS Software CDRs contain calling and called numbers, local and remote node names, data and time stamp, elapsed time, call failure class fields, and some vendor-specific attribute (VSA) fields. Each call through the CUBE is considered to have two call legs. Start and Stop records are generated for each call leg. These records can be sent to a RADIUS server or retrieved with Simple Network Management Protocol (SNMP) polling using the dial-control Management Information Base (MIB).

QoS Marking

TDM voice gateways originated IP packets and, therefore, could control the QoS markings on both the signaling and media VoIP packets entering your network for calls from the PSTN. With an end-to-end VoIP call over a SIP trunk, it's quite possible that the service provider preferred QoS markings are different from the ones you prefer, and, therefore, packets have to be remarked in both directions as the packets cross the border.

The CUBE is a back-to-back user agent and, therefore, has full control over packet marking in both directions and can be set either globally or based on destination. For example, if you have two SIP trunks to different providers and their choices of marking is different from each other and from your choice in the enterprise, the border element can remark these packets on a per-flow basis.

VoIP endpoints and call agents such as CUCM and CUCMExpress also have facilities to control and mark packets. These can be used directly if the enterprise markings are the same as the SP UNI markings, and an SBC can be used if markings need to be translated between the enterprise and the SP networks.

Security Considerations

The security concerns of TDM trunking, primarily toll fraud, exist equally on SIP trunking. In addition, SIP trunking exposes your network to IP level threats similar to data WAN or Internet access, such as denial of service (DOS).

For a hacker to gain access to your enterprise IP network via a TDM voice trunk is virtually impossible to do unless the TDM connection is specifically configured for modem dial-up access—and most voice trunks are not. Perpetrating a DOS attack on a TDM trunk is also highly unlikely as it is both expensive to do and requires large-scale autodialer equipment the average Internet hacker does not have access to. Launching these same attacks on IP addresses is significantly easier and open to a much larger pool of perpetrators because no sophisticated equipment is necessary, and the attacks can be launched for free from any Internet access connection.

When considering security on SIP trunks, you need to take into account different aspects of security. These aspects call for a series of features and capabilities to mitigate the potential threats. Security is always best deployed in a layered architecture, rather than a single box or feature that strives to protect against all possible attacks. Areas worth exploring for SIP trunk security include

- Determine the level of exposure on the SIP trunk, which depends on how it is deployed and who the provider is.

- Limit the devices that can contact your network via the SIP trunk. Mitigation capabilities include features such as access lists, hostname validation, and voice source group definitions.

- Hide your enterprise network addressing from the outside (which could be Internet-visible) and inspect the validity of traffic that enters your network. Mitigation techniques include network address translation (NAT), topology hiding, firewalls, and intrusion protection services (IPS).

- Determine protocol and session validity. Mitigation techniques include SIP port settings, SIP protocol inspection and termination, registration, and authentication methods.

- Lock down your SIP trunk against toll fraud access using the same methods you used on your TDM gateways.

- Control the privacy of sessions on the SIP trunk. Mitigation techniques involve the control of originator information available outside the enterprise network with the use of SIP privacy headers, SIP normalization, digit manipulation, and encryption methods of the signaling and the media streams (such as Transport Layer Security [TLS], Secure RTP, and the use of IPSec tunnels or virtual private networks (VPN) on the IP connections).

SIP Trunk Levels of Security Exposure

The level of security exposure depends on the characteristics of how the SIP trunk connects into your network and the strength of security protection your service provider offers.

Figure 7-2 illustrates four increasing levels of exposure depending on the connectivity method of your SIP trunk:

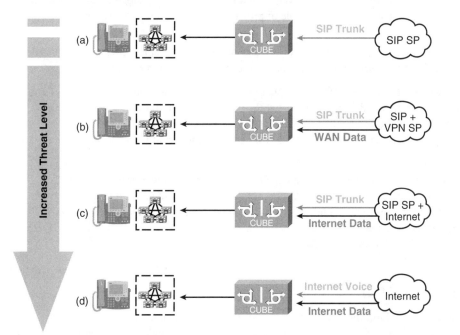

Figure 7-2   *Increasing Levels of Security Exposure*

- In model (a) the SIP trunk connects from a Tier 1 service provider with strong security over a dedicated physical connection into your network. No data traffic traverses this connection. With this model, your security exposure is low, and you can consider not having a firewall in addition to a border element on such a connection.

- In model (b) the SIP trunk connects from a Tier 1 service provider with strong security over a physical connection that carries both your voice and your VPN WAN data connection, such as an MPLS service. No Internet data traffic traverses this connection. With this model, your security exposure is still fairly low, and you might not need a firewall in addition to a border element on such a connection.

- In model (c) the SIP trunk connects from a service provider that offers both SIP trunking and Internet access on the same physical connection. This is often a cost-effective model for smaller businesses with no WAN data service between sites or that have only a single site. Regardless of the strength of security measures in the service provider's network, you are exposed to Internet attacks on this kind of connection, and you have to firewall in addition to deploying a border element to secure this type of connection.

- In model (d) there is no SIP trunk service offering, and you use plain Internet consumer voice access and Internet data from a general Internet service provider. This model is strongly discouraged for business-class voice access because there is no quality control on such a connection, and it is extremely exposed to all kinds of voice and data Internet attacks. Firewalling and border controlling alone are still not sufficient to make this model capable of providing business-quality voice services.

Many security features on both firewalls and border elements protect against attacks on SIP trunks. The following sections discuss these techniques in more detail.

A general best practice for SIP trunk security is always to use a border element to terminate a SIP trunk coming into your network. This can be an appliance function (such as deploying a dedicated CUBE), or it can be an integrated function, such as an IAD or CUCM Express device that acts as a border element and a routing or IP-PBX device in your network.

In addition to a border element, you can choose also to deploy a firewall. Again, this might be a separate appliance, or it might be integrated into a Cisco IOS router providing multiple functions to your business. Separate, dedicated devices tend to be the norm for larger enterprise and higher volume SIP trunks, whereas integrated devices tend to be the cost-effective solution for smaller sites or small business networks.

Access Lists (ACL)

Always strictly limit the devices that can access your SIP trunk, both from internal to your network and external to it. If you terminate your SIP trunk on a border element, you do not need all these security mitigation measures on every enterprise application, only on the border element. The border element itself should be set up to accept connections on the service provider side only from the provider's SBC, and on the enterprise side only from legitimate CUCM, IP-PBX, or other valid applications (for example, SIP proxies and meeting conference servers).

United States federal information reports that hackers are as frequently located inside your enterprise network as on the outside, and for that reason, it is imperative to lock down your border element on both sides so that rogue endpoints and applications inside your network cannot use the SIP trunk service for fraudulent calls. Similarly, rogue endpoints on the Internet should contact your SIP trunk. This configuration is illustrated in Figure 7-3.

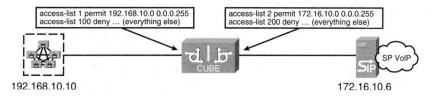

Figure 7-3 *Locking Down a SIP Trunk with ACLs*

Additionally, voice Source IP Groups can be used with the ACLs, as shown in Figure 7-3, to provide further restrictions on the devices that might originate SIP traffic to your border element. On devices in your network that should not run SIP traffic at all, the Control Plane Policing (CoPP) feature can be used to deny all SIP traffic.

CUCM has (by default) a feature that restricts traffic on a SIP trunk to be accepted only from the IP address configured on the SIP trunk.

Hostname Validation

You can use the hostname validation feature of the CUBE to restrict the valid hostnames that are accepted in the host portion of the SIP URI of an incoming SIP INVITE. Example 7-1 illustrates the commands used by this feature to enable calls only from the four hostnames listed.

Example 7-1 *Hostname Validation*

```
sip-ua
  permit hostname dns:example1.sip.com
  permit hostname dns:example2.sip.com
  permit hostname dns:example3.sip.com
  permit hostname dns:example4.sip.com
```

Security features often overlap to some extent, and it is a good practice to deploy these overlapping features because they provide layered security protection. Every layer might protect you against one particular attack that might have skirted around a single layer protection to exploit a weakness in a particular appliance, device, feature operation, or configuration.

NAT and Topology Hiding

Hiding the IP addresses of enterprise voice endpoints (such as those belonging to IP phones, call agents, and TDM voice gateways) from external view can in some cases be achieved with traditional NAT features. NAT adjusts the IP addressing of IP packet headers and some of the IP addresses appearing elsewhere in SIP packets, but generic NAT devices are Layer 3-capable only. Those that have Application Layer Gateways (ALG) have more sophisticated SIP awareness, but still, generally, might offer only suboptimal capabilities to translate deeply embedded IP addresses in SIP messaging.

It is therefore more secure to use a border element that is a full SIP back-to-back user agent (B2BUA) as the network demarcation offering 100 percent SIP packet inspection and address translation. The CUBE is a full SIP B2BUA and can therefore offer complete network address translation, usually referred to as topology hiding in this context to distinguish this function from appliance NAT devices. Both media and signaling flow through the CUBE and the service provider and off-net endpoints see only the addresses of the border element and never the addresses internal to your enterprise network.

Topology hiding is important to ensure that any attacks that might come from the service provider side can be directed only toward the border element, and the communications and call agents within your enterprise remain unaffected.

Figure 7-4 illustrates how topology hiding can be accomplished by using the CUBE.

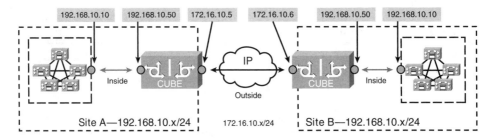

Figure 7-4   *Topology Hiding*

Firewalls

Many security features on both firewalls and border elements protect against attacks on SIP trunks. A certain amount of overlap occurs between the capabilities, especially true for the higher end firewalls with sophisticated SIP ALGs.

Generally you should deploy a firewall to provide generic IP protection against any kind of IP traffic, and your border element as a much more focused, voice-specific session protection function. For the least capable firewall devices, you should simply open pinholes for the traffic destined to the border element and have the border element do all the SIP inspection. For firewalls with SIP ALGs, there is some overlap in the inspection the firewall does and the inspection done by the border element. The border element always provides the most sophisticated layer of protection because it is a B2BUA whereas the firewall essentially inspects and passes through traffic but does not terminate it.

Functions that firewalls are particularly well suited to mitigate are Layers 2 and 3 inspection functions including:

- General IP DOS attacks

- Black hole routing

- TCP window control and dropping UDP packets

- Access lists, specifying what traffic is correct and allowed

- Optional SIP ALG for cursory SIP rogue and malformed packet inspection

- Optional SIP ALG protection against spikes of SIP calls (SIP-specific DOS)

More sophisticated SIP capabilities that some firewalls can have include

- Whitelist/blacklist filtering of SIP calls based on calling and called numbers

- Rate limiting of specific SIP methods to mitigate against SIP-specific DOS attacks

Firewalls are not as well suited to protecting against attacks launched from inside your network or doing session management at the level of deciding whether packets are arriving for valid sessions only, in valid sequences (or SIP dialogs), and for valid codecs or other negotiated parameters of the session. Some of the more sophisticated firewalls, such as the Cisco ASA product series or the Cisco IOS Firewall, have SIP ALGs that offer some protection services at protocol layers higher than Layer 3.

Specific functions a border element is well suited for include Layers 5 to 7 SIP inspection actions such as:

- Rejecting nonallowed calls and generating CDRs of call attempts for tracking

- Call limiting (only accept a certain number of calls)

- Codec limiting (only accept certain codecs)

- Call admission control to provide bandwidth protection

- Access lists specifying valid source and destination call agents

- Complete rogue and malformed SIP packet protection

- Digest authentication and hostname validation to ensure sessions are set up only between valid endpoints

- SIP registration to authenticate session originations

- SIP listening port configuration

Broadly, firewalls and border elements are deployed in one of two ways:

■ Separate devices in series

■ Integrated in a Cisco IOS device with collocated functions

Figure 7-5 provides six possible deployment models of firewalls and border elements.

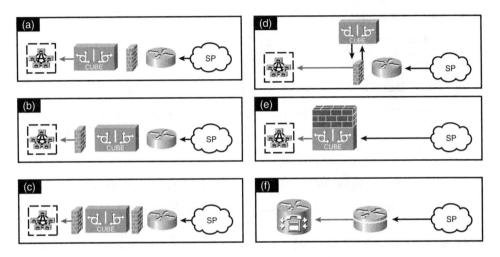

Figure 7-5　*Possible Firewall and Border Element Designs*

Models (a), (b), and (c) shown in Figure 7-5 are better suited to medium-to-large enterprises and high volume contact centers, and models (d), (e), and (f) are better suited to smaller businesses.

■ In model (a) the firewall appliance is on the outside of the border element. This is the recommended deployment model if you use separate devices for firewall services and a border element. This deployment generally makes sense for campus and data center locations where there is already a firewall present. This model also makes sense if the firewall is managed by the security team, whereas the border element is managed by the voice team. This is a mandatory model if the physical medium coming into the enterprise premises carries Internet traffic.

In this model, the firewall provides the first line of defense on all traffic arriving from the outside, passes the voice traffic to the border element for a Layer 7 inspection on the voice traffic. If the firewall has an ALG function, there is bound to be some overlap in functionality between the firewall and the border element. It is nevertheless recommended that you turn on both to get the fullest set of inspection and protection that you can, rather than having potential security holes between the appliances.

■ In model (b) the border element is on the outside of the firewall. This deployment model makes sense when the physical medium bringing the SIP trunk into your premises carries *only* SIP trunk traffic and nothing else. This means your data connections come in on a different physical path, onto different routers, and get firewalled entirely separately from the SIP trunk traffic. This model mandates that you trust your service provider's network to offer only clean SIP traffic to your enterprise.

■   In model (c) two firewalls are on either side of the border element. Some refer to this model as the one for the truly paranoid, but this is the classic design of a DMZ (demilitarized zone). It is not an uncommon design, especially in large financial, educational, and government institutions, or any other business particularly attractive to hackers.

■   Model (d) is a variation of model (c), where there are two virtual firewalls on either side of the border element, but one physical firewall device is used for the function, routing the unified communications (UC) traffic twice. This is a virtual DMZ design often used in video deployments where the CUBE is not only fronting a SIP trunk, but is also bringing in H.323 Internet video traffic and acting as a Cisco IOS Gatekeeper.

■   Model (e) provides a more cost-effective integrated deployment model for smaller sites or businesses where a separate firewall appliance does not already exist, is not desirable, or the cost is not justified. In this model the Cisco IOS router acts as both the CUBE and the firewall. Traffic flowing through this router is inspected first by the firewall and then handed to the border element for further processing. It is therefore conceptually similar to model (a).

■   Model (f) provides a lower end offering for commercial or small businesses (without IT departments) that do not want to carry the cost or the management of either a border element or a firewall. In this model, an integrated service from a service provider is purchased, and all security and demarcation issues is handled by the service provider. The service provider puts an IAD at the customer premises to connect to its IP-PBX or key system, such as CUCM Express. The IAD device will likely do NAT, perhaps basic firewalling, but essentially all the service provider's network and security are delivered as a managed service.

Security Protection at the SIP Protocol Level

SIP is a widely used and understood protocol and simple to create because it uses straight text encoding in its messages (unlike H.323 that uses ASN.1 encoding). This makes SIP an easy target for hackers. Many of the protocol attacks can be launched against H.323 as well, but very few incidents of this were in the industry because H.323 is not as accessible as SIP.

Several ways to protect your network against a variety of SIP protocol attacks include

■   Setting the SIP listening port

■   Using TLS for authentication

■   Using a border element B2BUA

- Using SIP normalization techniques to suppress or overwrite information in the SIP message such as the calling phone numbers, hostnames, or descriptive tags before a call enters the public network

- Using digit manipulation techniques to suppress or overwrite phone numbers before a call enters the public network

- Using SIP privacy settings to communicate the information within the SIP message that might or might not be used

Each of these areas is discussed in the following sections.

SIP Listening Port

Every Internet hacker knows the default SIP listen ports and can sweep them from any Internet location to find an open port to launch fraudulent calls, all while your business pays for them. One way to protect against this is to change the SIP listening port to a nondefault setting. It requires the service provider to set the complementary port on the provider edge SBC. This alone can protect you against the majority of hacker attacks launched against SIP port 5060.

Example 7-2 shows the commands needed to set the SIP listening port to a nondefault setting.

Example 7-2   *SIP Listening Port Setting*

```
voice service voip
 sip
   shutdown
voice service voip
 sip
   listen-port non-secure 2000 secure 2050
voice service voip
 sip
   no shutdown
```

Transport Layer Security (TLS)

Another way to protect against this attack is to use TLS (specified in IETF RFC-2246). TLS uses an authentication mechanism that ensures only valid endpoints connect to your SIP trunk, and if the authentication fails, the call is refused.

Although this is a good way to mitigate fraudulent SIP calls, none of the current SIP trunk offerings in the market include TLS as an option. Hopefully this situation will change.

Back-to-Back User Agent (B2BUA)

A B2BUA (such as the CUBE) terminates and reoriginates all calls before they enter your network. All SIP traffic passes through the SIP stack on the B2BUA twice (on ingress and egress) so that all malformed or rogue packets are dropped.

SIP Normalization

There are certain numbers, names, or other internal information you might want to populate informative displays on the endpoints in your network. When these calls exit over the SIP trunk to external destinations, you might not want all this information to remain in the SIP messaging, especially non-DID numbers used by your organization. You can use SIP normalization features to insert, delete, or change this kind of information in the SIP messaging on your border element.

Examples 7-3, 7-4, and 7-5 show how SIP normalization can be used on the CUBE to modify the *From* header in an INVITE to a **gateway@ip-address** format and to add the **phone-context=gateway** field to the *To* header of the INVITE. Example 7-3 shows the commands needed for the configuration; Example 7-4 shows the original SIP INVITE; and Example 7-5 shows the resulting INVITE after normalization has been applied.

Example 7-3 *SIP Normalizations Commands*

```
voice service voip
  sip
    sip-profiles 1
voice class sip-profiles 1
  request INVITE sip-header From modify "(<.*:)(.*@)" "\1gateway@"
  request INVITE sip-header To modify "<(.*)>" "<\1;phone-context=gateway>"
```

Example 7-4 *Original SIP INVITE*

```
INVITE sip:22220000205060 SIP/2.0

Via: SIP/2.0/UDP 9.13.24.6:5060;branch=z9hG4bK1AD9E2
Remote-Party-ID: "sipp " <sip:sipp@9.13.24.6>;party=calling;screen=no;privacy=off
From: "sipp "<sip:sipp@9.13.24.6>;tag=23C3F840-99A
To: <sip:2222000020@9.13.24.7>
Date: Thu, 30 Aug 2007 07:04:36 GMT
```

Example 7-5 *Normalized SIP INVITE*

```
INVITE sip:22220000205070 SIP/2.0

Via: SIP/2.0/UDP 9.13.24.7:5060;branch=z9hG4bK1191BFD
Remote-Party-ID: "sipp " <sip:sipp@9.13.24.7>;party=calling;screen=no;privacy=off
From: "sipp "<sip:gateway@9.13.24.7>;tag=1EDB2D94-11DD
```

continues

Example 7-5   *Normalized SIP INVITE (continued)*

```
To: <sip:2222000020@9.13.32.240;phone-context=gateway>
Date: Thu, 30 Aug 2007 07:04:36 GMT
```

Digit Manipulation

Another technique to suppress or change nonpublic numbers from exiting your network is to use digit manipulation techniques at the border of your network. For example, a non-DID number can be changed to your organization's basic public PSTN number if the call should go off-net.

SIP Privacy Methods

Various SIP specifications control the privacy of end user information in SIP messaging such that numbers and names can travel in the messaging but still be suppressed from delivery or display to the destination endpoint. Similar methods exist in ISDN when interconnecting to the traditional PSTN.

SIP specifications (and CUBE capabilities) of interest in this area include

■ The Privacy SIP header (RFC-3323) provides guidelines for withholding the identity of a person (and related personal information) from one or more parties in an exchange of SIP communications.

■ The P-Asserted-Identity (PAI) and P-Preferred-Identity (PPI) (RFC-3325) headers provide extensions that enable the communication of the identity of authenticated users and the application of existing SIP privacy mechanisms to communicating these identities.

If your applications are not SIP-capable, or if they do not insert these headers, you can have your border element insert (or change) the content of these headers as a call leaves your premises over the SIP trunk. The CUBE can also convert between the widely deployed Remote-Party-ID (RPID) header to and from PAI/PPI and Privacy headers.

Registration and Authentication

You can use SIP mechanisms to validate the originator of a SIP call and therefore provide a mechanism to reject SIP INVITEs that come from rogue endpoints. These mechanisms include

■ **Registration:** Some service provider SIP trunk offerings include a registration sequence enabling the enterprise edge to register explicitly with the provider's SIP softswitch. Some SIP applications are capable of this; if not you can have your CUBE do the registration on behalf of the endpoints behind it in the enterprise network.

■ **Digest Authentication (RFC-2617):** A SIP softswitch can challenge the INVITEs, and the originator must respond with credentials that are then authenticated by the SIP softswitch. Unlike a SIP registration sequence that happens once, the Digest

Authentication happens on every SIP INVITE. The CUBE can respond to Digest Authentication challenges with configured credentials.

Example 7-6 shows sample commands to configure the CUBE to do a SIP registration with credentials, and Example 7-7 shows the configuration for SIP Digest Authentication.

Example 7-6 *SIP Registration*

```
x(config)#sip-ua
x(config-sip-ua)#credentials username 1001 password cisco realm cisco.com

sip-ua
  registrar ipv4:172.16.193.97 expires 3600
  credentials username 1001 password 0822455D0A16 realm cisco.com
```

Example 7-7 *SIP Digest Authentication*

```
sip-ua
  authentication username xxx password yyy
```

Toll Fraud

Toll fraud has existed for as long as telephone networks have been in operation. This constitutes making unauthorized calls that someone else pays for. The perpetrator can be inside your network (for example, an employee making personal international calls) or an external hacker using your SIP trunk to make calls that your company pays for.

Ensure that whatever measures you took to combat toll fraud in your TDM PSTN access network are also implemented on your SIP trunk PSTN access network. Some of the common CUBE tools that enable you to mitigate toll fraud attacks include

- Use ACLs to enable explicit sources of calls and deny all other traffic.

- Apply explicit incoming and outgoing dial-peers to both Border Element interfaces to control the types and parameters of calls allowed through the network border. If an incoming dial-peer is not found for a call, the system default dial-peer 0 is used enabling all calls; to avoid this, specify explicit incoming dial-peers for valid call flows and deny all other calls.

- Use explicit destination-patterns on dial-peers (try to avoid using .T if you can) to block out disallowed off-net call destinations.

- Use translation rules to ensure only valid calling/called numbers are allowed. This allows you to add access codes dialing to gain entry to certain destinations (for example, international destinations). Your employees know these access codes, but off-net hackers do not.

- Use Tool Command Language (Tcl) or Voice Extensible Markup Language (VoiceXML) scripts to do database lookups or require PINs or authorization codes for additional validity checks to allow/deny call flows. This method protects against internal fraudulent calls.

■ Change the SIP listening port to something other than the default of 5060.

■ Close unused H.323 or SIP ports—if your Border Element is connected purely to a SIP trunk, there is no need for the H.323 ports to be open.

■ The Class of Restriction (COR) feature restricts call attempts based on both the incoming and outgoing dial-peers matched by the call.

Signaling and Media Encryption

Another area of security to consider is the privacy of communications, that is, how to keep hackers from recording calls or hijacking them and inserting or deleting segments. Several encryption features for voice call flows mitigate these types of attacks. Separate features for protection of the signaling traffic (TCP or UDP) and the media traffic (RTP) exist.

■ Signaling encryption can be achieved by IPsec tunnels (both TCP and UDP SIP traffic) or TLS (SIP TCP). You can use TLS just for authentication or also for encryption of the signaling stream.

■ You can achieve media encryption with Secure RTP (SRTP) (RFC-3711).

As the media encryption keys are exchanged in the signaling stream, there is no point in encrypting media without also encrypting the signaling. Only encrypting signaling is a valid option.

None of the current SIP trunk offerings in the market include TLS or SRTP as an option. Hopefully this situation will change. The CUBE can convert between encrypted communications (TLS/SRTP) on one side and nonencrypted (SIP/RTP) on the other side, so if your business can benefit from (or demands) encryption in the enterprise, you can still connect to a SIP trunk provider.

Session Management, Call Traffic Capacity, Bandwidth Control, and QoS

Managing simultaneous voice call capacity and IP bandwidth use is essential for providing consistent quality in enterprise communications. Areas regarding session management and CAC to be considered in the design of your network include

■ Trunk provisioning

■ Bandwidth adjustments and consumption

■ Call admission control

- QoS metrics, such as packet marking, delay, jitter, and echo
- Voice-quality monitoring

Trunk Provisioning

The capacity of a SIP trunk is normally defined by the number of simultaneous calls supported and the bandwidth provided for the trunk. An enterprise uses the same Erlang calculations traditionally used in a TDM environment to determine the number of simultaneous calls required on a SIP trunk.

Generally service providers offer a tiered service based on capacity. One of the major benefits of a SIP trunk is that as an enterprise's needs expand, the number of simultaneous calls can be readily expanded without changing the physical interconnection, or even without an increase in provisioned bandwidth, provided excess bandwidth is already available.

Bandwidth Adjustments and Consumption

Bandwidth consumption for IP call traffic inbound from the PSTN on a TDM gateway is easily predicted and controlled because the codec assignment is done by the gateway (or by the enterprise call agent such as CUCM). The use of a CUBE can ensure that this capability is maintained when an enterprise adds a SIP trunk to its communications infrastructure.

CAC policies and features are deployed in the enterprise network based on predictable patterns of codec use by calls (that is, typically G.711 for calls within a site on the LAN and G.729A for calls that traverse the WAN between sites). The bandwidth consumption of inbound SIP trunk calls is partly based on the service provider's configuration, but an enterprise can use a CUBE to influence codec selection (also called codec filtering or stripping) or to transcode streams in the codec selections the enterprise prefers to use.

Call Admission Control (CAC)

Gateways connecting to the PSTN through a TDM interface provide an implicit form of CAC in both directions (inbound and outbound) by virtue of the limited number of channels (or timeslots) physically available on the analog, BRI, T1, or E1 interface. No more calls can simultaneously arrive from the PSTN into the enterprise than there are timeslots available on the gateway TDM trunks, providing implicit call admission control.

With a SIP trunk entering your network on a physical GE connection (possibly fiber or OC3 transport within the service provider's network before hand-off to your network), nothing physical limits the number of calls that could enter or exit your network at any one time.

Top-tier service providers exert CAC control in their networks, and how much protection this offers your enterprise network depends on who your service provider is and how well the controls are implemented. But there is virtually no physical limit, and it is strongly recommended that you protect your own network with your own CAC controls at your Border Element (especially if you are considering a SIP trunk offering without an explicit SLA). This protects against occasional unplanned bursts or surges in legitimate traffic and against potential malicious Dos attack traffic. Lack of CAC control could overrun bandwidth on your network and adversely impact network operations.

One general problem with CAC implementations is that many policies are often based on simple *call-counting* mechanisms (such as the CUCM Locations CAC feature) as opposed to bandwidth-based mechanisms (such as Resource Reservation Protocol [RSVP]). It is therefore important to control not only the number of calls arriving through the SIP trunk, but also the codec assigned to the calls.

In addition to transcoding and codec filtering, a CUBE can support the CAC policy of the enterprise in the following two ways:

■ Limiting calls per dial peer (per destination)

■ Limiting calls based on memory and CPU

Limiting Calls per Dial-Peer

You can configure the **max-conn** command on both the inbound and outbound dial-peers of the CUBE to ensure that no more than the configured number of calls connects at one time. Each call, regardless of codec or the direction of the call, counts as one call.

When a call arrives at a dial-peer and the current number of calls in the connected state exceeds the configured amount, the SIP INVITE request is rejected with a 503 result code to indicate that the gateway is out of resources.

Example 7-7 shows how to configure CAC per dial-peer.

Example 7-7   *Using Dial-Peer CAC Mechanisms*

```
dial-peer voice 1 voip
  max-conn 2
```

Global Call Admission Control

The CUBE can also be configured to monitor calls on a global basis; that is, without regard of which dial-peer the call might be active on. This global CAC control can be done based on:

■ A global system count of calls

■ A CPU threshold (as a percentage)

■ A memory threshold (as a percentage)

■ Any combination of the preceding three metrics

The CUBE checks these configurations and metrics before it completes the processing of a SIP INVITE request. If system resources used exceed the configured amount, the CUBE returns a result code in the SIP INVITE request, indicating that the gateway is out of resources.

Example 7-8 shows how to configure global CAC.

Example 7-8 *Using Global CAC Mechanisms*

```
call threshold global total-calls low 20 high 24
call threshold global cpu-avg low 68 high 75
call threshold global total-mem low 75 high 80
call threshold interface Ethernet 0/1 int-calls low 5 high 2500
call treatment cause-code no-resource
call treatment on
```

The **call threshold global total-calls** command controls the total number of calls to be supported on the CUBE. The command tracks the number of calls, rejecting the 25th call and not accepting calls again until the total number of calls falls below 20. The **cpu-avg** and **total-mem** options rejects the calls if the CPU or memory of the border element exceed the given thresholds regardless of the actual active call count. The **call threshold interface** command limits the number of calls over a specific IP interface.

The **call treatment cause-code no-resource** command correlates (by default) to a SIP 503 Service Unavailable message sent when calls are rejected.

Quality of Service (QoS)

Cisco provides many methods of measuring and ensuring QoS in an enterprise IP network. You should always use these methods internally when designing a UC system, and you should also extend them to the interconnect point when using a SIP trunk to connect to a service provider. Consider several areas of QoS including:

- Traffic marking
- Delay and jitter
- Echo
- Congestion management

Traffic Marking

QoS on IP networks depends on the QoS marking on the IP packets. As with codec settings, QoS markings on voice signaling and media IP packets on IP call traffic inbound from the PSTN on a TDM gateway is easily predicted and controlled by the configuration on your gateway. On SIP trunks, the default packet markings are whatever the service provider sets them to and this might not be in line with your enterprise policies.

The CUBE can re-mark all media and signaling packets that enter you network or exit your network to comply with the SP UNI specification. Re-marking can be done on a per-dial-peer basis (that is, per voice call destination) or per interface (either ingress or egress or both).

Example 7-9 shows how to mark packets per dial-peer.

Example 7-9   *Marking QoS on a Dial-Peer*

```
dial-peer voice 40800011 voip
  destination-pattern 408.......
  session protocol sipv2
  session target ipv4 :10.10.1.1
  dtmf-relay rtp-nte
  ip qos dscp ef media
  ip qos dscp cs4 signaling
  no vad
```

Delay and Jitter

The telephone industry standard specified in ITU-T G.114 recommends the maximum desired one-way delay be no more than 150 milliseconds. With a round-trip delay of 300 milliseconds or more, users might experience annoying talk-over effects.

When using SIP trunks, you should consider the IP delay of *both* the enterprise and service provider networks. In some cases, centralized SIP trunk services cannot be effectively deployed because of the resulting increase in latency. A border element device at the customer premises is required to ensure that latency in the service provider network and enterprise network can be independently measured and controlled.

Echo

An echo is the audible leak-through of your own voice into your own receive (return) path. The source of echo might be a TDM loop in the call path or acoustic echo that applies to all-IP calls. Acoustic echo can come from improper acoustic insulation on the phone, headset, or speakerphone (all Cisco IP Phones have an acoustic echo canceller) and is common on PC-based softphones.

A border element demarcation point at a customer site can help you determine if a problem with echo is occurring at the customer premises or in the service provider's network.

Congestion Management

When using a single connection for both voice and data, you should carefully consider congestion management (for example, queuing techniques such as Low-Latency Queuing [LLQ]) and bandwidth allocation to prevent data traffic from affecting the voice quality of SIP trunk calls.

The end-to-end voice quality experience of your SIP trunk calls depend on congestion management techniques in both your network and in the service provider's delivery network to your premises. A enterprise border element can help you determine in which network jurisdiction a problem lies.

Voice-Quality Monitoring

To ensure business class voice quality within the enterprise network and to determine if a service provider is meeting an agreed-upon SLA, your enterprise should monitor some metrics. Each enterprise might choose to monitor different metrics, but an effective method of collecting the metrics independent from the service provider is important.

Table 7-1 describes some of the important metrics you can monitor. These metrics can be gathered by using various features previously discussed in this chapter in the "Statistics" and "Billing" sections. You can use these basic metrics from the network to calculate the more typical voice quality measurements such as Mean Opinion Score (MOS) or Perceptual Evaluation of Speech Quality (PESQ) to quantify with a single number the voice quality attained by the network.

Table 7-1   *Voice-Quality Monitoring Attributes*

Round-trip delay (RTD)	100–300 ms	The RTD is the delay for a packet sent from the originating endpoint at the customer location to the terminating endpoint at the service provider and back	This metric can be monitored through the RTD metric in Cisco IOS Software; it is provided per call and is also available through IP-SLA probes.
Jitter	50–100 ms	Jitter is a measurement of the change in the delay of one packet to another during a call.	Jitter is measured in the per-call statistics; the maximum jitter detected during the call is
Packet loss	1 percent or lower	Packet loss is the number of packets lost during any given call, including UDP and TCP packets.	This metric can be monitored by SNMP in Cisco IOS Software; it is provided per call and can also be tracked with IP-
Uptime	99.999 percent	Uptime is the percentage of time that a path is available for the customer to complete a call to the PSTN.	When uptime is measured, planned outages should be accounted for, and it should be measured as the number of unplanned minutes of outages and monitored with trouble

continues

Table 7-1   *Voice-Quality Monitoring Attributes (continued)*

Metric	Goal	Definition	Method to Monitor
Answer seizure rate (ASR) or call success rate (CSR)	Varies	The ASR can be recorded as the number of calls made divided by the number of calls that complete a voice path. This number varies greatly because of calling numbers that are unassigned or busy. CSR is the percentage of calls successfully completed through a service provider. The CSR rate should be more than 99 percent. The ASR rate is typically approximately 60 percent.	ASR can be measured by a summary of call activity at the end of the month. The specific value of ASR is not as important as whether there are large swings in the ASR from one month to another that might indicate a problem with end-to-end network connectivity.

Scalability and High Availability

One of the attractive cost benefits of SIP trunking is the technical ability to centralize PSTN access for the enterprise into a single large pipe. Doing so, however, creates several design considerations, including both scalability and high availability:

■ **Scalability:** Routing all calls from the entire enterprise over a single or a small number of centralized SIP trunk access points means that you are looking at a SIP trunk capacity of several hundred to several thousand connections for all enterprises except the really small ones.

This implies border handling session capacity equipment that often far outstrips any single TDM gateway that exists in the typical enterprise. Most enterprise gateways are in the 1 to 16 T1/E1 range that equates up to between 384 to 480 sessions. Even a T3 gateway, a relative rarity in the average enterprise, presents only 672 sessions.

Some of the redundancy schemes covered in the remainder of this section simultaneously address scalability mechanisms including higher-capacity equipment and load balancing over clusters of individual boxes.

■ **High Availability:** The more sessions that are concentrated into a single physical pipe, the larger the business impact to your organization of this single point of failure. For this reason few enterprises truly deploy a single SIP trunk entry point into their networks; there are almost always multiple points.

Redundancy also becomes a much more pressing consideration because of the potentially large session capacity of SIP trunks. TDM gateway redundancy amounted to alternative routing over a different gateway when there was a failure. But when a single failure can now easily impact more than a 1000 calls, and potentially the routing of all PSTN-destined calls, the need for mitigation of such a failure escalates.

You can deploy several strategies to protect against the business impact of a SIP trunk failure:

- Local and geographical SIP trunk redundancy

- Border element redundancy

- Load balancing and clustering

- PSTN TDM gateway failover

The handling for emergency calls that you decide on (see the "Emergency Calls" section earlier in this chapter) might affect considerations for the redundancy mechanisms discussed next.

Local and Geographical SIP Trunk Redundancy

For redundancy purposes there are almost always multiple SIP trunk entry points into an enterprise network even in a largely centralized design. This ensures that calls have alternative routing points if an equipment or building power failure occurs or a natural disaster in a particular region occurs. The only realistic alternative to multiple SIP trunk entry points is to have a single SIP trunk and maintain TDM gateway access to the PSTN for failover, a scenario discussed later in this section. For small, single-site businesses, cellular phone access might be a realistic alternative to a single SIP trunk, but this is rarely practical for a multisite enterprise of any size.

Consider three different areas of SIP trunk redundancy:

- **Local redundancy:** Most SIP trunk services offer at least two IP addresses. For local redundancy the physical medium is most likely shared and terminates into the same building on your premises. Local redundancy protects against equipment failure or power failure to a single piece of equipment. These two IP addresses should ideally terminate onto two redundant border elements. Most providers offer either a primary/secondary or a load-balancing scheme that the enterprise can choose from.

- **Geographic redundancy:** Most medium-to-large enterprises prefer to bring in the two IP addresses or perhaps two different SIP trunks (that is, four IP addresses, each SIP trunk with local redundancy) into two separate buildings, likely data centers, in two different geographies. This protects against natural disasters and buildingwide power or other outages.

■ **Service provider redundancy:** Some enterprises and contact centers get SIP trunks from two different providers, both for least-cost routing opportunities and for redundancy purposes. If one provider is having problems, the other provider's facilities can carry all traffic. This scheme is easy to implement for outbound traffic but harder (due to DID mapping) for inbound traffic.

Border Element Redundancy

SIP trunks terminate on the session border controller, or border elements, in the enterprise. These elements have to be redundant for high session capacity SIP trunks, both for scalability and high availability reasons. You can use various ways to provide redundancy for a particular border element platform (in addition to the local and geographic redundancy schemes already previously discussed):

■ In-box hardware redundancy

■ Box-to-box hardware redundancy

■ Clustering

In-Box Hardware Redundancy

In-box redundancy means duplicate processing components exist contained within the platform itself so that if one hardware component fails, another immediately takes over. In-box redundancy often includes components such as the CPU card, possibly the memory cards, I/O interface cards, and control and data plane forwarding engines.

The level of hardware redundancy the CUBE provides depends on the hardware platform on which the function is installed. The higher-end platforms offer more hardware redundancy than the lower-end platforms. In-box hardware redundancy is almost invariably seamless, also called stateful failover, so sessions are not dropped and end users on active calls are generally unaware that a hardware failover has occurred.

Box-to-Box Hardware Redundancy (1+1)

Box-to-box redundancy, or 1+1 redundancy, means there are duplicate platforms, acting and configured as a single one, in an active/standby arrangement with a keepalive mechanism between them. If the active hardware platform fails, the standby platform takes over.

One such method is the Hot Standby Router Protocol (HSRP) supported on Cisco IOS routers. With HSRP transparent hardware failover is possible while maintaining a single SIP trunk (that is, a single visible IP address) to the service provider. How well HSRP works in a particular deployment depends on the service provider IP addressing rules and the release of software deployed on the CUBE.

HSRP redundancy is not inherently stateful but can support stateful failover if the higher layers of software support application-level checkpointing and the basic router keepalive. The operation of this mechanism is shown in Figure 7-6.

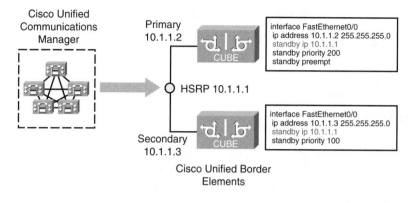

Cisco Unified
Communications
Manager

Primary
10.1.1.2

```
interface FastEthernet0/0
ip address 10.1.1.2 255.255.255.0
standby ip 10.1.1.1
standby priority 200
standby preempt
```

HSRP 10.1.1.1

```
interface FastEthernet0/0
ip address 10.1.1.3 255.255.255.0
standby ip 10.1.1.1
standby priority 100
```

Secondary
10.1.1.3

CUBE

CUBE

Cisco Unified Border
Elements

Figure 7-6   *Using HRSP for Redundancy*

Enterprise TDM gateways do not offer stateful failover redundancy because the session capacity per gateway is limited; therefore, the impact of a failure is limited. If an individual CUBE carries no more sessions than the average enterprise TDM gateway, there might not be a reason to expend the cost on deploying high-end hardware with stateful failover capability on the border element either. Instead, border element clustering can provide effective redundancy, as it does for TDM gateways.

Clustering (N+1)

Redundancy via clustering, or N+1 redundancy, means there are duplicate platforms independent of each other and each carries a fraction of the traffic, together providing a high session count SIP trunk. There is no state sharing or keepalives between the components, and if a single element is lost, some calls drop, but it is not the entire SIP trunk that goes down.

The CUBE can be deployed in a clustering architecture with load balancing over the individual components managed by the attached devices or by a SIP proxy element. (Load balancing methods are explored further in the next section.) A clustering architecture has the advantage of a pool of smaller elements, each of which can be taken out of service and upgraded without affecting the entire SIP trunk. The cluster can also be spread out over several buildings or geographic locations to enhance redundancy concerns about the impact of a power loss or a natural disaster on a building or data center.

Load Balancing

SIP trunks from providers usually come with two (sometimes more) IP addresses. As previously discussed, you might want to have multiple border elements fronting this SIP trunk for both redundancy and scalability benefits. If you choose a load-balancing algorithm (as opposed to a primary/secondary active/standby arrangement) for the multiple platforms forming the network border, some network entity is required to do load balancing across the possible destinations.

You can use multiple ways to implement SIP trunk load balancing:

- Service provider load balancing

- DNS

- CUCM route groups and route lists

- Cisco Unified SIP proxy

Service Provider Load Balancing

Many SIP trunk providers offer a choice of primary/secondary or load-balancing algorithm to the enterprise customer. If load balancing is chosen, this is implemented either on their SIP softswitch or their provider edge SBC.

Domain Name System (DNS)

You can use DNS SRV records (RFC-2782) to provide multiple IP address resolutions for the same hostname. In this way, the individual platforms in the border element cluster can be addressed dynamically using the information returned by DNS. The operation of this mechanism is shown in Figure 7-7.

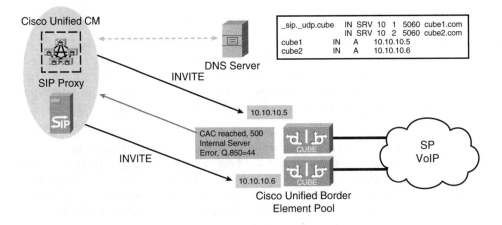

Figure 7-7   *Using DNS SRV for Load Balancing*

The attached SIP softswitch (this can be used either on the service provider side or on the enterprise side) queries DNS for the IP addresses of the border element. The originating softswitch uses these addresses to load balance traffic. If a call is presented to a CUBE that is overloaded (its configured CAC threshold has been reached), it returns a SIP 503 Internal Server Error, and the softswitch can use the next available address in the DNS SRV record.

DNS is not offered by all service provider SIP trunk offerings, but when it is, this is generally a good method of load balancing. Even when it is not offered, this mechanism can still be used to good effect on the enterprise side of the network border. This method is dependent on a predictable design of DNS server response time to ensure that post-dial delay (PDD) is minimal.

The DNS SRV mechanism can also be used for load-balancing calls outbound from the CUBE to an attached softswitch. If DNS is used for this call path, the SIP INVITE retry timer might need to be tuned to constrain PDD for outbound calls, as shown in Example 7-10.

Example 7-10   *SIP Retry Timers*

```
sip-ua
  retry-invite 2
```

CUCM Route Groups and Route Lists

When connecting a CUCM to a cluster of border elements for PSTN SIP trunk access, its Route Group and Route Lists constructs can be used to implement a load balancing algorithm for presenting calls outbound from the enterprise to the PSTN. Other SIP softswitches and IP-PBXs most likely have similar alternative routing capabilities that can be used in a similar manner. The operation of this mechanism is shown in Figure 7-8.

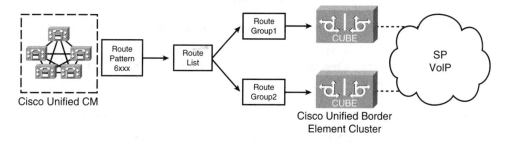

Figure 7-8   *CUCM Route Groups and Route Lists*

Configure a Route Group on CUCM pointing to each individual border element. Aggregate these Route Groups into a Route List that points to the SIP trunk. Configure a Route Pattern in the CUCM dial-plan to route calls of the appropriate dialed number patterns to this Route List. Configure CAC on the individual CUBEs to refuse calls under overload conditions, forcing CUCM to reroute to the next Route Group in the Route List.

Cisco Unified SIP Proxy

The Cisco Unified SIP Proxy can be used with a cluster of border elements as a logical large-scale SIP trunk network border interface to the attached softswitches. That is, the attached softswitches on both the service provider and enterprise sides are unaware of the individual elements, or the number of them, in the CUBE cluster. This is a handy mechanism when:

■   You build large-scale SIP trunks where the number of border elements exceed the two IP addresses given by your provider.

■   You want to grow the SIP trunk capacity over time without affecting the configurations of the attached softswitches on either side of the border.

The Cisco Unified SIP Proxy is responsible for the load balancing over the individual border elements, keeps track of their loads, and reroutes traffic when a particular element is overloaded or unavailable. The operation of this mechanism is shown in Figure 7-9.

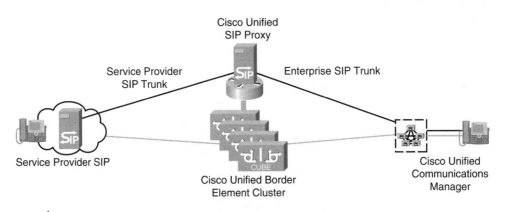

Figure 7-9   *Cisco Unified SIP Proxy and Border Element Cluster*

In addition to load balancing, the Cisco Unified SIP Proxy offers many benefits to the SIP trunk interconnect:

■   Hides the size of the border element pool from the attached softswitch configurations.

■   Offers policy-based SIP trunk call routing such as time-of-day and least-cost routing.

■   Offers powerful SIP Normalization capabilities.

■   Offers graceful service degradation for upgrades or maintenance of the border elements.

■   Offers an easy way to expand the capacity of your SIP trunk when your needs grow.

■   Offers intrinsic redundancy because there isn't a single border element but a cluster of them. (The SIP proxy itself must, of course, be deployed in a redundant configuration; otherwise, it becomes a single point of failure.)

PSTN TDM Gateway Failover

An easy and cost-effective way to provide redundancy and failover for a SIP trunk is simply to reroute calls to your already existing TDM gateways when the SIP trunk is not available or overloaded. This method provides a ready migration path while you ramp up SIP trunk traffic to full production and enables you more time to design and implement some of the other SIP trunk redundancy mechanisms in preparation for a future state where your network might no longer have TDM connectivity. The operation of this mechanism is shown in Figure 7-10.

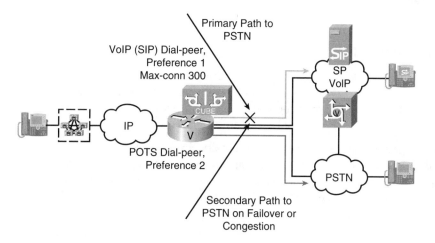

Figure 7-10   *SIP Trunk to PSTN Failover*

Configure call routing to use the SIP trunk as the primary method of access (using a higher preference dial-peer) and the TDM gateway as the secondary path (using a lower-preference dial-peer). You can use the same physical Cisco platform for both functions so that adding a SIP trunk to your PSTN gateway does not mean adding equipment to the network.

SIP Trunk Capacity Engineering

Part of the scalability assessment for your network is to determine how many concurrent sessions should be supported on the SIP trunk service offering that you get from a service provider. If you have current PSTN traffic statistics on your TDM gateways, this assessment is somewhat easier as the ratios of phones to trunks do not change with SIP trunking. But many enterprise networks do not have detailed current statistics of these call patterns.

SIP trunk session sizing is also affected if you choose a centralized model, as opposed to the distributed model of traditional TDM trunking where there is often oversubscription at each site. This oversubscription can be consolidated with a centralized SIP trunk facility, but you still have to engineer with some level of bursting of call traffic for unusual situations.

As a ballpark assessment, you can use the same method of estimating trunk (which is equivalent to a SIP trunk session) capacity as you used in the traditional voice traffic engineering exercises. An average enterprise business can use a 5:1 trunking ratio, meaning for every five phones, provision one trunk (SIP session). Enterprises that are primarily internally focused (for example research facilities or engineering departments) can use a 10:1 ratio. Contact center deployments should use a 1:1 ratio, and *phones* in this context include both live agents and automated ports serving Interactive Voice Response (IVR) front-end applications.

SIP Trunk Monitoring

Several generic IP mechanisms can monitor the health of a network element, such as an Internet Control Message Protocol (ICMP) Ping. Although these are useful, they provide only Layer 3 health. The SIP protocol specifies an Out-of-Dialog (OOD) Options Ping method in RFC-3261 that provides a Layer 7 health indication of a SIP endpoint.

The OOD Options Ping method can provide a health check for a SIP trunk and enables attached devices to reroute traffic upon a failure of any one element in the path. Note that it is a per-hop method and that several Pings might need to be configured to provide end-to-end failure detection on a SIP trunk. This method is illustrated in Figure 7-11.

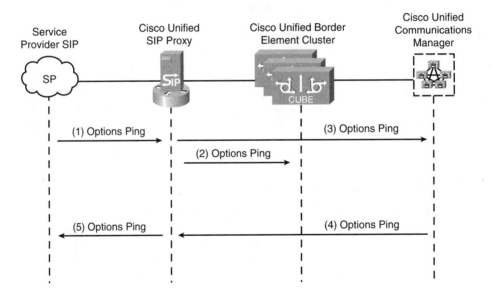

Figure 7-11   *SIP Trunk Monitoring Using Options Ping*

If the Options Ping between the elements fails (in the direction indicated in Figure 7-11), the following actions are taken:

Step 1.   The service provider fails over to the secondary IP address for the SIP trunk, if available, or reroutes calls destined to the enterprise.

Step 2.   The Cisco Unified SIP Proxy marks a border element as down and reroutes calls to alternative border elements in the cluster until it comes back up.

Step 3.   The Cisco Unified SIP Proxy marks CUCM as down and rejects incoming calls from the service provider.

Step 4.   When supported (a future capability), this path allows a CUCM to mark the SIP trunk as down and use its alternative routing logic to place outgoing calls.

Step 5.   The Cisco Unified SIP marks the SIP trunk to the service provider as down and rejects incoming calls from CUCM, enabling it to use its alternative routing logic to place outgoing calls. In the absence of (4), this is the method that indicates to the CUCM that the service provider SIP trunk is down.

Summary

SIP trunks are becoming an increasingly viable option for enterprises wanting to deploy IP-based PSTN access. This chapter highlighted many of the network design and implementation considerations you should work through while planning or installing a SIP trunk for production purposes in your network. Migrating to SIP trunking is a fundamental network change that should be accompanied by the appropriate level of planning and configuration and can require several phases of deployment.

In Chapter 8, another key area of network consideration—interworking and interoperability—is explored in further detail to round out the discussion of network design considerations regarding SIP trunking.

Further Reading

The following documents and references provide additional information on the topics covered in this chapter.

General

SIPConnect Forum: Focused on defining SP UNI compliance as a standard to ease interop requirements. http://www.sipforum.org/sipconnect.

Cisco IOS and Unified Border Element Documents

More information on TLS configuration for the CUBE can be found on Cisco.com. www.cisco.com/go/cube > Configure > Configuration Examples and TechNotes > Unified Border Element SIP TLS Configuration Example.

More SIP Normalization examples for the CUBE can be found on Cisco.com. www.cisco.com/go/cube > Configure > Configuration Examples and TechNotes > Unified Border Element (CUBE) Session Initiation Protocol (SIP) Normalization with SIP Profiles Configuration Example.

Voice Performance Statistics on Cisco Gateways. www.cisco.com/en/US/docs/ios/12_3t/12_3t4/feature/guide/gt_th.html.

IETF RFCs

Transport Layer Security (TLS) RFC-2246.
http://www.ietf.org/rfc/rfc2246.txt?number=2246.

A Privacy Mechanism for the Session Initiation Protocol (SIP) (RFC-3323).
http://www.ietf.org/rfc/rfc3323.txt?number=3323.

Private Extensions to the Session Initiation Protocol (SIP) for Asserted Identity within Trusted Networks (RFC-3325). http://www.ietf.org/rfc/rfc3325.txt?number=3325.

HTTP Authentication: Basic and Digest Access Authentication (RFC-2617).
http://www.ietf.org/rfc/rfc2617.txt?number=2617.

The Secure Real-Time Transport Protocol (SRTP) (RFC-3711).
http://www.ietf.org/rfc/rfc3711.txt?number=3711.

A DNS RR for specifying the location of services (DNS SRV) (RFC-2782).
http://www.ietf.org/rfc/rfc2782.txt?number=2782.

SIP: Session Initiation Protocol (RFC-3261).
http://www.ietf.org/rfc/rfc3261.txt?number=3261.

A Message Summary and Message Waiting Indication Event Package for the Session Initiation Protocol (SIP) (RFC-3842). http://www.ietf.org/rfc/rfc3842.txt?number=3842.

Chapter 8

Interworking

This chapter covers the following topics:

- Protocols

- Media

- Encryption interworking

Chapter 7, "Design and Implementation Considerations," discussed a series of network design and implementation considerations you should work through when connecting a service provider Session Initiation Protocol (SIP) trunk into your network. This chapter explores an additional set of considerations regarding interworking.

When all external Public Switched Telephone Network (PSTN) calls to the enterprise were Time Division Multiplexing (TDM) and only internal calls used IP, the enterprise network designer was in complete control of the following:

- Which IP user endpoints communicated with each other and the compatibility of the capabilities among these endpoints

- The H.323 and SIP protocols and vintages used between network elements

- The methods of interworking such as dual tone multi-frequency (DTMF), fax and codec choice, and packetization

When external PSTN calls arrive as IP calls using a SIP trunk, the enterprise no longer has direct control over any of these network elements. The protocol variations and media encoding methods of externally originated IP calls (such as the codec or DTMF-relay method chosen) might be incompatible with enterprise network components, or they might be undesirable because they violate call admission control (CAC) policies or cause difficulties with feature interoperability.

A border element device can help ease incompatibility and interoperability issues including:

- **Protocol interworking:** H.323, SIP, and variations of these

- **Media interworking:** DTMF and codec interworking

- **Fax and modem traffic interworking:** Negotiating between different fax and modem over IP transport mechanisms

- **Security interworking:** Connecting a network segment with encryption deployed to another network segment not yet capable of encryption

Protocols

All standards have variations when implemented by different vendors and by different software stacks in various applications. This is caused by variances in the interpretation of the standards, variances in vendor compliance to the standards, and by many optional elements in the standards specifications. These implementation variations cause interoperability difficulties between endpoints, applications, and other protocol-aware network devices.

Older standards such as H.323 and Integrated Services Digital Network (ISDN) have a maturity in the industry that has shaken out most of the interoperability issues between vendors. SIP is still a relatively new standard and is covered by many Request for Comments (RFC), and vendor compliance to, and interpretation of, these vary.

Protocol interworking areas to consider as your network migrates to SIP, or begins to use SIP trunking for PSTN access, include

- Applications

- Endpoints

- Service provider SIP Trunk Interworking—SP User-to-Network Interface (UNI)

- SIP Normalization

Applications

Enterprise networks today widely deploy H.323, whereas SIP applications and endpoints are slowly being phased in. Users cannot upgrade their entire network overnight, so this situation causes an almost perpetual state of *networks in transition* in which various protocols must be connected together.

As illustrated in Figure 8-1, several possible transitional situations might exist in your network:

- Older versions of Cisco Unified Communications Manager (CUCM) capable of only H.323

- Newer versions of CUCM that can reasonably be deployed with SIP

- Older IP-PBXs not capable of SIP without potentially expensive upgrades

- Newer SIP applications such as meeting servers, voice mail servers, and presence servers

- A shared SIP trunk for PSTN access used by all these applications

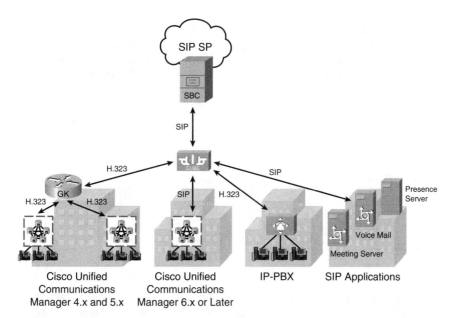

Figure 8-1 *H.323 and SIP Networks in Transition*

To interconnect these various H.323 and SIP applications, a border element can help by doing protocol translation of H.323 to SIP, or to normalize between different variations of SIP, and can also enable for the SIP trunk to the PSTN to be shared among these applications.

SIP Normalization is discussed in more detail in the later "SIP Normalization" section in this chapter, but other areas of H.323 and SIP protocol interworking to consider include H.323 slow-start and fast-start and SIP delayed offer (DO) and early offer (EO). SIP DO means no session description protocol (SDP) information specifying the session attributes such as codec choice is included in the initial INVITE for the call setup. SIP EO means an SDP is included in the initial call setup INVITE.

The Cisco Unified Border Element (CUBE) supports the protocol conversion combinations given in Table 8-1.

Endpoints

Similar to applications, you can find a large variety of SIP endpoints on the market with widely varying capabilities. As you start to deploy these in your network, they also might give rise to a need to normalize SIP messaging across the enterprise to ensure interoperability or predictability (for example, of the information included in various SIP headers that control how phone displays are rendered).

Service Provider SIP Trunk Interworking—SP UNI

IP access from a service provider almost always offers a SIP interface; although in rare cases, this interface might also be H.323. All *IP trunk for PSTN access* SP offerings that

Table 8-1   *CUBE Protocol Conversion Support*

Protocol	In-Leg	Out-Leg	Support
H.323–H.323	Fast Start	Fast Start	Bidirectional
	Slow Start	Slow Start	Bidirectional
	Fast Start	Slow Start	Bidirectional
H.323–SIP	Fast Start	Early Offer	Bidirectional
	Slow Start	Delayed Offer	Bidirectional
SIP–SIP	Early Offer	Early Offer	Bidirectional
	Delayed Offer	Delayed Offer	Bidirectional
	Delayed Offer	Early Offer	Unidirectional

became available in the past 2 years have been SIP, but a handful of older H.323 offerings in the installed base preceded the industry transition to SIP. These are no longer actively sold to new customers but exist in several current service provider networks.

Many enterprise networks have not yet migrated to SIP internally, and even for those who have the variation of SIP used by the enterprise's call agent might also not be of the same vintage, or compatible in message use, with the service provider's SIP offering for all call flows.

For example, there are variations in the use of the SIP REFER or REINVITE messages for modifying calls during a transfer. There are also multiple ways in SIP to put a call on hold and to resume it.

Because of these variations, SIP trunk service providers offer an explicit UNI specification of which message types, formats, and fields are valid on their service offering. For the enterprise to comply with this UNI, it is often easier to place a border element at the edge of the network to *normalize* all the variants from different enterprise applications and endpoints than to try to configure each individual application or endpoint to comply with the UNI. It is especially so if the enterprise connects to multiple different SIP trunk providers, perhaps for least-cost routing or for redundancy purposes.

Using a CUBE to interconnect to the SIP trunk also enables small businesses and enterprises to take advantage immediately of SIP trunk offerings, without requiring the rest of the network to be upgraded, or to be SIP-capable. The migration of the entire enterprise network to SIP can therefore be done in a timeline suitable to your business needs, while at the same time you can make SIP trunk services and benefits available to your user community. Industry efforts such as the SIPconnect forum (refer to http://www.sipforum.org/sipconnect for more information) strive to ease the collective migration to SIP, but the progress across the industry is slow, and business benefits can be accrued immediately if an interconnect device is used to resolve the interoperability problems.

SIP Normalization

The previous sections covered many reasons why it might be necessary to *manipulate* SIP messaging as it flows through your network or to a SIP trunk provider's network. In summary, SIP incompatibilities arise due to:

■ A device rejecting an unknown header (or value or parameter) instead of ignoring it

■ A device sending incorrect data in a SIP message

■ A device not implementing (or incorrectly implementing) protocol procedures

■ A device expecting an optional header value or parameter that can be implemented in multiple ways

■ A device sending a value or parameter that must be changed or suppressed before it leaves or enters the enterprise to comply with policies or the SP UNI

■ Variations in the SIP standards of how to achieve certain functions

■ Privacy settings that must often be set for calls that flow off-net but that are not necessary for internal-only calls

■ An application requiring an optional header for proper operation, and other applications or endpoints that do not implement that optional header

These incompatibilities often can be resolved with *SIP Normalization*: a blanket term describing the manipulation or customization of SIP messages by adding, modifying, or deleting certain elements within the messages. This manipulation can affect the content of the SIP headers or SDP headers.

Figure 8-2 shows two examples of SIP Normalization techniques:

■ In example (a), the user=phone tag is added to the SIP INVITE to comply with the needs of an application or SIP trunk provider on the outgoing side of the CUBE.

■ In example (b), the sip: Uniform Resource Identifier (URI) is changed to a **tel:** URI in the SIP INVITE to interoperate with an application requiring a **tel:** URI.

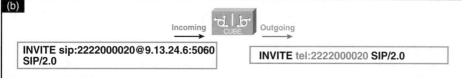

Figure 8-2 *SIP Normalization Examples*

Example 8-1 illustrates the regular expression commands configured to affect the SIP Normalization examples shown in Figure 8-2.

Example 8-1   *SIP Normalization Commands*

```
(a)
voice class sip-profiles 100
   request INVITE sip-header SIP-Req-URI modify "; SIP/2.0" ";user=phone SIP/2.0"
   request REINVITE sip-header SIP-Req-URI modify "; SIP/2.0" ";user=phone SIP/2.0"
(b)
voice class sip-profiles 100
   request INVITE sip-header SIP-Req-URI modify "sip:(.*)@[^ ]+" "tel:\1"
   request INVITE sip-header From modify "<sip:(.*)@.*>" "<tel:\1>"
   request INVITE sip-header To modify "<sip:(.*)@.*>" "<tel:\1>"
```

Example 8-2 shows a number of additional examples that **add** an element to a SIP message.

- In example (a), a b=AS:4000 SDP header for the video-media line is added to INVITE messages.

- In example (b), a Retry-After SIP header is added to 480 Temporarily Not Available response message.

- In example (c), a user=phone field is added to SIP URI of INVITE and REINVITE messages.

- In example (d), a User-Agent SIP header is added to 200 response messages.

Example 8-2   *SIP Normalization Add Examples*

```
(a)
voice class sip-profiles 100
  request INVITE sdp-header Video-Bandwidth-Info add "b=AS:4000"
(b)
voice class sip-profiles 100
  response 480 sip-header Retry-After add "Retry-After: 60"
(c)
voice class sip-profiles 100
  request INVITE sip-header SIP-Req-URI modify "; SIP/2.0" ";user=phone SIP/2.0"
  request REINVITE sip-header SIP-Req-URI modify "; SIP/2.0" ";user=phone SIP/2.0"
(d)
voice class sip-profiles 100
  response 200 sip-header User-Agent add "User-Agent: CiscoSystems-SIP-GW-UA"
```

Example 8-3 shows a number of additional examples that **remove** an element from a SIP message.

■   In example (a), the Cisco-Guid SIP header is removed from all requests and responses.

■   In example (b), the Reason SIP header is removed from all BYE and CANCEL messages.

■   In example (c), the Server SIP header is removed from all 100 and 180 responses.

Example 8-3   *SIP Normalization Remove Examples*

```
(a)
voice class sip-profiles 100
  request ANY sip-header Cisco-Guid remove
  response ANY sip-header Cisco-Guid remove
(b)
voice class sip-profiles 100
  request BYE sip-header Reason remove
  request CANCEL sip-header Reason remove
(c)
voice class sip-profiles 100
  response 100 sip-header Server remove
  response 180 sip-header Server remove
```

Example 8-4 shows a number of additional examples that **Modify** an element of a SIP message.

■   In example (a), the From: SIP header is changed to the gateway@gw-ip-address format in INVITE messages; for example, 2222000020@9.13.24.7 is changed to gateway@9.13.24.7.

■   In example (b), the CiscoSystems-SIP-GW-UserAgent SDP header is replaced with "-" in the o= line of INVITE messages.

■   In example (c), a sip URL is converted to a tel URL in all INVITE messages; for example, from sip:22220000205060 to tel:2222000020.

Example 8-4   *SIP Normalization Modify Examples*

```
(a)
voice class sip-profiles 100
  request INVITE sip-header From modify "(<.*:)(.*@)" "\1gateway@"
(b)
voice class sip-profiles 100
  request INVITE sdp-header Session-Owner modify "CiscoSystems-SIP-GW-UserAgent" "-"
```

continues

Example 8-4   *(continued)*

```
(c)
voice class sip-profiles 100
  request INVITE sip-header SIP-Req-URI modify "sip:(.*)@[^ ]+" "tel:\1"
  request INVITE sip-header From modify "<sip:(.*)@.*>" "<tel:\1>"
  request INVITE sip-header To modify "<sip:(.*)@.*>" "<tel:\1>"
```

The preceding examples provided an illustration of the command line interface syntax used by the CUBE to do SIP message manipulation. Additional examples and descriptions of the feature can be found on Cisco.com at www.cisco.com/go/cube, "Configure," "Configuration Examples and TechNotes."

Media

The speech path, or Real-Time Transport Protocol (RTP) stream, of an IP call typically flows directly between the communicating endpoints, requiring that the endpoints support a common set of capabilities for voice or video encoding.

These streams can be encoded in myriad ways and still be standards-compliant, and it is likely that your enterprise endpoints support only a subset of these methods, or that you want to deploy only a subset of them to ensure that the interconnect policies of your network are met.

Media interworking areas to consider as your network migrates to end-to-end IP, or start to use SIP trunking for PSTN access, include

- DTMF digits

- Codecs, including transcoding and transrating

- Fax and modem traffic

DTMF

DTMF digits can be transported in numerous ways in both H.323 and SIP. How DTMF digits are exchanged between endpoints and applications often requires conversion or translation between these methods.

DTMF Relay

For G.711 streams DTMF digits can reasonably be carried in-band as tones within the speech path itself, but for low bit-rate codecs such as G.729 and Internet Low-Bitrate Codec (iLBC) the encoding algorithm distorts the DTMF frequencies to the point that

DTMF recognizing success rates with voice mail and interactive voice response (IVR) systems become unacceptably low. For this reason DTMF relay methods are predominant in Voice over IP (VoIP) streams.

DTMF relay means that the DTMF tones are encoded in a manner different from voice sample encoding and are re-created as clear tones at the destination endpoint by its local Digital Signal Processor (DSP). That way, network transport does not distort the frequencies of the tones. Some DTMF relay methods encode just the tone pressed by the originator; others also encode the duration of the tone, enabling higher accuracy in play-out at the destination endpoint.

Although a handful of SIP trunk providers offer in-band tones (that is, DTMF carried as audible tones inside the G.711 speech path) and therefore avoid encoding of DTMF in any of the relay mechanisms, the vast majority of providers use RFC-2833 encoding as the DTMF relay method.

DTMF Relay Methods

H.323 offers three common methods of DTMF relay:

- H.245 Alphanumeric
- H.245 Signal
- RFC-2833

SIP offers four common methods of DTMF relay:

- SIP NOTIFY
- RFC-2833
- Key Press Markup Language (KPML) (RFC-4730)
- SIP INFO

Both H.323 and SIP additionally enable in-band tones (G.711) for DTMF and the DTMF relay methods listed previously.

Although the SIP NOTIFY and SIP INFO methods are specified in the SIP standards (RFC-3265 and RFC-2976, respectively), these are generic methods and not particular to carrying DTMF relay. The RFCs do not specify how to use them for DTMF relay, and therefore any implementation of these methods for DTMF relay should be considered vendor-specific.

RFC-2833 is a well-known specification for both SIP and H.323 DTMF relay, and virtually all vendors implement this. The RFC has been superseded by RFC-4733, which is currently not yet commonly implemented.

DTMF Relay Conversion

A back-to-back user agent (such as that offered by the CUBE) at the edge of your network terminating the external SIP trunk session and reoriginating an internal SIP (or H.323) session can convert these DTMF mechanisms. The same border element can also convert between these mechanisms to provide interworking between different endpoints or applications within your network.

Example 8-5 shows the configuration of DTMF relay options available on Cisco IOS dial-peers.

Example 8-5   *DTMF Relay Configuration Commands*

```
dial-peer voice 10 voip
 description example
 destination-pattern 408555.
 session protocol sipv2
 session target ipv4:10.10.10.1
 dtmf-relay rtp-nte
 no vad


router(config-dial-peer)# dtmf-relay ?
  h245-alphanumeric  DTMF Relay via H245 Alphanumeric IE
  h245-signal        DTMF Relay via H245 Signal IE
  rtp-nte            RTP Named Telephone Event RFC 2833
  sip-kpml           DTMF Relay via KPML over SIP SUBCRIBE/NOTIFY
  sip-notify         DTMF Relay via SIP NOTIFY messages
```

Most DTMF relay mechanisms travel in the signaling path and are therefore available for manipulation by all call agents, soft switches, and proxies. RFC-2833 DTMF relay, however, travels in the media path, as does any in-band tones. Manipulating these forms of DTMF is available only to network elements that handle the media path. Interpreting (that is, capturing and converting) in-band tones to DTMF relay requires a DSP on the CUBE. All other DTMF mechanisms can be converted in software only.

Codecs

Codecs specify how to encode and decode speech using various parameters and compression techniques. Common codecs in use for VoIP include G.711 and G.729. Narrowband codecs encode speech in the range 400 Hz to 3500 Hz, whereas wideband codecs such as G.722 encode 50 to 7000 Hz thereby offering much higher fidelity voice quality. Newer narrowband codecs such as (internet Low Bitrate Codec (iLBC) has better voice quality resiliency over networks with packet loss than the traditional G.711 and G.729A codecs, but it is not currently widely supported or used.

Wideband codecs are becoming increasingly popular in end-to-end VoIP systems because the traditional PSTN (generally capable of nothing better than G.711) could not provide high fidelity voice. With SIP trunking this *lowest common denominator* limitation has been removed. Most current SIP trunk providers do not yet offer wideband codecs as a commercial offering, but this is bound to appear in the not-too-distant future.

Consider several aspects of codecs in network interworking scenarios:

- Payload types

- Codec filtering or stripping

- Transcoding (meaning to change the codec used by a single voice call in the middle of the stream; for example, one endpoint uses G.711 whereas the other endpoint on the same call uses G.729A, and a device in the middle of the stream transcodes the RTP stream from G.711 to G.729A)

- Transrating (meaning to change the packetization period of the codec of a single call in the middle of the stream; for example, one endpoint uses G.729A 20 ms whereas the other endpoint on the same call uses G.729A 30 ms, and a device in the middle of the stream transrates the RTP stream from G.729 20 ms to G.729A 30 ms packetization)

Payload Types

All the different voice and video codecs and ancillary traffic such as DTMF relay and voice-band data (for example fax and modem) are indicated in the RTP protocol by a designated payload type. Payload types assigned by the standards are given in RFC-1890 and RFC-3551. The range between 96 to 127 is unassigned and listed as *dynamic*, which means vendor implementations can use these as they prefer. This is the range where incompatibilities occur and where it becomes important to configure or convert (when configuration is not possible or desired) between a payload type for a specific type of traffic.

Example 8-6 shows an example of explicit mappings of payload-types on a Cisco IOS dial-peer. Payload-type 96 is used by default for fax by Cisco IOS code. However, Cisco Telepresence systems also use this by default for the Advanced Audio Coding Low Delay (AAC-LD) codec. The configuration here assigns 96 to the Telepresence AAC-LD codec and maps fax to payload type 110 instead.

Example 8-6   *Payload Type Configuration Commands*

```
dial-peer voice 11 voip
 description payload-type conversion
 destination-pattern 408555.
 rtp payload-type cisco-codec-fax-ind 110
 rtp payload-type cisco-codec-aacld 96
 rtp payload-type cisco-codec-video-h264 112
 session protocol sipv2
 session target ipv4:10.10.10.1
 dtmf-relay rtp-nte
 no vad
```

Example 8-7 shows the payload types assigned in Cisco IOS in the 96 to 127 range and the keywords that can be used to change the assignment if needed.

Example 8-7   *Payload Type Options in Cisco IOS*

```
c2851-cube2(config-dial-peer)#rtp payload-type ?
  cisco-cas-payload            Cisco CAS RTP payload
  cisco-clear-channel          Cisco clear channel RTP payload
  cisco-codec-aacld            Cisco codec AACLD
  cisco-codec-fax-ack          Cisco codec fax ack
  cisco-codec-fax-ind          Cisco codec fax indication
  cisco-codec-gsmamrnb         Cisco codec GSM AMR Narrow Band
  cisco-codec-ilbc             Cisco codec iLBC
  cisco-codec-video-h263+      RTP video codec H263+ payload type
  cisco-codec-video-h264       RTP video codec H264 payload type
  cisco-fax-relay              Cisco fax relay
  cisco-pcm-switch-over-alaw   Cisco RTP PCM codec switch over ind (a-law)
  cisco-pcm-switch-over-ulaw   Cisco RTP PCM codec switch over ind (u-law)
  cisco-rtp-dtmf-relay         cisco-rtp dtmf relay
  comfort-noise                RTP comfort noise payload type
  g726r16                      Using dynamic payload for g726r16 in H323 - SIP
interop
  g726r24                      Using dynamic payload for g726r24 in H323 - SIP
interop
  lmr-tone                     Land Mobile Radio Tone Event
  nse                          Named Signaling Event
  nte                          Named Telephone Event
nte-tone                       Named Telephone Tone Event
```

Codec Filtering or Stripping

The term *codec filtering* or *codec stripping* denotes a network border function in which the list of valid codecs that can be negotiated by the endpoints on a call are limited or manipulated.

Figure 8-3 shows how the CUBE can provide a codec filtering function. The incoming dial-peer on the left is configured as *codec transparent* that enables all codecs offered by the endpoint. The outgoing dial-peer on the right, however, lists G.711 explicitly, and therefore the outgoing H.323 or SIP call setup contains only G.711 as a codec offer. The terminating endpoint on the right can support more than G.711, but because G.711 is the only codec offered to it, it accepts the call with this codec.

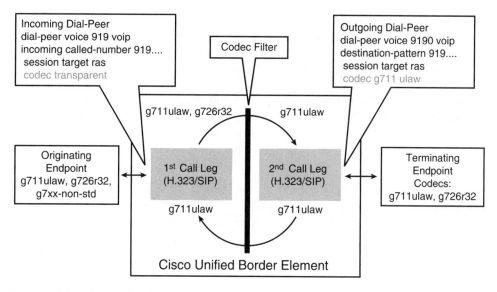

Figure 8-3 *Codec Filtering*

Example 8-8 shows filtering of the higher bandwidth codecs by dial-peer 1. With this configuration, codecs other than those specified are disallowed by calls matching dial-peer 1 for routing.

Example 8-8 *Codec Filtering Configuration Commands*

```
voice class codec 1
  codec preference 1 g729br8
  codec preference 2 g723r53
  codec preference 3 g723r68
!
dial-peer voice 1 voip
  voice-class codec 1
```

Transcoding

Codec filtering restricts or controls the codec that can be negotiated by the endpoints. The resulting call uses a single codec end-to-end. Another network interworking option is transcoding where a larger selection of external codecs can be enabled even if they are incompatible with the codecs you want to use internally on your network. With transcoding you change the codec at the network border so that two different codecs are used on different legs of the call.

The mechanism of transcoding is illustrated in Figure 8-4. One half of the call uses G.711 whereas the other half uses G.729. DSPs are required for transcoding, and you should generally attempt to avoid transcoding between two low-bitrate codecs because the voice quality might become impaired to the point of causing end user dissatisfaction. Transcoding between a high-bitrate codec (such as G.711 or G.722) and a low-bitrate codec (such as G.729 or iLBC) is common practice and results in acceptable voice quality. However, transcoding a single call multiple times or transcoding between two low-bitrate codecs (such as G.729A and iLBC) usually results in poor voice quality and should be avoided. Transcoding for contact center calls should also generally be avoided because voice quality is of the utmost importance in providing a superior caller experience when interacting with a contact center customer service application.

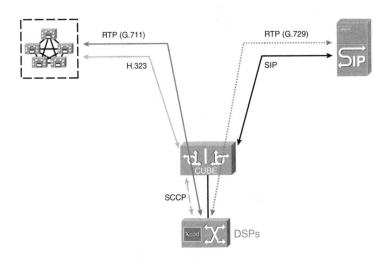

Figure 8-4   *Codec Transcoding*

Transrating

The codec (such as G.711 or G.729) specifies the speech sampling rate, encoding algorithm, and compression technique used to encode the voice. But it does not specify how many of the voice samples should be packed into a single IP packet. For example, the sampling rate for G.711 is 5 ms, but a typical packetization rate is 20 ms so that four samples are packaged per IP packet. Similarly G.729 has a sampling rate of 10 ms so that a packetization rate of 30 ms would contain three samples per packet.

The packetization rate can usually be configured on applications, endpoints, and network elements. The ranges supported by different endpoints might not overlap, or different packetization rates on different network segments might be desirable for bandwidth control or policy reasons.

Codec transrating—that is, changing the number of voice samples per packet, also referred to as codec repacketization—is another codec interworking function that a border element can perform in your network. The time directive in the SDP of a SIP message specifies the packetization rate of the codec.

Fax and Modem Traffic

The ability to send modem and fax calls over SIP trunks is an important consideration for both the service provider and enterprise. Enterprises that cannot achieve adequate fax and modem call success over SIP trunks should maintain these services over their traditional TDM PSTN trunks.

Fax calls terminated by a SIP trunk service provider might have slightly lower speeds than TDM trunks and might support fewer native fax protocols. For example, Super Group 3 (SG3) fax and color faxing cannot be completed over SIP trunks at present. Cisco voice gateways provide mechanisms to transmit SG3 fax calls over SIP trunks using G3.

There are two common ways of transmitting fax over IP:

■ Fax Relay (T.38)

■ Fax passthrough or G.711 Fax

T.38 as a Fax Method for SIP Trunks

T.38 is a standard for implementing faxing over an IP network. For T.38 fax calls to work over a SIP trunk, both the originating and terminating endpoints must support T.38 faxing.

T.38 fax is more resilient to delay, jitter, and loss on an IP network than a fax pass-through method. The T.38 configuration can replicate both the low-speed V.21 and the high-speed T4 traffic generated with a fax. The replication of packets can aid in providing a higher fax success rate when using unified communications (UC) SIP trunks.

A T.38 capability is indicated in the SDP, and the negotiation can occur through a REINVITE request or by using a named signaling event (NSE) in the RTP stream. The NSE option is supported by Cisco voice gateways and the CUBE. Cisco products implement the User Datagram Protocol (UDP) as the transport layer for T.38 fax.

Fax Pass-Through as a Fax Method for SIP Trunks

Fax pass-through involves the originating and terminating gateways changing their codec to G.711 and fixing the jitter buffer (to a recommended 200 ms) to send fax information in-band in the speech path. Fax pass-through consumes more bandwidth than T.38 Fax Relay and is generally used only to ease interoperability to non-T.38 capable endpoints. After the fax tone is detected, the upspeed request to the G.711 codec for fax pass-through mode can be signaled using a SIP REINVITE request or using NSE. The NSE option is supported by Cisco voice gateways and the CUBE.

Modem Traffic

Modem calls are less and less prevalent as many data communications systems move to using pure IP. However, modems are still used in many retail locations for credit card validation systems (point of sale) and across enterprises for monitoring and triggering security and alarm systems. The main disadvantage of carrying a modem call over an IP network is the absence of a TDM clock, and therefore high-speed 56 Kbps connections cannot be achieved. Connection speeds of 28.8 Kbps are achievable when the IP network has no jitter or packet loss.

Modem traffic can, like fax, be transported over IP networks as either pass-through or relay traffic. SIP trunk providers do not offer modem relay mechanisms, so the only current method to carry modem over SIP trunks is as in-band G.711 traffic. For better call success rates, it is recommended to keep modem traffic on TDM PSTN connections until industry interworking for modem over IP improves or until modem applications become native IP applications and no longer need traditional TDM modem technology.

Encryption Interworking

Border element security features were covered in Chapter 7, including signaling (with Transport Layer Security [TLS]) and media encryption (with Secure RTP [SRTP]). The remaining interworking issue in the security category to discuss is how to interoperate between a network segment that is capable of TLS or SRTP to a segment that is not.

Figure 8-5 illustrates three scenarios where such interworking might be desirable:

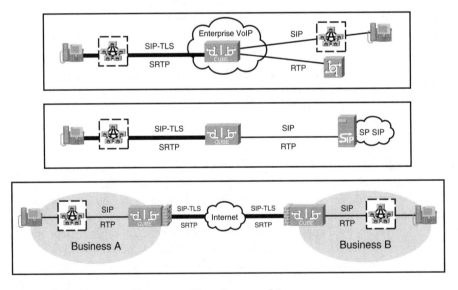

Figure 8-5   *Secure to Nonsecure Zone Interworking*

- **Intra-enterprise application interworking:** Connecting SRTP-capable CUCM clusters with other non-SRTP-capable clusters or other applications.

- **SIP trunk interworking:** Connecting an SRTP-capable CUCM or enterprise domain with a SIP trunk that does not offer SRTP as a service.

- **Business-to-business interconnect:** The public segment between the two enterprises are protected with encryption while neither of the enterprises themselves have deployed encryption.

Numerous combinations of TLS and SRTP interworking might be desirable. Often only the signaling is encrypted (TLS), but the media is not. The opposite is technically possible—which is to encrypt the media (SRTP) but not the signaling—but this makes no sense to deploy because it is does not produce any security. The SRTP keys are exchanged in the signaling streams, so unless the signaling path is secured, there is no point in encrypting the media.

Figure 8-6 illustrates five different TLS/SRTP interworking scenarios:

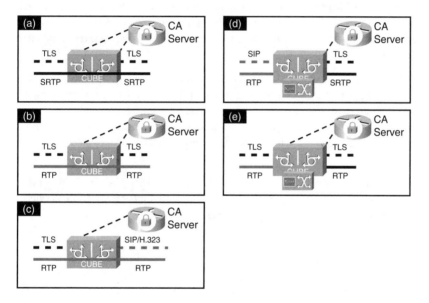

Figure 8-6   *TLS/SRTP Interworking Options*

- **Both legs TLS; SRTP passthrough (a):** The signaling of both legs of the call is encrypted with TLS and are terminated on the border element. The SRTP packets are passed through as is. The border element rewrites the IP headers of the SRTP packets, but does not examine the encrypted payload. The border element passes through the SRTP keys between the endpoints, but it is not involved in key management or decryption or encryption of the media.

- **Both legs TLS; no media encryption (b):** The signaling of both legs of the call is encrypted with TLS and is terminated on the border element. The media is not encrypted, and the RTP packets are passed through as is.

- **One leg TLS; no media encryption (c):** The signaling of one leg of the call is encrypted with TLS and is terminated on the border element. The media is not encrypted, and the RTP packets are passed through as is.

■ **One leg TLS and SRTP; no encryption on the other leg (d):** The signaling of one leg of the call is encrypted with TLS and is terminated on the border element. The media of the same leg is encrypted with SRTP and terminated (that is, decrypted) on the border element. The other leg of the call has no signaling or media encryption.

■ **Both legs TLS; one leg media encryption (e):** The signaling of both legs of the call is encrypted with TLS and is terminated on the border element. The media of one leg is encrypted with SRTP and terminated (that is, decrypted) on the border element. The other leg of the call has media encryption.

Summary

This chapter along with Chapter 7 focused on key areas of network design considerations you should work through while planning or installing a SIP trunk for production purposes in your network. This chapter elaborated specifically on interworking and interoperability areas for SIP trunking.

H.323 and SIP interworking and ways to normalize SIP messaging to aid interworking of applications speaking, or preferring, different dialects of SIP is discussed. Interworking in the media path including different DTMF relay methods; different codecs and different fax methods are also covered. Completing the discussion is information on signaling and media encryption methods and ways to interwork encrypted and nonencrypted network segments.

Chapter 9, "Questions to Ask of a Service Provider Offering and SBC Vendor," shifts the focus to areas to explore with your service provider when looking for a SIP trunk service and guides you on how to evaluate different offerings.

Further Reading

The following documents and references provide additional information on the topics covered in this chapter.

CUBE Documents

Examples on SIP Normalization configuration for the CUBE can be found on Cisco.com. www.cisco.com/go/cube > Configure > Configuration Examples and TechNotes > Unified Border Element (CUBE) Session Initiation Protocol (SIP) Normalization with SIP Profiles Configuration Example.

An example of transcoding configuration on the CUBE can be found on Cisco.com. www.cisco.com/go/cube > Configure > Configuration Examples and TechNotes > Unified Border Element Transcoding Configuration Example.

An example of TLS configuration on the CUBE can be found on Cisco.com. www.cisco.com/go/cube > Configure > Configuration Examples and TechNotes > Unified Border Element SIP TLS Configuration Example.

RTP Profile for Audio and Video Conferences with Minimal Control (RFC-1890). http://www.ietf.org/rfc/rfc1890.txt?number=1890.

RTP Payload for DTMF Digits, Telephony Tones, and Telephony Signals (RFC-2833). http://www.ietf.org/rfc/rfc2833.txt?number=2833.

The SIP INFO Method (RFC-2976). http://www.ietf.org/rfc/rfc2976.txt?number=2976.

Session Initiation Protocol (SIP)-Specific Event Notification (RFC-3265). http://www.ietf.org/rfc/rfc3265.txt?number=3265.

RTP Profile for Audio and Video Conferences with Minimal Control (RFC-3551). http://www.ietf.org/rfc/rfc3551.txt?number=3551.

A Session Initiation Protocol (SIP) Event Package for Key Press Stimulus (KPML) (RFC-4730). http://www.ietf.org/rfc/rfc4730.txt?number=4730.

RTP Payload for DTMF Digits, Telephony Tones, and Telephony Signals (RFC-4733). http://www.ietf.org/rfc/rfc4733.txt?number=4733.

Chapter 9

Questions to Ask of a Service Provider Offering and an SBC Vendor

This chapter covers the following topics:

■ Technical requirements

■ Delivery, documentation, and support

■ Quality

■ Business

■ Cost

This chapter explains the questions you should ask your service providers and Session Border Controller (SBC) vendors before you deploy Session Initiation Protocol (SIP) trunks and SBC into your network. It also explains the possible proper answers for the questions. The chapter also discusses the different issues and concerns you need to resolve and the different options you need to examine, and it guides you through selecting the right partners for SIP trunks and SBC.

Expectations of SBC are mostly set by the design of your network. However, it is important to understand the detail features that might be incorporated into your Request For Proposal (RFP). This chapter might not cover every single component of your RFP, but it does cover most of the requirements.

Technical Requirements

The following technical items need to be answered during the process of selecting SIP providers and SBC vendors:

■ Session management

■ Interworking support

■ Demarcation

- Security

- Operations and management

- System specification

- Performance/sizing

Now, let's look into the details of each area.

Session Management

As the SBC is used mostly to connect SIP networks, some SIP-specific requirements need to be answered by the SBC vendor and SIP service provider.

Signaling/Media Protocol

The SBC should support multiple IP Telephony/Voice over IP (VoIP) protocols such as H.323, SIP, SIP-T, SIP-I, and Media Gateway Control Protocol (MGCP). SBC vendors can list the versions supported for the following protocols:

- H.323

- SIP

- SIP-T

- MGCP

- MGCP+

- H.248

- H.248+

Operational Modes Support

An SBC can be operated in different modes. In general, enterprises see the SBC as a Back to Back User Agent (B2BUA) to enable centralized call management, interworking with alternative networks, management, monitoring of the entire call state, and so on. You can check with your SBC vendors about the following modes of operations:

- B2BUA peering

- B2BUA access

- IMS P-CSCF

- Transaction stateful proxy mode

- Session stateful proxy mode

- Stateless proxy mode

- NAT traversal mode

SIP Features

You can put the following SIP-specific features in your RFP. Vendors might not support all the features, but you can pick some of them according to your needs:

- IMS SIP capabilities

    - RFC-3455 headers and procedures

        - ☐ P-Associated-URI

        - ☐ P-Charging-Vector

        - ☐ P-Charging-Function-Address

        - ☐ P-Called-Party-ID

        - ☐ P-Visited-Network-ID

        - ☐ P-Access-Network-Info

    - RFC-3608

        - ☐ Service Route

    - RFC-3327

        - ☐ Path header

- SIP Privacy (RFCs 3324, 3325, and 3326)

    - RFC-3325

        - ☐ P-Asserted-ID for session agents

        - ☐ P-Preferred-ID

- Multiple SIP ports per SIP interface (for example, port 5060 plus alternative listening ports)

- SIP L5 NAT/Topology hiding

- SIP dialogue transparency

- SIP media release intrarealm

- SIP media release intranetwork

- SIP distributed media release (multiple SDs)

- SIP media release behind the same IP address

- SIP RFC-2833 relay

- SIP proxy modes: redirect, proxy, or record route modes

- SIP Redirect processing modes: recurs, proxy, or tunnel
- SIP strict routing
- SIP loose routing
- SIP contact modes: m-address, strict, or loose routing
- Configurable SIP timers (global)
- Configurable SIP timers per realm
- Extended (fine-grained) configurable SIP timers and counters
- Tel URI support
- SIP-to-Tel URI conversion
- SIP status code mapping—per session agent
- SIP transit of unrecognized headers
- SIP Forced unregistration
- SIP configurable locally generated response codes by Session Agent
- SIP configurable locally generated response codes
- SIP RFC-3326 Reason w/Cause
- SIP Port mapping
- SIP selective PAI stripping per SIP interface
- SIP max message size filtering
- SIP media release across network interfaces
- Codec Reordering
- SDP Anonymization
- Aggregate Session Constraints (per SIP interface)
- SIP forced Hosted NAT Traversal (HNT)
- SIP restricted latching
- SIP Symmetric latching
- SIP server failover—timeout cache
- Implicit SERVICE ROUTE—SIP requests follow REGISTRATION
- SIP midcall reregistration following SERVICE ROUTE
- P-CSCF failure—timeout cache and forward based on DNS
- SIP Contact header encoding option
- Surrogate registration (IMS)—IMS aggregate endpoint support

- SIP transport selection/backoff

- Implicit service route enhancements

- SDP-Response early media suppression

- SIP configurable response recursion

- SIP Privacy enhancements

- SIP early media suppression—fraud prevention

- SIP overload registration protection (avalanche restart protection)

- SIP Header Manipulation Rule support for regular expressions

- SIP CAC enhancement support for media release

- Registration event package NAT

- CAC, media policing, ToS for non-AVT types

- SDP—codec filtering and reordering

- SIP interface response map

- SIP response manipulation

- Header Manipulation Rule capability for SIP response code changing

- SIP dialogue move between TCP connections

- P-CSCF load balancing for midcall Uas

- SIP resource priority header (GETS)

- Session agent status based on SIP response

- SIP session agent ping response code settings

- Session router—session agent constraints

- SIP Retry-After Support

- Session Agent Group recursion control

- SIP method transaction stats

- SIP INFO to RFC-2833 DTMF interworking

- SIP response map per sip-interface

- SIP TCP keepalive support

- SIP TCP implicit connection reuse and dialog/transaction changes

- SIP SDP public IP encoding for upstream policy control

- SIP: Session Agent—configurable interval to reopen TCP connection

SIP Methods

SIP uses Methods/Requests and corresponding Responses to establish a call session. Here are the requests and responses defined for SIP:

SIP Requests: There are six basic request/method types:

- INVITE = Establishes a session

- ACK = Confirms an INVITE request

- BYE = Ends a session

- CANCEL = Cancels establishing of a session

- REGISTER = Communicates user location (hostname, IP)

- OPTIONS = Communicates information about the capabilities of the calling and receiving SIP phones

SIP responses: SIP Requests are answered with SIP responses, of which there are six classes:

- 1xx = Informational responses, such as 180, which means ringing

- 2xx = Success responses

- 3xx = Redirection responses

- 4xx = Request failures

- 5xx = Server errors

- 6xx = Global failures

You need to include the following requirements as part of SIP Methods in your RFP:

- RFC-3261: ACK, BYE, CANCEL, INVITE, OPTIONS, REGISTER

- PRACK (RFC-3262): Reliability of provisional responses in SIP

- SUBSCRIBE (RFC-3265): SIP Specific Event Notification

- NOTIFY (RFC-3265): SIP Specific Event Notification

- PUBLISH (RFC-3903): SIP Extension for Event State Publication

- INFO (RFC-2976): SIP INFO method

- UPDATE (RFC-3311): SIP UPDATE method

- MESSAGE (RFC-3428)

- REFER (RFC-3515) SIP Refer Method

IETF and General SIP Support

The Internet Engineering Task Force (IETF) works with a lot of RFCs (Request For Comments) in the general SIP-related area. Check the following RFCs for your RFP:

- RFC-3261
- B2BUA as defined in RFC-3261
- RFC-1889 (RTP)
- RFC-2833 (Telephone Event)
- RFC-2976 (Info)
- RFC-3204 (MIME Support)
- RFC-3312 (Preconditions)
- RFC-3313 (Media Authorization)
- RFC-3326 (Reason Field)
- RFC-3327 (Path)
- RFC-3329 (Security Mechanism)
- RFC-3420 (Sipfrag)
- RFC-3262 (PRACK)
- RFC-3264 (Offer/Answer)
- RFC-3265 (SUBSCRIBE/NOTIFY)
- RFC-3311 (UPDATE)
- RFC-3323 (Privacy)
- RFC-3325 (Private Extensions)
- RFC-3372 (SIP-T)
- RFC-3407 (SDP Simple Capability Declaration)
- RFC-3428 (SIP Extension for Instant Messaging)
- RFC-3515 (REFER)
- RFC-3551 (RTP Profiles for Audio and Video)
- RFC-3581 (SIP Extension for Symmetric Response Routing)
- RFC-3608 (Service Route Discovery)
- RFC-3680 (Event Package Registration)
- RFC-3840 (Indicating User Agent Capabilities)
- RFC-3842 (Message Waiting Indication)

- RFC-3853 (S/MIME Advanced Encryption)

- RFC-3891 ('Replaces' Header)

- RFC-3892 (Referred by Mechanism)

- RFC-3903 (Event State Publication)

- RFC-3911 ('Join' Header)

- RFC-3966 (URLs for Telephone Calls)

- RFC-4028 (Session Timers)

- RFC-4566 (SDP)

Session Timers

Session Timer is a keepalive mechanism for SIP sessions. User Agents (UA) send periodic re-INVITE or UPDATE requests to keep the session alive. The interval for the session refresh requests is determined through a negotiation mechanism. If a session refresh request is not received before the interval passes, the session is considered terminated. You need to check with your SBC vendors to see if it supports following timers:

- Media supervision/fault timers (initial, subsequent, and max session)

- Signaling (SIP max session timer)

Quality of Service

Quality of Service (QoS) is a significant issue in VoIP network. The concept is how to guarantee that packet traffic for a voice or other media connection will not be delayed or dropped due to interference from other lower priority traffic. You need to know how the SBC behaves with latency, jitter, packet loss, and burstiness of the network:

- Does the product support Bandwidth Policing—Per Flow (RTP)?

- Does the product support RTCP?

- Does the product support DSCP/Diffserv?

- Does the product support QoS reporting?

- Does the product support Session Admission Control (SAC) or CAC?

- Does the product support IEEE 802.3p/q?

- Does the product support Echo cancellation?

- Does the product support Delay monitoring?

- Does the product support Jitter monitoring?

■   Does the product support packet loss monitoring?

■   Does the product support Voice Activity Detection (VAD)?

Interworking Support

Interworking is one of the primary functions of an SBC. As an SBC sits at the edge of the network, it has to ensure that different kinds of signaling, coder-decoder (codec), DTMF (dual-tone multifrequency), security measures, and so on work seamlessly between incoming and outgoing sessions. We identify the major interworking topics here. But because we are experiencing significant new developments in the field of unified communications (UC), you might need to check the latest developments to ensure the interworking. Usually the vendors release new software to update their interworking features. You can check the basic interworking features (discussed in the following sections) during your RFP process.

Codecs Support

Codec plays an important role in the UC network. You might need to change your network parameters (CPU capability, bandwidth, Digital Signaling Processing, and so on) to accommodate different kinds of audio and video codecs. Moreover, you might see new codecs in the market while designing and deploying your network. Recently, we have seen two new codecs—internet Low Bitrate Codec (iLBC) and internet Speech Audio Codec (iSAC)—developed by Global IP Solutions (GIPS). These have received very good responses in the industry. Both the codecs work better than other existing codecs in the network with packet loss.

Here is the list of questions to check the support of different kind of codecs and related technologies. You may see new codecs in video technology in near future, as video is the most demanding area in the collaboration space. So, you can add more questions if you want.

■   Does the product support G.711?

■   Does the product support G.722?

■   Does the product support G.723?

■   Does the product support G.729 (G.729A, G.729B)?

■   Does the product support G.722?

■   Does the product support AMR-NB?

■   Does the product support video codecs: H.261, H.263, H.264?

■   Does the product support iLBC?

■   Does the product support iSAC?

■   Does the product support Media Codec Transcoding (G.711 to G.729, and so on)?

- Does the product support Media Codec Negotiation?

- Does the product support Media Codec Prioritization?

- Does the product support Secure Real-Time Transport Protocol (SRTP) and SRTP to RTP conversion?

- Does the product support RTCP?

- Does the product support MIME type (RFC-3555)?

SIP to H.323 Interworking Support

SIP is a standard protocol introduced by the IETF in 1999 to carry VoIP. Because it was created by the IETF, it approaches voice and multimedia from the Internet or IP perspective. H.323 emerged around 1996, and as an International Telecommunication Union standard was designed from a telecommunications perspective. Both standards have the same objective—to enable voice and multimedia convergence with IP protocols.

Although we are talking about SIP trunking, there are existing networks with the H.323 protocol. Both H.323 and SIP use RTP/RTCP and SRTP to transport the media. But if we look into the basic call signaling, call setup, message definition, message encoding, load sharing, load balancing, addressing, address resolution, capability negotiation, conferencing, multicast signaling, authentication, encryption, and so on, they are different. So, when you place an SBC to interwork between your SIP and H.323 network, you need to make sure the product support has a minimum of the following criteria:

- Full support for H.323 version 4 interworking to SIP

- H.323 Fast Start (FS)—SIP and vice versa

- H.323 Slow Start (SS)—SIP and vice versa

- Support of H.245 tunneling in Interworking Function (IWF)

- H.323 Annex-E support for UDP signaling

- Q.931 port can be specified by SBC

- H.245 UII to RFC-2833 DTMF interworking

- Transparent RFC-2833 support

- Support of call hold using Empty the terminal capabilities set

- Support of call transfer using the Empty terminal capabilities set

- Support of conference call using the Empty terminal capabilities set

- SBC can act in Gatekeeper proxy mode

- SBC can act as a virtual gateway

- Q.850 Cause to H.323 Release Complete Reason

- Codec mapping supported

- SIP Redirects can be mapped to an H.323 LRQ

- SIP Info and DTMF UII management capabilities

- Support of midsession media change

- Early media support

- Ringback support for IWF sessions

- Media release, or antitromboning, for IWF calls

- Support for Privacy in IWF calls

- SIP Trunk URI compliancy for IWF calls including trunk group routing

- Manipulation of SIP headers allowed in IWF calls

Other Interworking Support

A few more interworking-related issues could not be grouped in the previous sections, which are also critical for your network and good to put into the RFP:

- DTMF interworking

- SIP over TCP to SIP over User Diagram Protocol (UDP) interworking

- IPSEC to non-IPSEC interworking

- RTP to SRTP interworking

- IPv4 to IPv6 interworking

- SIP-T to SIP-T interworking

- TLS to non-TLS interworking

- FAX capability: T38 ITU standard fax protocol over IP network

Demarcation

An SBC separates your internal network from the external network. This is kind of a wall between these two networks. When you connect your UC system via SIP, there is a possibility to expose your whole network to the external world. SBC protects you from that risk. You need to check with your SBC vendor about the demarcation issues discussed in the following sections.

Topology Hiding

The SBC must have the capability to hide your whole IP topology information (at both Layers 3 and 5) when interworking between the public and private interfaces. It should include a guarantee that not a single IP address can be leaked within the L5 headers.

When a user connects to the outside network, its IP address and port needs to be properly translated to protect its identity. The SBC should support the complete infrastructure topology, hiding at all protocol layers for confidentiality, attacking prevention security, and modifying, removing, or inserting call signaling application headers and fields.

NAT Traversal

NAT breaks end-to-end connectivity. Most NAT behavior-based techniques bypass enterprise security policies. We prefer the techniques that explicitly cooperate with NAT and firewalls, enabling NAT traversal while still enabling marshalling at the NAT to enforce enterprise security policies. Many techniques exist, but no single method works in every situation because NAT behavior is not standardized. You can check at least the following support in the SBC:

- Does the product support NAT Traversal of the near end firewall?

- Does the product support NAT Traversal of the far end firewall?

Session Routing

Session routing is an integral part of session management. The routing database and routing engine needs to perform some basic functions so that your SIP network can accommodate flexible call routing features as needed. You should check with your vendor whether the product supports the following routing features:

- Calling/From and Called/To address-based routing

- Least cost routing (time of day, day of week, cost)

- Answer Seizure Ratio (ASR)-based routing

- Routing by codec—traffic grooming

- Route advance/route hunting (SIP)

- Local policy route recursion override

- Configurable route recursion based on SIP response

- Routing capability based on source IP address

- Ability to act on redirect/REFER

- Trusted calling party name (CNAM) services

- Ability to run ENUM query

Accounting and Billing

The SBC should capture and generate the correct data for accounting and billing purposes. You also need to capture session data to protect against theft and abuse of service. You need to check with your SBC vendor to find whether the product supports the following accounting features:

- Real-time events

- Local CDR storage with FTP push

- CDR Redundancy for locally stored CDRs

- Start, Stop, and Interim (Intermediate) events

- RADIUS attribute filtering

- RADIUS server load balancing

- QoS statistics (jitter, latency, packet loss, total packets, and total octets)

- Media flow attributes (realm, IP addresses, codec, and so on)

- Basic call attributes

Security

Secure Unified Communications is becoming increasingly important as the adoption of IP telephony accelerates and the growing popularity of VoIP makes it a target for attacks. Your network will experience denial of service (DOS) attacks, hijacking of calls, eaves-dropping, man-in-the-middle attacks, toll fraud, spam, malicious attachments, malformed messages from overloading resources, and many other unwanted issues. You need to use tight security measurements so that you can keep the integrity of your network.

Security itself is a wide open element. Nothing can guarantee the security of your network; rather it can minimize the risk. In the following sections, we identify and address the security measurements. You might need to add more questions to comply with the security policy of your organization.

Privacy

You can ensure the privacy of the signaling and the media in many ways. Encryption is one of the proven ways to achieve the privacy. Check the product to understand the following privacy issues and answers to these questions:

- Does the product support TLS for Signaling Encryption (AES 256 encryption)?

- Does the product support MTLS for Signaling Encryption?

- Does the product support SRTP for Media Encryption?

- Does the product support IPSEC?

- Does the product allow for Encryption on one side and nonencryption on the other (including enforcement)?

- Does the product support User-level privacy (for example, caller ID, P-asserted identity)?

Firewall Integration

You might not deploy SIP trunk without a firewall. But the big problem with SIP is that it uses a wide range of ports to transmit media. If you keep all these ports open into your firewall, your network is open for vulnerability. We see firewalls that can open pinholes intelligently. You can check with your SBC vendor, too.

- Closing and opening media pinholes on a session-by-session basis.

- By default, all pinholes should be closed. Pinholes should not be opened until explicitly configured or signaled via session initiation.

- Pinholes for a session should be closed immediately after the appropriate session termination signaling.

Threat Protection

Any IP network is always subject to certain levels of threats. You cannot stop it; instead, you need to take protection measures to safeguard your network. One interesting thing to know is that most of the attacks come from inside the network. Put the following questions in your RFP and see how the SBC handles those attacks:

- Does the product support DoS protection?

- Does the product support DDoS protection?

- Does the product enable trusted/authenticated users access while under DoS attack?

- Does the product support blocking L3/4 attacks (for example, TCP, SYN, ICMP, fragments, IP spoofing, and so on)?

- Does the product support blocking L5 attacks (for example, SIP signaling floods, malformed messages, Rogue RTP Detection, and so on)?

- Does the product support blocking spoofing, masquerading, and toll fraud?

- Does the product support blocking and verify anomalous behavior?

- Does the product support virus protection?

- Does the product support Spam over Internet Telephony (SPIT) attacks?

- Does the product support auto and manual threat signature updates?

- Does the product implement real-time caller verification to protect against script-based attacks?

Policy

You will always put some policy into the network, but your SBC might not implement those. We see some good policy servers that keep all policies in the central location and execute them locally in the SBC. Even if you are not deploying any centralized policy server, you need to answer the following questions before selecting the right SBC for you:

- Does the product support Media Policing?

- Does the product support Signaling Policing?

- Does the product support Domain-level and User-level blacklists?

- Does the product support granular call admission control policies?

- Does the product support policy-based call routing?

- Does the product support digit and header manipulation?

- Does the product provide support for full E.164 addressing (including the +)?

- Does the product categorize and police traffic based on originating network?

- Does the product categorize and police traffic based on SIP domain?

- Does the product categorize and police traffic based on originating user?

- Does the product categorize and police traffic based on originating user groups?

- Does the product categorize and police traffic based on originating device?

- Does the product categorize and police traffic based on time of day?

Access Control

Controlling the access of your network is another security measure. You need to authenticate the user before accessing any resources and then authorize that user to use the resources at different levels. Check with your SBC vendors about the following questions about access control mechanism:

- Does the product support Secure Sockets Layer (SSL)/TLS X.509 root certificate mutual authentication?

- Does the product support RFC-3280 public key infrastructure?

- Does the product support SIP digest authentication?

- Does the product support granular CAC policies?

- Does the product support clientless RSA (Rivest, Shamir, and Adleman first publicly described it) two-factor authentication?

Operations and Management

After you deploy the network with an SBC, you need to run and manage it every day. You will be using some methods, procedures, and tools that pertain to the operation, administration, maintenance, and provisioning of the systems. Data for network management is collected through several mechanisms, including agents installed on infrastructure, synthetic monitoring, logs of activity, sniffers, and real-user monitoring. In the past network management mainly consisted of monitoring whether devices were up or down; today performance management has become a crucial part of the IT team's role that brings about a host of challenges—especially for large organizations. The Operation and Maintenance function must be capable of performing the following functions:

- Event/alarm management

- Configuration management

- Performance management

- Security management

- Fault management

These functions are discussed in the following sections.

Event/Alarm Management

Alarms need to be presented to the Network Management System (NMS) platform, via software programs and tools for easy presentation and interpretation, for easy maintenance and to locate faults of all managed elements of the SBC system. Events shall be logged for future inspection and remedial actions.

Configuration Management

The Operating and Management (O&M) module must provide real-time configuration access to manage software loading, version tracking, and support for addition, deletion, and change of network element parameters. The O&M module needs to support software installation and upgrade.

Performance Management

The O&M module must provide tools (such as Simple Network Management Protocol (SNMP), command-line interface, XML, COBRA, and so on) for the collection of statistics and call and session information into a logging file for the SBC. The data must be viewed using tabular or graphical reports on the Graphical User Interface (GUI) terminal.

Security Management

The O&M module must provide password and login access to the system to prevent any unauthorized access to the system. It needs to have the capability of providing at least two-level access profiles with provision for field-definable of the privileges for each.

Fault Management

The O&M module must provide the capability to query and change device states and provide control for system diagnostics. It needs to monitor different protocols in real time.

Other Questions about Operations and Management

- Does the product support being managed by an external element management system (EMS)?

- Does the product support configuration and management via a GUI such as Hypertext Transfer Protocol with security (HTTPS)?

- Does the product support configuration and management via CLI (SSHv2)?

- Does the product support a separate management interface?

- Does the product support Admin Auth Terminal Access Controller Access-Control System (TACACS+)?

- Does the product support Admin Auth Remote Authentication Dial-In User Service (RADIUS)?

- Does the product support Admin Auth Lightweight Directory Access Protocol (LDAP)?

- Does the product support a minimum of two levels of access (super user and read/write)?

- Does the product support multiple remote syslog destinations?

- Does the product support session Call Detail Records (CDR) with the capability to export these records through automation, syslog, or SNMP? Information in CDR should contain at a minimum DNIS (DID), ANI, start/stop time, duration, min/ave/max MOS, origination IP, and destination IP.

- Does the product support system backups via the management GUI/CLI?

- Does the product support periodic backups to redundant backup servers via onboard automation or script?

- Does the product support system restores via the management GUI/CLI?

- Does the product support SNMP v2/v3?

- Does the product provide a list showing Management Information Bases (MIB) and OIDs for your product?

- Does the product support the Remote Network Monitoring (RMON)?

- Does the product support Link Layer Discovery Protocol (LLDP)?

- Does the product support Real-time Alarming monitoring via the management GUI/CLI?

- Does the product support Real-time Monitoring via the management GUI/CLI?

- Does the product support Scripting (CLI, API, XML, and SAS)?

- Does the product support alarming for Mean Opinion Score (MOS) below a configurable threshold during call?

- Does the product support Packet Capture capability via the management GUI/CLI for such items as signaling and messaging?

System Specification

When you are deciding on the right SBC, you need to check the system specifications of that device, too. Vendors build products differently. The physical characteristics of the SBC can vary based on the size and capacity of the box. Moreover, the connectivity, hardware, processing power, energy savings, and other things should be considered. Ask the following questions:

- Does the product support 100/1000-Mb Ethernet Ports—Copper?

- Does the product support 1000-Mb Ethernet Ports—Fiber?

- Does the product support Internal AC Power Supply (110/240 v) auto sensing for voltage range?

- What is the local routing table entry size?

- Does the product have a dedicated Encryption Acceleration Hardware?

- Does the product support having a private IP address on its public-facing port?

- Does the product have a security-hardened operating system suitable for deployment in the Demilitarized Zone (DMZ)?

- Does the product support IPv6?

- Does the product support SIP routing for trunks?

Performance/Sizing

You might find a feature-rich SBC, but it might not perform the way you want. For example, you might look for an SBC that can support 500 simultaneous calls, but the vendor does not support 500 calls in a single box. You also need to be careful about the word "session" and "call." Some vendors specify their capacity as total sessions. But, a complete call needs two sessions. So, you need to half their numbers to find the right capacity of that SBC. You can judge the performance of the SBC by the following three criteria:

- Availability

- Load balancing

- Performance

We use different parameters to find the right size of your SBC. You might need to adjust the following questions based on your own needs.

Availability

First, you need to decide whether you need a high-available SBC. Also consider the price of the SBC. High-available and high-redundant systems are usually expansive. Moreover, you can achieve redundancy in many different ways, which were previously discussed in this book. Following are some basic considerations when you are looking for a high-available SBC:

- Does the product support Geographical Diverse High availability?

- Does the product support Local Redundancy Active/Standby with stateful failover?

- Does the product support Local Redundancy Active/Active with stateful failover?

- Does the product support Clustering for Scalability?

- Does the product support zero downtime and zero call interruption during system upgrade when deployed in high availability model?

- Does the product support Redundant Hot Swappable Power Supplies?

- Does the product support Redundant Cooling Fans?

Load Balancing

- Even though you might deploy a high-available redundant SBC, you might need to load balance your calls among multiple locations for many reasons. And you can check with your SBC vendor how it implements the load-balancing features among those sites. Following are load-balancing options (SIP and H.323):

  - Hunt

  - Round robin

  - Least busy

  - Proportional

- Automatic recursion within session agent group or among the dial-peers.

- In a SIP trunking configuration with multiple service providers, the ability to distribute the incoming traffic from the other carrier to the various call agents.

- In a SIP trunking configuration with multiple service providers, the ability to distribute the out-going traffic from the internal call-agents/endpoints to the various carriers.

- Can the number of routes attempted in a lookup be configured to set a max threshold?

- In a SIP configuration, describe in detail what mechanism the SBC platform has for determining that a call-agent is reachable and active. Also, describe the SBC platform behavior when it determines that a particular call-agent is either not reachable or not active.

- Describe methods for terminating a recursion of multiple routes in local routing tables, or in response to messages including a list of multiple destinations (such as a SIP 3xx).

- Can the SBC perform call routing decisions based on QoS metric calculations on a per segment and per next-hop basis?

- Describe any ENUM capabilities including local route table storage.

Performance

The system should meet performance features in the design process and the equipment performance. Ask these questions to determine if your system meets the following:

- How much latency is added by the product for unencrypted signaling traffic?

- How much latency is added by the product for encrypted signaling traffic?

- How much latency is added by the product for unencrypted media traffic?

- How much latency is added by the product for encrypted media traffic?

- Is the product capacity constrained by licensing?

- What is the pricing model for connections, encryption, and any other licensing features not standard and unlimited with the system?

- Which model platform would support 1000 users with 250 simultaneous sessions?

- What are the environmental size, btu, power, and so on of this previously listed model?

- Which model platform would support 10,000 users with 2000 simultaneous sessions?

- What are the environmental size, btu, power, and so on of this previously listed model?

- Which model platform would support 50,000 users with 10,000 simultaneous sessions?

- What are the environmental size, btu, power, and so on of this previously listed model?

- The SBC should have the capability to show call duration.

- SBC should provide a report for every call and summaries to daily, weekly, monthly, and yearly statistics. This report also should present Attempt, Fail, BHCA, and MHT information.

- The CPU and memory (RAM) utilization should not exceed 70 percent while working at the maximum BHCA.

Delivery, Documentation, and Support

So far, we have discussed all the technical issues to prepare a good RFP for an SBC. But this is not good enough to select a vendor for your next generation unified communication solution. You need to know the vendor's capability in running the business, its delivery mechanism, and its support systems. In this section of the RFP, we identify the questions you need to ask for the following major items:

- Delivery of the systems

- Documentation and training

- Product support system

Delivery

It is important to know how the system will be delivered to your place, especially when you have multiple locations. In general, account teams or partners handle the customers. Some companies engage dedicated account teams depending on the size of your business and its needs. In addition, if you have multiple international offices, things become even more complicated. We prepared the following questions assuming that you have a large operation in many places worldwide. You can tailor these questions according to your needs:

- Does the bidder offer a dedicated Account Manager (AM)? If so, will AM confirm each order with the end user to ensure delivery accuracy?

- Does the bidder have individual AMs per region, per country, or a single global account manager?

- Does the bidder provide a dedicated global AM to assist with large-scale projects, regional coordination, and so on?

- Does the bidder offer an online quoting/ordering tool with real-time pricing and lead-time capabilities?

- Does the bidder's online quoting tool have the capability to save, edit, or process quotes into orders?

- Are there other areas that the bidder has a relationship with your company that might enhance the bidder's ability to effectively service this account?

- Ask the bidder to describe how it would ensure/guarantee the capability to meet the requirements in the Statement of Work. Would the bidder agree to incorporate a Service Level Agreement (SLA) of applicable remedies contract.

- Ask bidder to describe the lifecycle of delivery, from receipt of the purchase order (PO) to the delivery of the product/service.

- Ask the bidder to describe the lifecycle of Quotes, from request to delivery of the quote.

- Ask the bidder to describe its process for handling change requests including its flexibility.

- Your company might require an accurate weekly Order Status on a regional/country basis. What methodology does the bidder employ to provide the order status?

- Does the bidder offer an online order status tool or method by which to track the orders?

- Does the bidder offer any Product Expediting services, that is, distribution sourcing, staging, stocking, and pre-ordering? If there is an additional fee for these services, ask them to include this on the bidder's Rate Sheet.

- What is the expected deployment/rollout period?

- Ask them to describe the installation/setup process and deployment process.

- What reporting capabilities are available? Request a description.

Documentation and Training

Documentation and training are issues of a mission-critical system such as the SBC. The vendor might help you install and configure the box, but you need to train your people to manage it properly. A good product comes with good documentation. You can put the following questions into your RFP to make sure the vendor is providing you the right set of documents and training:

- Does the bidder have any online resources available such as documentation and a knowledge base about the products and services?

- Ask the bidder to describe training to be provided with deployment.

- Ask the bidder to describe training manuals, documentation, training visual aides, and so on.

- Ask the bidder to describe the support system including support levels detailing inclusions.

- Describe follow-up training potentially required.

Support

Things will go wrong for sure. The product might fail, the system might not accommodate the load, or it might not function during any adverse situation. You might need to face some emergency situations. We all know about this. But the important issue is how you handle it and how your vendor stands by you when you really need them. Some vendors can offer you 24/7 support. You can imagine how much productivity could be lost if your SBC goes down for a few hours. We have compiled generic support questionnaires. You might need to add more based on the need of your application.

- Does the bidder provide a dedicated Support Contract Team to assist with managing the Support Contract globally?

- Ask the bidder to describe the support escalation process and point of contact.

- Ask the bidder to describe in-country product/service deployment and support for global availability.

- Ask the bidder to describe the escalation path for issue resolution.

- Does the bidder agree to make every effort to effectively manage the Support Offering Contract, for example, consolidation, recommendations, reporting, and management capabilities?

- Ask the bidder to describe the professional services offered by the bidder.

- Ask the bidder to describe available technical assistance (if applicable). Is assistance available by phone 24/7? Can calls be logged electronically?

- Does the bidder offer phone support in multiple languages? If so, ask for detail-specific language offerings including any additional costs on the Bidder Rate Sheet.

- Does the bidder offer any variations of the Support Offering?

- Does the bidder offer any value-added services in combination with the Support Offering?

- Nonemergency issues need to be addressed within 24 hours; emergency issues need to be addressed immediately. The selected bidder needs to log and provide monthly reporting on issues to your procurement team. Will the bidder meet this requirement?

- Ask the bidder to provide detail on any SLAs needed for support, different levels, and so on, attaching a matrix if needed.

- Ask the bidder to provide examples of innovation in finding new approaches to solving operational or commercial problems.

- Does the bidder employ any processes to monitor and track customer satisfaction? If so, ask the bidder to describe and provide examples of items measured.

- Does the bidder offer secure, centralized, and customized reporting?

- What experience does the bidder have in the area of offering support to customers similar in size and business focus to your company?

- Is all or any part of the Professional Services provided through an outsourcer or third-party provider?

- If the answer is yes to the previous question, how does the bidder select and review the performance of its subcontractors and suppliers?

Quality

In engineering and manufacturing, quality control is used in developing systems to ensure products or services are designed and produced to meet or exceed customer requirements. There are defined rules and regulations to produce goods that ensure the quality. Different kinds of industry certifications are also available that show the vendors' credibility to manufacture the specific product. For example, ISO 9001 certification ensures that the manufacture has a set of procedures that covers all key processes in the business; it keeps adequate records checks output for defects, with appropriate and corrective action where necessary, and facilitates continual improvement. ISO 9000 is an international standard that many companies use to ensure that their quality assurance system is in place and effective. Conformance to ISO 9000 is said to guarantee that a company delivers quality products and services.

Some engineering companies go through a quality assurance process of establishing evidence that provides a high degree of assurance that a product, service, or system accomplishes its intended requirements. And sometimes some equipment needs compliance with different regulatory bodies and environmental organizations. But it is important to realize also that quality is determined by the intended users, clients, or customers, not by society in general: It is not the same as "expensive" or "high quality." Even goods with low prices can be considered quality items if they meet a market need.

We have categorized the quality control mechanism in two broad areas:

- Quality assurance

- Certification

The following quality-related items need to be addressed during the process of selecting SIP providers and SBC vendors.

Quality Assurance

Quality assurance (QA) refers to planned and systematic production processes that provide confidence in a product's suitability for its intended purpose. It is a set of activities intended to ensure that products satisfy customer requirements in a systematic, reliable fashion. QA cannot absolutely guarantee the production of quality products, unfortunately, but makes this more likely. Therefore, you can check the following items with the vendor who will be supplying your SBC:

- Ask them to list and describe all quality certifications held by the bidder.

- Has the bidder achieved ISO accreditation? If so, when was it last renewed?

- Ask the bidder to describe its policy and process for changing management.

- Can the bidder provide accurate delivery estimates on a weekly regional/country basis?

- Ask the bidder to describe the inspection process for ensuring a high-quality finished product. Also, ask the bidder to describe corrective actions taken if a substandard product is shipped.

- Ask the bidder to describe the process to handle defects and policy/procedures for corrective action.

- Ask the bidder to describe the methodology for tracking failure/defect rates, including inclusion of templates. Ask the bidder to provide examples of typical failure/defect rates for product/services similar to those described in this sourcing engagement.

- What methods might the bidder employ to resolve a customer satisfaction issue with you?

Certification

Certification is the process of certifying that a certain product has passed performance and quality assurance tests or qualification requirements stipulated in regulations, or that it complies with a set of regulations governing quality and minimum performance requirements. Because SIP trunks are a new phenomena in the industry, you might depend of some test results and certification process run by third party so that you know all the standards are maintained in their development.

Some service providers test the SBC with their existing network before they deploy it into the customer network. These might give you some level of comfort to buy the product. Here, we have compiled some questions for you:

- Which SIP trunk providers are product Interoperability Test (IOT) Certified?

- Which call servers are product IOT Certified?

- Is your product IOT Certified with any IP-PBX? If yes, ask for detailed information.

- Which SIP phones are product IOT Certified?

- Which SCCP phones are product IOT Certified?

- Does your company provide a managed service solution? If so, ask it to describe.

Business

In the whole process of bidding, you must check the business experience of the bidder. There are lot of companies (especially startups) that are coming into the market with brilliant ideas and products. But, they may not sustain the business for a long period of time. You need to decide whether you can take a risk on any new company that might not stay in the market for a long time. If the company cannot sustain, your network will fall into severe risk. You might not find the right people to support the product. Moreover there will be no growth or roadmap of that product. That's why you need to check the bidder's business background and capabilities.

In the last few years, we have seen many startup companies building SBC products. And today when we look back, most of them are gone or bought by their competitors. As the industry is still building new features on SIP, you need to check the following two things about the vendor:

- Bidder background

- Bidder references

We have compiled a lot of questions to verify the bidders' business background and references. Please use these tools to measure their background before you select any of them.

Bidder Background

The bidder should provide the following details and background information for its company:

- Bidder trading name.

- Bidder tax ID/ABN and VAT number.

- Date the bidder company established.

- Names, titles, and background of senior leadership, including longevity, experience, title, and so on.

- Ownership (public, private, partnership, and so on).

- Total number of employees, with a breakdown by region and country.

- Company ownership, impending changes in ownership.

- Business philosophy and mission statement.

- Geographic locations.

- Financial report.

- URL of the bidder website.

- Name of general insurer.

- Professional indemnity insurance policy number and expiration date.

- Public and professional insurance policy number and expiration date.

- List all financial applications used to run the bidder's business.

- Description of any litigation in which the bidder or any bidder partners currently involved.

- List and brief background of contractors, subcontractors, or partners utilized by the bidder for the services described herein.

- Documented awards or certifications granted to the bidder for work that relates to this RFP. Copies of reports or certifications should also be attached.

- The bidder proposed account team titles, responsibilities, contact information, and organization chart.

- The name of the dedicated national/global account representative from the account management team who would be accountable and responsible for this bid.

- The name of the single point of contact from account management team for billing issues.

- The name of the technical point of contact for all technical or support issues.

- The primary benefits that the company would derive from selecting the bidder, for example, strategic alliances you might have and your network, and such.

- Is there an active corporate social responsibility or similar program?

- Request a list and description of environmental certifications.

- Detail of three largest competitors with similar products/services to those requested in this sourcing engagement.

- Internal auditing procedures in place to monitor internal activities to ensure conformance to standard processes.

- Detail the percentage of business driven by the products/services specified in this sourcing engagement.

- List organizations' significant environmental impacts, for example, carbon emissions, energy usage, waste, and so on. Describe as fully as possible.

- The main environmental impacts, as a result of the provision of goods/services, such as resource consumption of goods, emissions from transport, and so forth. Describe as fully as possible.

- Details of any third-party verification of good environmental performance (including ISO14001 or equivalent). If this is unavailable, detail any future plans to achieve certification.

- Description of regularly used financial metrics used to measure the market strength and health of the company.

- Company initiatives to minimize an environmental impact.

- Standards and implementation process for data protection and information security.

- Advise if any prompt payment discount options are available. Any bidder offered discount would be factored into the proposal evaluation process.

You can also ask the following questions to identify bidder strengths in other areas:

- Does the bidder's ownership fall into any of the following categories: a) minority-owned business? b) woman-owned business? and c) disable veteran-owned business? If yes, has the bidder been certified as such, and if so, by which organization?

- If the bidder does not qualify as a WMDVBE, does the bidder have a supplier diversity program and a set spending goals with minority-, woman-, or disabled veteran-owned businesses?

- If the bidder has a supplier diversity program and set spending goals with minority-, woman-, or disabled veteran-owned businesses, provide the respondent's supplier diversity program contact information.

- Will the bidder be utilizing a reseller to fulfill the orders if awarded this RFP? If so, provide documentation describing the length of relationship with the reseller, number of the bidder's clients currently utilizing a reseller, and so on.

- Does the bidder (and reseller) accept local purchase orders in local currency (with in-country ordering and receiving tools)?

- Can the bidder (and reseller) accept electronic purchase orders?

- Can the bidder (and reseller) offer a flexible settlement method, accepting both corporate credit card and the purchase order?

- Fees are billed in arrears as services are performed or at the end of each month, or for Goods, fees will be billed upon shipment. The invoice must be billed in the purchase order currency and by the named entity on the purchase order. Can the bidder comply with this request?

Bidder References

You can ask your vendor to provide a list of references that can be contacted for a candid discussion about specific service offerings. Ask the vendor to provide a minimum of three references summarizing the following:

- **Reference No. 1:** Contact name, title, company name, address, phone number, fax number, and email address. Brief overviews of the services, including any unique services provided to the reference company, contract period, and spend amount. List any special projects the bidder might have managed for the reference company. Letters of recommendation might be used as a substitute.

- **Reference No. 2:** Contact name, title, company name, address, phone number, fax number, and email address. Brief overviews of the services, including any unique services provided to the reference company, contract period, and spend amount. List any special projects the bidder might have managed for the reference company. Letters of recommendation can be used as a substitute.

- **Reference No. 3:** Contact name, title, company name, address, phone number, fax number, and email address. Brief overviews of the services, including any unique services provided to the reference company, contract period, and spend amount. List any special projects the bidder might have managed for the reference company. Letters of recommendation can be used as a substitute.

Cost

The following cost-related questions need to be answered during the process of selecting SIP providers and SBC vendors.

All rates must meet the requirements as defined in the Statement of Work and be applicable for all locations worldwide. If the bidder needs to specify pricing specific to a region or area, the bidder is required to notate the currency, country/region, support levels, pricing, and any other regional differences:

- Describe the bidder's process and commitment to drive continuous cost reductions.

- Open policy: Is the bidder willing to disclose cost structure and profit margins? If so, please include.

- Is the bidder willing to dedicate resources to joint cost-reduction initiatives?

- Is the bidder open to consortium arrangements between multiple customers?

- How will the bidder regulate price changes over multiple years? What type of guarantees (ties to price index, and so on) can be made to ensure prices will not increase beyond reasonable expectations?

- Does the bidder offer trade-in credit for the competitors' products and services? Are there specific limitations?

- All rates quoted in the bidder Rate Sheets must be good for one year and include update requests.

- Is there additional cost associated with support and technical assistance? If so, please provide details on the bidder's Rate Sheet.

- Does the bidder offer discounts for purchasing multiple years upfront?

- Is the bidder willing to engage in an incentive/discount structure if the agreed-upon volume targets are met?

- Is the bidder willing to share cost drivers within the business?

Summary

In this chapter, we tried to provide most of the information to prepare a RFP for your enterprise. This chapter assumes you have a large enterprise with many offices in different parts of the world. It is a challenging task to prepare a good RFP for such a large organization covering all areas to include technology, quality, delivery, business, costs, and so on. We intentionally chose a larger enterprise to show you the complexity of the bidding system. Some smaller enterprises might not go through such a detailed process to select their SBC vendor; however, you might need to add even more clauses that are specific to your organization. At the end of the day, this is your network, and you have to make the judgment.

Further Reading

The following document provides additional information on the topics covered in this chapter:

- IETF RFC: The RFC repository maintained by the IETF Secretariat. http://www.ietf.org/rfc.html.

Chapter 10

Deployment Scenarios

This chapter covers the following topics:

- Enterprise SIP Trunk for PSTN access
- SMB SIP Trunk for PSTN access
- Additional deployment variations
- Troubleshooting

Part 2 of this book provided detailed coverage of all the planning activities, Session Initial Protocol (SIP) trunk models, SIP trunk evaluation questions, and interworking and network design information necessary to prepare for a SIP trunk installation into your network.

The chapters in Part 3 look much more closely at the actual deployment and implementation of a SIP trunk and the configurations necessary to interconnect equipment and networks. This chapter covers configurations for the typical SIP trunk deployment scenarios and helpful implementation notes for each of these.

The connectivity and features needed in different deployment scenarios vary. SIP trunk deployments covered in this chapter are shown in Figure 10-1, including the following:

- Enterprise SIP Trunk for Public Switched Telephone Network (PSTN) Access
- Small-Medium Business (SMB) SIP Trunk for PSTN Access

Enterprise SIP Trunk for PSTN Access

There are already many SIP trunk service provider (SP) globally offering services, and undoubtedly, more will add services as time goes by. The offerings vary from one another, so it is difficult to give a single configuration that enables implementation of a SIP trunk with any SP. Two interoperability examples are given in the following sections. These examples are AT&T and Verizon because they were two of the first to market with a business-class offering and are therefore more known quantities at this time. Even if you connect to a different provider's offering, reading through these configurations can be helpful for the type of configuration commands you might require to configure your border element to interconnect with the SP of your choice.

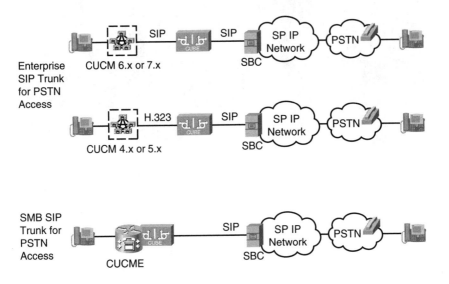

Figure 10-1 *SIP Trunk Deployment Scenarios*

- The following implementations are discussed in this section:

- Connecting Cisco Unified Communications Manager (CUCM) using SIP to an AT&T FlexReach SIP trunk

- Connecting CUCM using SIP to a Verizon SIP trunk

- Connecting CUCM using H.323 to a SIP trunk

- Connecting multiple Internet Protocol Private Branch Exchanges (IP-PBX) in the enterprise using H.323 and SIP to a shared SIP trunk

- Connecting a contact center to a SIP trunk

Cisco UCM SIP to an AT&T FlexReach SIP Trunk

When using CUCM 6.0 or later, the use of SIP (rather than H.323) is recommended to interconnect to a SP SIP trunk, as shown in Figure 10-2.

Example 10-1 shows the Cisco Unified Border Element (CUBE) configuration connecting to CUCM 7.0 on the inside and an AT&T FlexReach SIP trunk on the outside. CUBE 1.2 Internet Operation System (IOS) 12.4(22)T is used in this example. The following SIP trunk features were tested on this configuration:

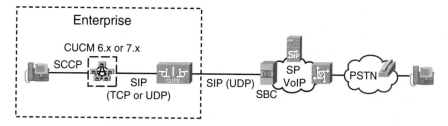

Figure 10-2 *CUCM to SIP Trunk Interconnect Using SIP*

- SIP trunk voice calls using G.729 codec

- Calling name display

- Intrasite call transfer

- Call hold and resume

- Call forward all, call forward busy, and call forward no answer

- Dual-tone multi-frequency (DTMF) relay using Request for Comments (RFC) 2833

- Fax using T.38 or G.711 passthrough

- CUBE performing Delayed-Offer-to-Early-Offer conversion of the initial SIP INVITE

Example 10-1 *Cisco UCM SIP to CUBE to an AT&T FlexReach SIP Trunk*

```
voice-card 0 (1)
  dspfarm
  dsp services dspfarm
!
voice service voip
  address-hiding (2)
  allow-connections sip to sip (3)
  redirect ip2ip
  fax protocol t38 ls-redundancy 0 hs-redundancy 0 fallback pass-through
g711ulaw (4)
  sip
    header-passing error-passthru (5)
    midcall-signaling passthru (6)
    g729 annexb-all (7)
!
voice class codec 1 (8)
  codec preference 1 g729r8
  codec preference 2 g711ulaw
!
```

continues

Example 10-1   *continued*

```
voice class sip-profiles 1
  request INVITE sip-header Diversion modify "<sip:(.*)@(.*)>"
"<sip:732320\1@\2> (9)
!
interface GigabitEthernet0/0 (10)
  description Inside towards CUCM
  ip address 172.X.X.X 255.255.255.0
  duplex auto
!
interface GigabitEthernet0/1 (11)
  description Outside towards SIP Trunk
  ip address 99.X.X.X 255.255.255.0
  duplex auto
!
sccp local GigabitEthernet0/1 (12)
sccp ccm 172.X.X.X identifier 1 version 7.0
sccp
!
sccp ccm group 1
  associate ccm 1 priority 1
  associate profile 1 register cfb0018185bb7a1
!
dspfarm profile 1 conference (12)
  codec g711ulaw
  codec g711alaw
  codec g729ar8
  codec g729abr8
  codec g729r8
  codec g729br8
  maximum sessions 6
  associate application SCCP
!
dial-peer voice 1999 voip (13)
  description CUCM to AT&T
  destination-pattern 1[1-9,1-9,1-9].......
  rtp payload-type nse 99 (14)
  rtp payload-type nte 100 (15)
  voice-class codec 1 (16)
  voice-class sip early-offer forced (17)
  voice-class sip profiles 1 (18)
  session protocol sipv2
  session target ipv4:207.Y.Y.Y (19)
  incoming called-number 1.......... (20)
  dtmf-relay rtp-nte (21)
```

```
    fax-relay sg3-to-g3
    fax rate 14400
    fax protocol t38 ls-redundancy 0 hs-redundancy 0 fallback pass-through
g711ulaw (22)
!
dial-peer voice 732111 voip (23)
    description AT&T to CUCM
    destination-pattern 732.......
    rtp payload-type nse 99
    rtp payload-type nte 100
    voice-class codec 1
    voice-class sip profiles 1
    session protocol sipv2
    voice-class sip dtmf-relay force rtp-nte (24)
    session target ipv4:172.X.X.X
    incoming called-number 732320....
    dtmf-relay rtp-nte
    fax-relay sg3-to-g3
    fax protocol t38 ls-redundancy 0 hs-redundancy 0 fallback pass-through g711ulaw
!
sip-ua
    retry invite 2 (25)
    no remote-party-id
```

Note the following:

1. This command enables Digital Signal Processing (DSP) resources on the router to register to CUCM to be used for conferencing of G.729 SIP trunk participants.

2. This command enables IP address hiding between the private network (CUCM side) and the public network (AT&T IP Flex-reach).

3. This command enables CUBE (IP-to-IP voice communication).

4. This command enables T.38 fax at a global level, meaning all Voice over IP (VoIP) dial-peers not configured for a specific fax protocol utilizes this setting. Set this command instead to **fax protocol pass-through g711ulaw** to use G.711 as the fax protocol.

5. This command enables for SIP error messages to pass through CUBE end-to-end without modification.

6. This command must be enabled at a global level to maintain integrity of SIP signaling between the AT&T network and CUCM.

7. This command enables CUBE to negotiate all flavors of the G.729 codec and must be configured to interoperate seamlessly with AT&T's network.

8. This command enables multiple codec support and performs codec filtering required for correct interoperability between AT&T's SIP network and CUCM.

9. This SIP profile expands the Diversion header number from a four-digit extension to a full ten-digit DID number to obtain interoperability with users on certain AT&T network service offerings during call-forward call scenarios.

10. Inside interface facing CUCM.

11. Outside interface facing AT&T Flexreach network.

12. These commands configure DSP resources for CUCM conferencing.

13. This is the dial-peer routing calls from the enterprise CUCM to AT&T. To configure a redundant outgoing dial-peer toward a second (backup) AT&T border element, create a second dial-peer with the same configuration values, except set the **session target** to the backup AT&T border element's IP address, and set the **preference** command under both dial-peers as appropriate (load balancing or primary/secondary).

14. This command frees up payload type value 100 to assign it to RFC-2833 DTMF (nte).

15. This command assigns payload type value 100 to nte (RFC-2833 DTMF).

16. Assigns voice class codec 1 settings to the dial-peer (codec support and filtering).

17. This command enables delay offer (DO) to early offer (EO) conversion for the initial SIP INVITE message of calls matched by this dial-peer.

18. This command enables the SIP profile 1 conversion given earlier in the configuration for calls matching this dial-peer.

19. This command sets the SIP target IP address for outgoing calls.

20. This command assigns dial-peer properties to incoming calls matching this called number.

21. This command enables DTMF relay using RFC-2833 for calls matching this dial-peer.

22. This command is an example of how to configure T.38 fax on a per dial-peer basis, overriding the global configuration done earlier.

23. This is the dial-peer routing calls from AT&T to the enterprise CUCM. To route calls from CUBE to multiple CUCMs in the enterprise, create multiple dial-peers with the same configuration values, except set the **session target** to the alternate CUCMs. Calls can be routed to different clusters based on dial-plan (change the **destination-pattern** appropriately) or load-balanced across SIP trunk to different CUCM servers in the same cluster.

24. This command forces the configured NTE payload type value (in this case the 100 value) for incoming calls to CUCM. This command is used to synchronize RFC-2833 DTMF dynamic payload-type values with the various components in the AT&T network. The majority of the network components support this, but some older configurations might still use other values such as 96. In cases where an incoming SIP INVITE from AT&T to CUCM carries a payload-type value other than 100, the CUBE command **voice-class sip dtmf-relay force rtp-nte** forces the configured payload-type under the dial-peer back to AT&T in the 200OK SDP message. This

enables the PSTN user to have the correct DTMF capability to navigate through auto-attendant or IVR services.

25. This command should be enabled when failover dial-peers are configured (for example, when using a CUCM cluster instead of a single CUCM IP address for all SIP calls).

CUCM to a Verizon SIP Trunk

Example 10-2 shows the CUBE configuration connecting to CUCM 6.1.2 on the inside and a Verizon SIP trunk on the outside. CUBE 1.2 (IOS 12.4(20)T) is used in this example. The following SIP trunk features were tested on this configuration:

- SIP trunk voice calls using G.729 codec

- Locating SIP servers using Domain Name Server (DNS) Service Location (SRV) and A records

- DTMF relay using RFC-2833

- Fax using G.711 passthrough

- CUBE performing Delayed-Offer-to-Early-Offer conversion of the initial SIP INVITE

Example 10-2 *CUCM SIP to CUBE to a Verizon SIP Trunk*

```
voice-card 0  (1)
  dspfarm
  dsp services dspfarm
!
voice service voip
  allow-connections sip to sip  (2)
  fax protocol pass-through g711ulaw
  sip
    early-offer forced  (3)
    midcall-signaling passthru  (4)
!
voice class codec 1
  codec preference 1 g729r8 bytes 20
  codec preference 2 g711ulaw bytes 160
!
voice translation-rule 8
  rule 2 /^8\(.*\)/ /\1/
voice translation-rule 9
  rule 2 /^9\(.*\)/ /\1/
!
voice translation-profile DIGITSTRIP-8  (5)
  translate called 8
```

continues

Example 10-2   *continued*

```
voice translation-profile DIGITSTRIP-9 (6)
translate called 9
!
interface GigabitEthernet0/0 (7)
  description Inside interface to CUCM
  ip address 192.X.X.X 255.255.255.0
  ip virtual-reassembly
  load-interval 30
!
interface GigabitEthernet0/1 (8)
  description Outside interface to Vz
  ip address X.X.X.X 255.255.255.X
  ip virtual-reassembly
  load-interval 600
!
call threshold global cpu-avg low 68 high 75 (9)
call threshold global total-mem low 75 high 85 (9)
call threshold global total-calls low 9 high 11 (9)
!
voice-port 0/1/0 (10)
  no non-linear
  playout-delay maximum 120
  playout-delay nominal 15
  playout-delay minimum low
  timeouts interdigit 2
  timeouts call-disconnect 3
  timing digit 300
  caller-id enable
!
voice-port 0/1/1
!
sccp local GigabitEthernet0/0
sccp ccm 192.168.0.6 identifier 2 priority 2 version 5.0.1
sccp ccm 192.168.0.4 identifier 5 priority 1 version 5.0.1
sccp
!
sccp ccm group 10
  associate ccm 5 priority 1
  associate ccm 2 priority 2
  associate profile 12 register CON001193484810 (11)
!
dspfarm profile 12 conference (11)
  description conference bridge
  codec g711ulaw
```

```
   codec g711alaw
   codec g729ar8
   codec g729abr8
   codec g729r8
   codec g729br8
   maximum sessions 10
   associate application SCCP
!
dial-peer voice 10 pots
   description dial '9' for outbound calls
   preference 1
   service session
   destination-pattern 10XX
   fax rate disable
   port 0/1/0
!
dial-peer voice 100 voip
   description OUTBOUND G729 Voice SIP calls to VzB
   translation-profile outgoing DIGITSTRIP-9 (12)
   destination-pattern 9T (13)
   voice-class codec 1
   voice-class sip early-offer forced (14)
   session protocol sipv2
   session target sip-server
   dtmf-relay rtp-nte (15)
   no vad
!
dial-peer voice 101 voip
   description INBOUND G729 Voice SIP calls from VzB
   voice-class codec 1
   session protocol sipv2
   session target sip-server
   incoming called-number 1... (16)
   dtmf-relay rtp-nte
   no vad
!
dial-peer voice 200 voip
   description inbound FAX dial peer from VZ
   session protocol sipv2
   session target sip-server
   incoming called-number 1018 (17)
   codec g711ulaw (18)
   fax rate disable (19)
   no vad
```

continues

Example 10-2 *continued*

```
 !
dial-peer voice 201 voip
   description outbound FAX calls to VZ
   translation-profile outgoing DIGITSTRIP-8 (20)
   destination-pattern 8T (21)
   voice-class sip early-offer forced
   session protocol sipv2
   session target sip-server
   codec g711ulaw
   fax rate disable
   no vad
 !
dial-peer voice 300 voip
   description To/From CUCM subscriber for FAX Calls
   preference 2
   destination-pattern 1018
   session protocol sipv2
   session target ipv4:192.168.0.4
   incoming called-number 8T (22)
 !
dial-peer voice 301 voip
   description To/From CUCM publisher for FAX Calls
   preference 5
   destination-pattern 1018
   session protocol sipv2
   session target ipv4:192.168.0.6 (23)
   incoming called-number 8T
   codec g711ulaw
   fax rate disable
   no vad
 !
dial-peer Voice 401 voip
   description To/From CUCM subscriber for Voice
   preference 2
   destination-pattern 1...
   voice-class codec 1
   session protocol sipv2
   session target ipv4:192.168.0.4
   incoming called-number 9T (24)
   fax rate disable
   no vad
 !
dial-peer Voice 411 voip
   description To/From CUCM publisher for Voice
```

```
   preference 5
   destination-pattern 1...
   voice-class codec 1
   session protocol sipv2
   session target ipv4:192.168.0.6 (25)
   incoming called-number 9T
   dtmf-relay rtp-nte
   no vad
!
sip-ua
   retry invite 2
   retry bye 2
   retry cancel 2
   sip-server dns:sip.server.com (26)
   g729-annexb override
```

Note the following:

1. These commands define DSP resources for CUCM's use (conferencing).

2. This command enables SIP-to-SIP call processing.

3. Use this command to force CUBE to send an early offer (SIP INVITE with SDP) on the outgoing leg toward Verizon.

4. This command enables support for SIP Supplementary Services (only used for SIP-to-SIP Calls).

5. This command strips the leading "8" from outgoing called numbers.

6. This command strips the leading "9" from outgoing called numbers.

7. This command defines the inside interface facing CUCM. No SIP bind command is configured; SIP is sourced from both interfaces.

8. This command defines the outside interface facing Verizon network. No SIP bind command is configured; SIP is sourced from both interfaces.

9. These commands define global call admission control (CAC) based on resource utilization.

10. This command defines an optional Foreign eXchange Station or Subscriber (FXS) port for locally connected fax devices.

11. These commands define DSP resources for CUCM conferencing for G.729 SIP trunk calls.

12. This command strips the leading "9" from the outgoing called number.

13. This command matches outbound calls from CUCM with leading "9."

14. This command does Delay-Offer to Early-Offer SIP interworking.

15. This command configures DTMF relay using RFC-2833.

16. This command enables CUBE to set configuration parameters for incoming calls. This ensures that both legs of the SIP call use matching codecs.

17. This command matches the inbound call-leg for fax calls. This ensures that both legs of the SIP call use matching codecs.

18. This command forces the use of G.711 for fax calls.

19. This command disables fax relay capability. Fax passthrough is the supported fax method.

20. This command strips the leading "8" from outbound fax calls.

21. This command matches outbound fax calls from CUCM with a leading "8."

22. This command enables CUBE to set configuration parameters for outgoing calls based on the received called number. This ensures that both legs of the SIP call use matching codecs.

23. This command defines an alternate SIP trunk for redundant connections to the CUCM cluster.

24. This command enables CUBE to set configuration parameters for outgoing calls based on the received called number. This ensures that both legs of the SIP call use matching codecs.

25. This command defines an alternate SIP trunk for redundant connections to the CUCM cluster.

26. This command defines a SIP Proxy fully qualified domain name (FQDN) for outbound SIP calls to Verizon.

Cisco UCM H.323 Interconnect

When using CUCM 3.x, 4.x, or 5.x, using H.323 is the only practical choice to interconnect to a SP SIP trunk, as shown in Figure 10-3.

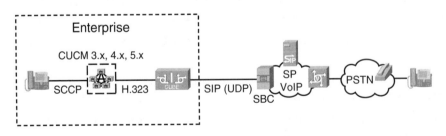

Figure 10-3 *CUCM to SIP Trunk Interconnect Using H.323*

When using H.323 to an older CUCM, the SIP side facing the SP's network is the same as shown in Examples 10-1 and 10-2. It is only the interconnection (dial-peer) to the CUCM

that changes. Initiating a SIP Early Offer to the SP SIP trunk requires that CUCM initiates an H.323 FastStart. Initiating an H.323 FastStart, in turn, requires that CUCM makes
use of a Media Termination Point (MTP).

Example 10-3 shows the CUBE configuration connecting to CUCM using H.323. CUCM
4.2 and CUBE 1.0 (IOS 12.4(11)T) are used in this example.

Example 10-3   *H.323 CUCM to SIP Trunk Interconnect*

```
voice service voip
  allow-connections h323 to sip (1)
  allow-connections sip to h323 (1)
  fax protocol t38 ls-redundancy 0 hs-redundancy 0 fallback pass-through g711ulaw
  h323
    h225 connect-passthru
!
voice class codec 1
  codec preference 1 g729br8
  codec preference 2 g711ulaw
!
interface GigabitEthernet0/0
  description Inside towards CUCM
  ip address 172.x.x.x 255.255.255.0
  duplex auto
!
interface GigabitEthernet0/1
  description Outside towards SIP Trunk
  ip address x.x.x.x 255.255.255.0
  duplex auto
!
sccp local GigabitEthernet0/0 (2)
sccp ccm 172.x.x.x identifier 1 version 4.1
sccp
!
sccp ccm group 1 (2)
  associate ccm 1 priority 1
  associate profile 1 register MTP0013C4037300
!
dspfarm profile 1 mtp (2)
 codec g729br8
 maximum sessions software 10
 associate application SCCP
!
dial-peer voice 1 voip
  description Calls toward CUCM
  destination-pattern 1...
```

continues

Example 10-3   *continued*

```
voice-class codec 1
session target ipv4:172.x.x.x
dtmf-relay rtp-nte (3)
```

Note the following:

1. These commands enable CUBE's H.323-SIP interworking capability.

2. CUCM 4.2 requires an MTP for H.323 FastStart calls, which in turn is required for SIP Early-Offer calls toward the SP SIP Trunk. These statements define a collocated MTP on CUBE.

3. This command specifies RFC-2833 for H.323. The H.245 mechanisms can also be used, for example, **dtmf-relay h245-signal**.

Sharing a SIP Trunk Across the Enterprise

One of the many benefits of a border element is that it enables you to share a single SIP trunk among different CUCM and IP-PBXs at your site. It also enables you to connect to different vintages of these IP-PBXs using either the H.323 or SIP protocols.

Figure 10-4 shows how to share a SIP Trunk across three CUCMs and two IP-PBXs at a site.

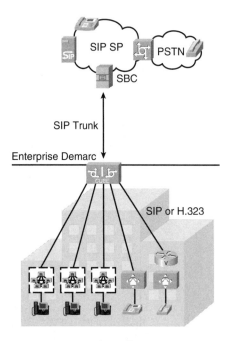

Figure 10-4 *Sharing a SIP Trunk Across the Enterprise*

Example 10-4 shows the additional configuration required to connect to the CUCMs and IP-PBXs shown in Figure 10-4. The SIP side facing the SP's network remains the same, as shown in Examples 10-1 and 10-2.

Example 10-4   *Sharing a SIP Trunk Across the Enterprise*

```
voice service voip
  address-hiding
  allow-connections h323 to sip
  allow-connections sip to h323
  allow-connections sip to sip
  fax protocol t38 ls-redundancy 0 hs-redundancy 0 fallback pass-through g711ulaw
  h323
    h225 connect-passthru
  sip
    header-passing error-passthru
    midcall-signaling passthru
    g729 annexb-all
!
voice class codec 1
  codec preference 1 g729br8
  codec preference 2 g711ulaw
!
interface GigabitEthernet0/0
  description Inside towards CUCM
  ip address 172.x.x.x 255.255.255.0
  duplex auto
!
interface GigabitEthernet0/1
  description Outside towards SIP Trunk
  ip address x.x.x.x 255.255.255.0
  duplex auto
!
dial-peer voice 701 voip
  description SP to CUCM-1 with SIP
  destination-pattern 701.......
  voice-class codec 1
  session protocol sipv2
  session target ipv4:172.X.X.1
  dtmf-relay rtp-nte
!
dial-peer voice 710 voip
  description SP to CUCM-2 with SIP
  destination-pattern 710.......
  voice-class codec 1
```

continues

Example 10-4 *continued*

```
   session protocol sipv2
   session target ipv4:172.X.X.2
   dtmf-relay rtp-nte
!
dial-peer voice 720 voip
   description SP to CUCM-3 with H.323
   destination-pattern 720.......
   voice-class codec 1
   session target ipv4:172.x.x.3
   dtmf-relay rtp-nte
!
dial-peer voice 730 voip
   description SP to PBX-4 with SIP
   destination-pattern 730.......
   voice-class codec 1
   session protocol sipv2
   session target ipv4:172.X.X.4
   dtmf-relay rtp-nte
!
dial-peer voice 740 voip
   description SP to PBX-5 with H.323
   destination-pattern 740.......
   voice-class codec 1
   session target ipv4:172.x.x.5
   dtmf-relay rtp-nte
```

Contact Center SIP Trunk Interconnect

There are broadly two deployment options for PSTN access in Contact Center scenarios. These exist regardless of whether the PSTN access is via traditional Time Division Multiplexing (TDM) trunks or SIP trunks:

- In large sites, typically centralized deployments, the PSTN *ingress* gateways are usually dedicated to the task and the Voice Extensible Markup Language (VoiceXML) browser capabilities that Cisco Voice Portal (CVP) uses to provide interactive voice response (IVR) services residing on dedicated VoiceXML gateways that are separate from the platform where the PSTN trunks terminate.

- In smaller sites, typically remote offices in a distributed network architecture, the same Cisco IOS platform serves as both PSTN gateway and VoiceXML browser gateway.

When SIP trunking is used for PSTN access into a contact center, the same architectures apply. The CUBE terminating the SIP trunk might be dedicated to the task or might serve as the VoiceXML browser for CVP. This is shown in Figure 10-5.

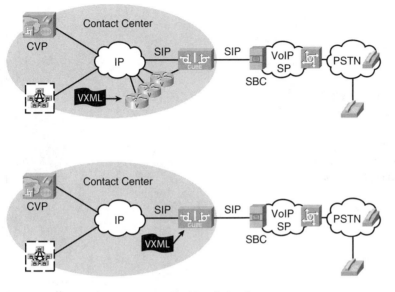

Figure 10-5   *Contact Center SIP Trunk Deployments*

Example 10-5 gives the configuration of a CUBE deployed in the *integrated* scenario shown in Figure 10-5, that is, the SIP trunk from the PSTN terminates on the same platform where VoiceXML services are provided.

If you use the dedicated deployment scenario in the top part of Figure 10-5 (a separate platform hosting the VoiceXML capability from the CUBE terminating your SIP trunks), the CUBE configuration looks exactly the same as in Examples 10-1 and 10-2.

Example 10-5   *Contact Center SIP Trunk Deployments*

```
voice-card 2 [1]
 dsp services dspfarm
!
voice-card 3 [1]
 dsp services dspfarm
!
voice rtp send-recv
!
voice service voip
  h323
  emptycapability
  allow-connections h323 to sip
  allow-connections sip to h323
  allow-connections sip to sip
  signaling forward unconditional [2]
```

continues

Example 10-5   *continued*

```
  sip
    rel1xx disable
    header-passing
!
voice class uri NUANCE sip
  pattern NUANCE@nuance-host
!
voice class codec 1
  codec preference 1 g711ulaw
  codec preference 2 g729r8
!
voice translation-rule 1
  rule 1 /6505552.../ /71006/
!
voice translation-profile myprofile
  translate called 1
!
ivr prompt memory 15000
ivr prompt streamed none
!
application (3)
  service collect_transfer_bridged flash:SelfService.tcl
    paramspace english language en
    paramspace english index 0
    paramspace english location flash
    param SelfService-port 7000
    paramspace english prefix en
    param SelfService-app collect_transfer_bridged
    param PrimaryVXMLServer 10.1.34.2
!
  service collect_transfer flash:SelfService.tcl
    paramspace english index 0
    paramspace english language en
    paramspace english location flash
    param SelfService-app collectdigits_transfer
    paramspace english prefix en
    param SelfService-port 7000
    param PrimaryVXMLServer 10.1.34.2
!
  service new-call flash:bootstrap.vxml
    paramspace english index 0
    paramspace english language en
    paramspace english location flash:
    paramspace english prefix en
```

```
!
  service Secure flash:SelfService.tcl
    param SelfService-SSL 1
    param PrimaryVXMLServer 10.1.34.2
    paramspace english index 0
    paramspace english language en
    paramspace english location flash
    paramspace english prefix en
    param SelfService-port 7443
    param SelfService-app Test_GD_DTMF_60sec
!
  service SelfService flash:SelfServiceBootstrap.vxml
    paramspace english language en
    paramspace english index 0
    paramspace english location flash:
    paramspace english prefix en
!
  service ringtone flash:ringtone.tcl
    paramspace english index 0
    paramspace english language en
    paramspace english location flash
    paramspace english prefix en
!
  service Error flash:Error.tcl
    paramspace english language en
    paramspace english index 0
    paramspace english location flash
    paramspace english prefix en
!
  service bootstrap flash:bootstrap.tcl
    paramspace english language en
    paramspace english index 0
    paramspace english location flash
    param serverssl 1
    paramspace english prefix en
!
  service handoff flash:handoff.tcl
    paramspace english index 0
    paramspace english language en
    paramspace english location flash:
    paramspace english prefix en
!
mrcp client timeout connect 20
vxml tree memory 128
```

continues

Example 10-5   *continued*

```
vxml version 2.0
!
interface GigabitEthernet0/0
  ip address 172.x.x.x 255.255.0.0
  duplex full
!
interface GigabitEthernet0/1
  ip address 99.x.x.x 255.255.0.0
  duplex full
!
no ip http server
no ip http secure-server
!
sccp local GigabitEthernet0/0
sccp ccm x.x.x.x identifier 1 version 5.0.1 (4)
sccp
!
sccp ccm group 1
  associate ccm 1 priority 1
  associate profile 1 register XCD000bbecadcf1 (4)
  keepalive retries 5
!
dspfarm profile 1 transcode (1)
  codec g711ulaw
  codec g711alaw
  codec g729ar8
  codec g729abr8
  codec g729r8
  maximum sessions 144
  associate application SCCP
!
dial-peer voice 200 voip (5)
  description Incoming dial-peer for all calls
  incoming called-number 6505552...
  dtmf-relay rtp-nte
  no vad
!
dial-peer voice 700 voip (6)
  description Outgoing Call to Cisco Unified Presence Server and CVP
  translation-profile outgoing myprofile (7)
  destination-pattern 6505552...
  session protocol sipv2
  session target ipv4:172.x.x.x (8)
  dtmf-relay rtp-nte
```

```
   codec g711ulaw (9)
   no vad
!
dial-peer voice 9292 voip (10)
  description SIP Error
  service Error
  incoming called-number 92T
  codec g711ulaw
!
dial-peer voice 9191 voip (10)
  description SIP Ringtone
  service ringtone
  incoming called-number 91T
  codec g711ulaw
!
dial-peer voice 888999 voip (11)
  service bootstrap
  incoming called-number 888999T
  dtmf-relay rtp-nte
  codec g711ulaw
!
sip-ua
!
telephony-service (12)
  sdspfarm units 5
  sdspfarm transcode sessions 20
  sdspfarm tag 1 XCD000bbecadcf1
  max-ephones 6
  ip source-address x.x.x.x port 2000 (13)
```

Note the following:

1. These commands define DSPs on the router chassis to be used for Media Resources (specifically, in this configuration, for transcoding).

2. This command enables passing User-to-User Information (UUI) parameters via Generic Transparency Descriptor (GTD) from the SIP trunk to CVP.

3. The series of commands starting here are the base (bootstrap) definition of the Tcl and VoiceXML scripts used by CVP for IVR control of the call. These are the same scripts used for CVP deployments on TDM PSTN gateways.

4. This command points to the IP address of the local CUBE router itself (the IP address assigned to the GigabitEthernet0/0 interface) and defines transcoding resources under local control of CUBE.

5. This is the incoming dial-peer matching all calls from the SIP trunk.

6. This is the outgoing dial-peer routing calls to the SIP proxy and on to CVP.

7. The Dialed Number Identification Service (DNIS) of the call is translated to 71006 before sending call to CVP to trigger the appropriate service for the call.

8. The IP address of the Cisco Unified Proxy Server (UPS) proxy is used as the session target for call setup.

9. G.711 is used for all contact center calls. If the incoming SIP trunk call is G.729, this codec mismatch triggers CUBE to engage transcoding resources (defined earlier in the configuration) for the call.

10. Additional dial-peers to trigger some of the call and error control Tcl scripts that CVP uses on the gateway.

11. The dial-peer tag "888999" corresponds to the LABEL configured on the ICM. This label is known as the "Voice Response Unit (VRU) transfer label" and is returned to the CVP call server (and eventually to the CUBE via the SIP proxy) by ICM for VRU treatment.

12. This block of commands defines CUBE as a transcoding controller, and the DSP resources defined earlier (see Note 1 earlier in this list) will be used when transcoding is required for a call.

13. The IP address in this command is that of the local CUBE router itself (the IP address assigned to the GigabitEthernet0/0 interface).

SMB SIP Trunk for PSTN Access

For an SMB there is usually no need for a dedicated session border controller device to connect to a SIP trunk; SIP trunk traffic levels do not warrant it, nor is it cost-effective to have a separate appliance.

It is usually sufficient to use a smaller device with integrated SIP routing capability, unsophisticated session border control functions, and firewalling capability. However, SMB owners should carefully think through their SIP trunk connectivity, because the physical connection is much more likely to be shared with Internet access than the SIP trunk connection of a large enterprise. A shared access medium poses significantly higher security exposure than a dedicated SIP trunk and must be protected against.

Figure 10-6 depicts two common SMB deployments: one with a traditional TDM keysystem or PBX, the other with an IP-PBX. Unlike the enterprise offerings, the SMB services are most often not pure SIP trunk offerings; they are instead managed services that most likely include the PBX (or at least the connectivity to it where the business might manage their own PBX) and offer full business communications connectivity for the company including Internet access, data connectivity to other sites (for larger businesses with multiple sites), and SIP trunk access for PSTN calls.

Example 10-6 provides a configuration of a Cisco IOS router configured with Cisco Unified Communications Manager Express (CME) as the managed IP-PBX, integrated voice mail and auto-attendant (offered by Cisco Unity Express), SIP trunk access, fire-wall, and Internet access via a Digital Subscriber Line (DSL) uplink. This configuration represents a Cisco IOS router running 12.4(15)T software.

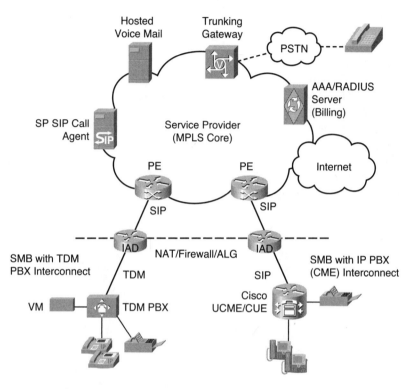

Figure 10-6 *SMB SIP Trunk Deployments*

Example 10-6 *CME Interconnect with SIP Trunk*

```
no ip dhcp use vrf connected
ip dhcp ping timeout 10000
!
ip dhcp pool IPPBX11Ph1 (1)
host x.40.x.x 255.255.255.0
client-identifier 0100.0ab8.4a03.0b
default-router x.40.x.1
option 150 ip x.40.x.1
!
ip dhcp class test
!
ip dhcp update dns
ip domain lookup source-interface Loopback0
```

continues

Example 10-6   *continued*

```
ip domain name example.com
ip name-server x.x.x.x
ip name-server x.x.x.x
!
ip inspect name mh_fw_rule dns (2)
ip inspect name mh_fw_rule ftp
ip inspect name mh_fw_rule http
ip inspect name mh_fw_rule https
ip inspect name mh_fw_rule icmp
ip inspect name mh_fw_rule imap
ip inspect name mh_fw_rule pop3
ip inspect name mh_fw_rule rcmd
ip inspect name mh_fw_rule esmtp
ip inspect name mh_fw_rule sqlnet
ip inspect name mh_fw_rule tftp
ip inspect name mh_fw_rule sip
ip inspect name mh_fw_rule h323
ip inspect name mh_fw_rule tcp
ip inspect name mh_fw_rule udp
!
voice-card 0
  dspfarm
  dsp services dspfarm
!
voice service voip
  allow-connections sip to sip (3)
  no supplementary-service sip refer
  fax protocol t38 ls-redundancy 0 hs-redundancy 0 fallback pass-through g711ulaw
  sip
    bind control source-interface Loopback0
    bind media source-interface Loopback0
    min-se 90
    registrar server expires max 3600 min 3600
    localhost dns:example.net
!
controller DSL 0/0/0 (4)
  mode atm
  line-term cpe
  line-mode 4-wire enhanced
  line-rate 4608
!
class-map match-any media
  match protocol rtp
  match ip precedence 5
```

```
class-map match-any signaling
  match protocol sip
  match ip precedence 4
!
policy-map SIP_QOS
  class signaling
    bandwidth percent 4
  class media
    priority percent 90
!
interface Loopback0
  ip address x.10.x.x 255.255.255.255
!
interface GigabitEthernet0/1
  ip address x.40.x.x 255.255.255.0
  duplex auto
!
interface ATM0/0/0
  ip address x.80.x.x 255.255.255.252
  ip inspect mh_fw_rule in (5)
  ip access-group lp_wan_acl out (6)
  ip ospf 150 area 0
  service-policy output SIP_QOS
  logging event atm pvc state
  logging event atm pvc autoppp
  logging event subif-link-status
  no atm ilmi-keepalive
  cdp enable
  pvc 0/100
  protocol ip x.80.x.x broadcast
  cbr 4608
!
interface Service-Engine1/0 (7)
  ip unnumbered GigabitEthernet0/1
  service-module ip address x.40.x.x 255.255.255.0
  service-module ip default-gateway x.40.x.x
!
ip access-list extended lp_wan_acl (8)
permit tcp any any established
permit ahp any any
permit esp any any
permit udp any any eq non500-isakmp
permit udp any any eq isakmp
permit ospf any any
```

continues

Example 10-6   *continued*

```
permit udp any eq 5060 any
permit udp any any eq 5060
permit udp any range 16384 32767 any
permit udp any any range 16384 32767
permit udp any eq domain any
permit tcp any any eq 5060
permit tcp any eq 5060 any
permit tcp any any eq 443
permit tcp any any eq 22
permit icmp any host 10.80.80.69 echo-reply
permit icmp any host 10.80.80.69 time-exceeded
permit icmp any host 10.80.80.69 unreachable
permit icmp any host 10.10.11.64 echo-reply
permit icmp any host 10.10.11.64 time-exceeded
permit icmp any host 10.10.11.64 unreachable
!
voice-port 1/0/0
voice-port 1/0/1
!
dial-peer voice 1 voip (9)
  description Incoming Calls
  answer-address .T
  session protocol sipv2
  incoming called-number .T
  dtmf-relay rtp-nte digit-drop
  codec g711ulaw
  fax-relay ecm disable
  ip qos dscp cs5 media
  ip qos dscp cs5 signaling
  no vad
!
dial-peer voice 102 voip (10)
  description ** Outgoing calls to SIP trunk **
  destination-pattern 9[0-1][2-9]..[2-9]......
  voice-class codec 1
  voice-class sip dtmf-relay force rtp-nte
  session protocol sipv2
  session target sip-server (11)
  dtmf-relay rtp-nte
  ip qos dscp cs5 media
  ip qos dscp cs4 signaling
  no vad
!
dial-peer voice 103 voip (12)
```

```
   description ** 911 outgoing call to SIP trunk **
   destination-pattern 911
   voice-class codec 1
   voice-class sip dtmf-relay force rtp-nte
   session protocol sipv2
   session target sip-server (11)
   dtmf-relay rtp-nte
   ip qos dscp cs5 media
   ip qos dscp cs4 signaling
   no vad
!
dial-peer voice 26 voip
   description ** Cisco Unity Express number **
   destination-pattern 2000
   b2bua
   session protocol sipv2
   session target ipv4: 10.40.50.100
   dtmf-relay sip-notify
   codec g711ulaw
   no vad
!
dial-peer voice 27 voip
   description ** Cisco Unity Express auto attendant number **
   translation-profile outgoing PSTN_CallForwarding
   destination-pattern 2100
   b2bua
   session protocol sipv2
   session target ipv4: 10.40.50.100
   dtmf-relay sip-notify
   codec g711ulaw
   no vad
!
dial-peer voice 100 pots (13)
   description PSTN-FXO
   destination-pattern 9.T
   port 1/0/0
!
dial-peer voice 101 pots (13)
   description PSTN-FXO
   destination-pattern 9.T
   port 1/0/1
!
sip-ua
   authentication username myuser password YYYYYY (14)
```

continues

Example 10-6   *continued*

```
  no remote-party-id
  retry invite 2
  retry register 2
  retry options 0
  timers connect 100
  registrar dns:example.net expires 3600 (14)
  sip-server dns:example.net (15)
  host-registrar (14)
!
telephony-service (16)
  sdspfarm units 5
  sdspfarm transcode sessions 10
  sdspfarm tag 1 XCD111122223333
  load 7910 P00403020214
  load 7960-7940 P00307020300
  load 7971 SCCP70.8-0-3S.loads
  load 7970 SCCP70.8-0-3S.loads
  load 7912 CP7912010200SCCP031023A
  max-ephones 40
  max-dn 50
  ip source-address 10.40.50.1 port 2000
  voicemail 2000
  system message LP-2811-CME11
  dialplan-pattern 1 408555.... extension-length 4
  max-conferences 10 gain -6
  call-forward pattern .T
  call-forward system redirecting-expanded
  moh music-on-hold.au
  transfer-system full-consult
  transfer-pattern .T
  create cnf-files version-stamp Jan 01 2002 00:00:00
!
ephone-dn 1 dual-line
  number 2001 secondary 4085552001 no-reg primary
  label 4085552001
  description 40855520XX
  name 4085552001
!
ephone 1
  device-security-mode none
  mac-address 000A.B84A.030B
  codec g729r8
  type 7970
  keep-conference endcall
  button 2:2
```

Note the following:

1. This section defines the DHCP Configuration for CME phone endpoints.

2. This section defines the inbound Cisco IOS Firewall configuration rules (**mh_fw_rule**).

3. This command enables CUBE SIP trunking services.

4. This is the SP (Internet) uplink.

5. These commands apply the firewall inspect policy **mh_fw_rule** to inbound traffic.

6. These commands apply the firewall inspect policy **wan_acl** out to outbound traffic.

7. This section defines the Cisco Unity Express interface for voice mail and auto-attendant services.

8. This section defines the outbound Cisco IOS Firewall configuration rules (**lp_wan_acl**).

9. This is the dial-peer for incoming SIP trunk calls.

10. This is the dial-peer for outgoing SIP trunk calls.

11. This points to the SP's SIP call agent.

12. This is the dial-peer for outgoing 911 calls over the SIP trunk.

13. These are the backup FXO trunks to use for emergency call access if the SIP trunk is down.

14. This is the SIP registration information for the CME to register with the SP's SIP call agent. This enables the SIP call agent to do direct inward dial (DID) call routing.

15. This defines the SP's SIP call agent.

16. The remainder of the configuration is for CME and its endpoints (that is, the IP-PBX configuration).

Example 10-7 provides a configuration of a Cisco IOS router used purely as an Integrated Access Device (IAD) connecting the SP's service on the outside and to a privately owned keysystem or PBX on the inside. This configuration represents a Cisco IOS router running 12.4(15)T software.

Example 10-7   *IAD Interconnect with SIP Trunk*

```
card type e1 1
!
```

continues

Example 10-7   *continued*

```
network-clock-participate wic 0
network-clock-participate E1 1/0
network-clock-participate E1 1/1
network-clock-select 1 E1 1/1
!
! Firewall rule configuration
!
ip inspect name mh_fw_rule dns (1)
ip inspect name mh_fw_rule ftp
ip inspect name mh_fw_rule http
ip inspect name mh_fw_rule https
ip inspect name mh_fw_rule icmp
ip inspect name mh_fw_rule imap
ip inspect name mh_fw_rule pop3
ip inspect name mh_fw_rule rcmd
ip inspect name mh_fw_rule esmtp
ip inspect name mh_fw_rule sqlnet
ip inspect name mh_fw_rule tftp
ip inspect name mh_fw_rule sip
ip inspect name mh_fw_rule h323
ip inspect name mh_fw_rule tcp
ip inspect name mh_fw_rule udp
!
isdn switch-type primary-qsig (3)
voice-card 0
!
voice service voip
  fax protocol t38 ls-redundancy 0 hs-redundancy 0 fallback pass-through g711ulaw
  sip (2)
    bind control source-interface Loopback0
    bind media source-interface Loopback0
!
controller E1 1/0
  framing NO-CRC4
  clock source internal
  pri-group timeslots 1-31 (3)
!
controller E1 1/1
  framing NO-CRC4
  channel-group 0 timeslots 1-31 (4)
!
class-map match-any IMIX
  match ip precedence 1
class-map match-any VOICE
```

```
   match ip precedence 5
class-map match-any SIG
   match ip precedence 3
 !
policy-map mypm
   class VOICE
      priority percent 55
   class SIG
      priority percent 20
   class IMIX
      priority percent 20
 !
interface Loopback0
   ip address 10.x.x.x 255.255.255.255
 !
interface FastEthernet0/1
   ip address 192.x.x.x 255.255.255.0
   ip nat inside (5)
   ip virtual-reassembly
 !
interface Serial1/0:15 (3)
   no ip address
   encapsulation hdlc
   no logging event link-status
   isdn switch-type primary-qsig
   isdn protocol-emulate network
   isdn incoming-voice voice
 !
interface Serial1/1:0
   ip address 10.x.x.x 255.255.255.252
   ip access-group wan_acl in (6)
   ip nat outside (6)
   ip inspect mh_fw_rule out (6)
   ip virtual-reassembly
   encapsulation ppp
   service-policy output mypm (6)
 !
ip nat pool mydata 10.x.x.x 70.x.x.x prefix-length 24 (7)
ip nat inside source list 70 pool mydata
ip nat outside source static 10.x.x.x 192.x.x.x
 !
ip access-list extended wan_acl (8)
permit tcp any any established
permit ahp any any
```

continues

Example 10-7   *continued*

```
permit esp any any
permit eigrp any any
permit udp any any eq non500-isakmp
permit udp any any eq isakmp
permit udp any eq 5060 any
permit udp any any eq 5060
permit udp any range 16384 32767 any
permit udp any any range 16384 32767
permit udp any eq domain any
permit tcp any any eq 5060
permit tcp any eq 5060 any
permit tcp any any eq 443
permit tcp any any eq 22
permit icmp any host 10.1.1.2 echo-reply
permit icmp any host 10.1.1.2 time-exceeded
permit icmp any host 10.1.1.2 unreachable
permit icmp any host 10.0.0.2 echo-reply
permit icmp any host 10.0.0.2 time-exceeded
permit icmp any host 10.0.0.2 unreachable
deny ip any any
access-list 70 permit 192.168.16.0 0.0.0.255
access-list 101 permit ip 10.1.0.0 0.0.0.255 any
!
voice-port 1/0:15
!
dial-peer voice 1 pots (9)
   destination-pattern 510555....
   incoming called-number 732555....
   no digit-strip
   direct-inward-dial
   port 1/0:15
!
dial-peer voice 2 voip (10)
   max-conn 12
   destination-pattern 732999....
   session protocol sipv2
   session target ipv4:10.x.x.x
   incoming called-number 510111....
   dtmf-relay rtp-nte
   codec g711ulaw
   fax rate 14400
   ip qos dscp cs5 media
   ip qos dscp cs3 signaling
   no vad
```

Note the following:

1. This block of commands defines the Cisco IOS Firewall rules.

2. This command defines the SIP parameters for the SIP trunk.

3. These commands define the connection to the PBX.

4. This command defines the data interface to the SP network.

5. This command enables NAT on the inside interface.

6. This defines the data connection to the SP network. NAT and firewall services are enabled, and the *mypm* quality of service (QoS) policy is assigned to the serial uplink.

7. These commands define the NAT translation.

8. These commands define the firewall inspection.

9. A single Plain Old Telephony Service (POTS) dial peer points all incoming calls to the trunk to the PBX. The destination pattern configuration should be adjusted to allow all calls to be routed to the PBX. The **no-digit-strip** command enables all dialed digits to pass to the PBX for call routing to the phone extensions.

10. A single VoIP dial peer points all outgoing calls to the SP's SIP call agent over the SIP trunk. A maximum of 12 simultaneous calls are enabled in this configuration. This is just an example and should be configured based on the number of concurrent calls the SLA allows.

Additional Deployment Variations

So far this chapter has provided near-complete configurations of CUBE or a Cisco TDM gateway (in the case of the IAD connected to a TDM PBX) to connect on the outside to various SIP trunk deployments and on the inside to the enterprise or SMB's PBX or IP-PBX equipment.

Using these basic SIP trunk configurations with the additional configuration excerpts given in this section allows you to customize the configurations for a wide variety of specific deployments in your network. This section provides additional configuration information on the following deployments:

■ CUBE collocated with SRST

■ CUBE doing transcoding on a SIP trunk

■ CUBE collocated with the integrated Cisco IOS Firewall

■ CUBE with Tcl Scripting for additional customized call routing or treatment

■ CUBE with SIP TLS to CUCM

- CUBE allowing Telepresence Business-to-Business interconnect

- Miscellaneous other helpful configurations

CUBE with SRST

CUBE can be used for centralized or distributed SIP trunking deployments. In a centralized deployment, CUBE likely carries high traffic and is dedicated to the function of being a session border controller.

In a distributed deployment where the SIP trunk terminates directly into a remote or branch office, the SIP trunk traffic level is generally much lower, and it is usually not cost-effective to dedicate an appliance to the SIP trunk function. In such a deployment, the Cisco IOS router already present in that remote or branch site can terminate the SIP trunk and function as the SRST router for the same site.

Example 10-8 shows a configuration of CUBE and SRST on the same router. This configuration uses Cisco IOS 12.4(20)T1 Software.

Example 10-8   *CUBE and SRST Configuration*

```
voice service voip (1)
  address-hiding
  allow-connections sip to sip
  no supplementary-service sip moved-temporarily
  no supplementary-service sip refer
  supplementary-service media-renegotiate
  fax protocol pass-through g711ulaw
  sip
    min-se 90
    header-passing error-passthru
    midcall-signaling passthru
!
dial-peer voice 2000 voip (2)
  description *** Incoming Dial-Peer ***
  codec g729r8
  session protocol sipv2
  incoming called-number 6T
  dtmf-relay rtp-nte digit-drop
  no vad
!
dial-peer voice 2001 voip (2)
  description *** Outgoing Dial-Peer ***
  destination-pattern .T
  codec g729r8
  voice-class sip early-offer forced
  session protocol sipv2
```

```
      session target ipv4:x.x.x.x
      dtmf-relay rtp-nte digit-drop
      no vad
   !
   sip-ua (3)
      authentication username yyyyy password 7 xxxxxxxxxx
      retry invite 2
      retry response 5
      retry bye 2
      retry cancel 2
      retry register 10
      retry options 1
   !
   call-manager-fallback (4)
      video
      max-conferences 10 gain -6
      transfer-system full-consult
      log table max-size 1000
      ip source-address 10.x.x.x port 2000
      max-ephones 50
      max-dn 50
      dialplan-pattern 1 415555.... extension-length 4
      transfer-pattern .T
```

Note the following:

1. This block of commands represent typical CUBE configuration.

2. These commands define the SIP trunk incoming and outgoing dial-peers.

3. This command defines the SIP User Agent attributes.

4. This command defines the SRST parameters.

CUBE Transcoding

When a SIP trunk enters a private network, there might not be an end-to-end common codec that can be negotiated between the endpoints. If so, transcoding is required at the border. Transcoding can be triggered on CUBE by the mismatch of codecs on the inside and outside interfaces. DSP resources must be available on the CUBE platform to perform the transcoding function.

Example 10-9 shows a CUBE transcoding configuration.

Example 10-9 *CUBE Transcoding*

```
voice-card 1 (1)
```

continues

Example 10-9   *continued*

```
   dspfarm
   dsp services dspfarm
!
interface GigabitEthernet0/0
   ip address 10.x.x.x 255.255.255.0 (2)
!
sccp local GigabitEthernet0/0 (3)
sccp ccm 10.x.x.x identifier 1 version 4.0 (4)
sccp
!
sccp ccm group 1 (5)
   associate ccm 1 priority 1
   associate profile 1 register TRANS12345
   keepalive retries 1
   keepalive timeout 10
   switchover method immediate
   switchback method immediate
!
dspfarm profile 1 transcode (6)
   codec g711ulaw
   codec g711alaw
   codec g729ar8
   codec g729abr8
   codec g729r8
   codec g729br8
   maximum sessions 18
   associate application SCCP
!
telephony-service (7)
 max-ephones 2
 max-dn 2
 ip source-address 10.x.x.x port 2000 (8)
 sdspfarm units 1
 sdspfarm transcode sessions 128
 sdspfarm tag 1 TRANS12345
```

Note the following:

1. These commands define the DSPs on the platform to be available for services such as conferencing and transcoding.

2. This command defines the IP address of CUBE.

3. This block of commands defines the controlling call agent for the DSP resources. Although the command language uses CUCM terminology, the controlling call agent can be CUCM, CUBE, or CME.

4. For CUBE to be the controlling call agent of the transcoding DSP resources, this IP address must match the IP address in (2).

5. This block of commands is the same regardless of whether CUCM, CME, or CUBE is the controlling call agent. These commands instruct the DSP resources to register with the call agent.

6. These commands define the codecs and the number of sessions the transcoding DSPs can service.

7. These commands turn on local call agent control of transcoding. This configuration is the same for either CUBE or CME as the controlling call agent.

8. This IP address must match the IP address in (2).

CUBE with Integrated Cisco IOS Firewall

The Cisco IOS Zone-Based Firewall (ZBFW) has the capability (starting in 12.4[20T]) to inspect locally sourced traffic and router transit traffic. CUBE creates locally sourced traffic on the router as it is a back-to-back user agent (B2BUA) and terminates and re-originates the H.323 and SIP call streams routed by it.

Example 10-10 shows a sample configuration of how the ZBFW inspection policies can be used with CUBE to provide a layered security approach where the firewall inspects the traffic first, before handing it off to the Layer 7 SIP User Agent (CUBE) application for additional security checks and call routing.

Example 10-10   *CUBE and Cisco IOS ZBFW Configuration*

```
voice service voip (1)
  address-hiding
  allow-connections sip to sip
  sip
    session transport tcp
    rel1xx disable
    header-passing
    midcall-signaling passthru
!
class-map type inspect match-any SIP-inbound (2)
  match protocol sip
class-map type inspect sip match-any sip_rfc3261_2 (3)
  match request method message
  match request method subscribe
  match request method notify
class-map type inspect sip match-any sip_rfc3261 (4)
  match request method invite
  match request method ack
  match request method register
```

continues

Example 10-10   *continued*

```
   match request method bye
   match request method cancel
   match request method options
!
policy-map type inspect sip dpi_policy (5)
  class type inspect sip sip_rfc3261
    rate-limit 16
  class type inspect sip sip_rfc3261_2
policy-map type inspect sip-policy-inbound (6)
  class type inspect SIP-inbound
    inspect
    service-policy sip dpi_policy
  class class-default
    drop
!
zone security zout (7)
zone security zin
zone-pair security self-to-out source self destination zout
  service-policy type inspect sip-policy-inbound
zone-pair security out-to-self source zout destination self
  service-policy type inspect sip-policy-inbound
zone-pair security self-to-zin source self destination zin
  service-policy type inspect sip-policy-inbound
zone-pair security zin-to-self source zin destination self
  service-policy type inspect sip-policy-inbound
!
interface GigabitEthernet0/0
  description Inside interface
  ip address 10.x.x.x 255.255.255.0
  zone-member security zin (8)
!
interface GigabitEthernet0/1
  description Outside interface
  ip address 200.x.x.x 255.255.255.252
  zone-member security zout (9)
!
dial-peer voice 910 voip (10)
  destination-pattern .T
```

Notes:

1. This block of commands provides the global CUBE configuration.

2. These commands define the *SIP-inbound* FW class of traffic. It matches all SIP traffic. Later policies define the actions to take on traffic that matches these criteria.

3. These commands define the *rfc3261_2* FW class of traffic. It matches the SIP methods specified. Later policies define the actions to take on traffic that matches these criteria.

4. These commands define the *rfc3261* FW class of traffic. It matches the SIP methods specified. Later policies define the actions to take on traffic that matches these criteria.

5. This section of commands defines the *dpi_policy* FW policy, which does rate limiting on SIP traffic defined in the *sip_rfc3261* class, and SIP inspection on the traffic defined in the *sip_rfc3261_2* class.

6. This section of commands defines the *sip-policy-inbound* FW policy, which inspects the SIP traffic that matches the *SIP-inbound* class and drops all other non-matching traffic.

7. This section of commands defines the ZBFW zones and inspection policies. Whenever traffic flows between the zones, the applicable inspection policy is executed on the traffic. In this example, the *sip-policy-inbound* policy is used for traffic in all directions. You could also define different policies for the different directions of traffic.

8. The interface facing the inside of the network is assigned to the *zin* zone.

9. The interface facing the outside of the network is assigned to the *zout* zone.

10. The remainder of the typical CUBE configuration (dial-peers) follows here.

CUBE with Tcl Scripting

Tcl scripting is a general Cisco IOS unified communication (UC) capability that provides powerful means of intercepting, manipulating, controlling call routing, treatment, and information associated with calls. Tcl scripts are generally attached to dial-peers so that any application using dial-peers (such as CUBE) can be customized by using Tcl scripts.

Example 10-11 provides a configuration segment where a Tcl script was used to determine if a call is audio only or video and audio and have CUBE send the appropriate Session Description Protocol (SDP) for the call that arrives at CUBE without an SDP altogether. The steps in the example are as follows:

■ CUCM sends a Delayed Offer (without an SDP) SIP INVITE toward CUBE using the SIP CONTACT header (as per RFC 3840) to indicate endpoint video capability.

■ CUBE converts the Delayed Offer INVITE into an Early Offer (requiring an SDP).

■ The Tcl script on CUBE examines the original INVITE for video capabilities in the CONTACT header, and if present, the outgoing Early Offer INVITE contains both video and audio capabilities in the SDP. Otherwise, the Early Offer INVITE has only an audio SDP.

This configuration example uses CUCM 6.1 and CUBE IOS 12.4(20)T Software.

Example 10-11   *CUBE with Tcl Scripting*

```
voice service voip
  allow-connections sip to sip
  sip
    header-passing
!
voice class codec 1 (1)
  codec preference 1 g711ulaw bytes 160
  codec preference 2 g729r8 bytes 20
!
voice class codec 2 (2)
 codec preference 1 g711ulaw bytes 160
 video codec h264
!
voice translation-rule 1
 rule 1 /^3\(.*\)/ /\1/
!
voice translation-profile video
 translate called 1
!
application (3)
  service redirige tftp://192.x.x.x/video.tcl
  param prefix 3
!
dial-peer voice 1 voip (4)
  service redirige
  session protocol sipv2
  incoming called-number .
  codec g711ulaw
!
dial-peer voice 2 voip (5)
  destination-pattern 6........
  voice-class codec 1
  voice-class sip early-offer forced
  session protocol sipv2
  session target ipv4:192.x.x.x
!
dial-peer voice 3 voip (6)
  description video
  translation-profile outgoing video
  destination-pattern 36........
  voice-class codec 2
  voice-class sip early-offer forced
  session protocol sipv2
  session target ipv4:192.x.x.x
```

Notes:

1. Defines the codecs included in the SDP of an audio only call.

2. Defines the codec included in the SDP of a video call.

3. Defines the Tcl script and its parameters to the system.

4. Defines an incoming dial-peer that matches all calls from CUCM. The Tcl script is
    attached to this dial-peer and examines the CONTACT header of the INVITE
    received before the call is routed to match outgoing dial-peers. If the call is audio
    only, it does nothing and sends the call on to match an outgoing dial-peer. If video is
    specified in the CONTACT header, the Tcl script modifies the dialed number by
    prepending a "3" to the string, forcing the call to match a different outgoing dial-
    peer.

5. This section defines the dial-peer that sends out outgoing audio-only calls (with
    codecs from voice-class 1). Calls unaltered by the Tcl script match this outgoing
    dial-peer.

6. This section defines the dial-peer that sends out outgoing video call (with codecs
    from voice-class 2). Calls altered by the Tcl script (prepended 3 in the dial string)
    match this outgoing dial-peer. A translation rule removes the "3" from the dialed
    string before the call exits on the SIP trunk.

Example 10-12 shows the incoming (with no SDP) and outgoing (with SDP) INVITES on
CUBE for a call that is audio only.

Example 10-12   *Audio-only INVITE*

```
INVITE from Cisco UCM to Cisco UBE:
INVITE sip:6802005345060 SIP/2.0
To: <sip:680200534@192.x.x.x>
Contact: <sip:1004@192.168.10.207:5060:transport=tcp>


INVITE from Cisco UBE to the SIP Trunk:
INVITE sip:680200534@192.X.X.X:5060 SIP/2.0
m=audio 18978 RTP/AVP 0 18 19
a=rtpmap:0 PCMU/8000
a=rtpmap:18 G729/8000
a=fmtp:18 annexb=no
a=rtpmap:19 CN/8000
```

Example 10-13 shows the incoming (with no SDP) and outgoing INVITES (with SDP) on
CUBE for a video call.

Example 10-13 *Video INVITE*

```
INVITE from Cisco UCM to Cisco UBE:
INVITE sip:680200534@192.X.X.X:5060 SIP/2.0

Contact: <sip:1004@192.X.X.X:5060;transport=tcp>;video;audio


INVITE from Cisco UBE to the SIP Trunk:
INVITE sip:680200534@192.X.X.X:5060 SIP/2.0
m=audio 16972 RTP/AVP 0 19
a=rtpmap:0 PCMU/8000
a=rtpmap:19 CN/8000
a=ptime:20
m=video 17792 RTP/AVP 119
a=rtpmap:119 H264/90000
```

CUBE Using SIP TLS to CUCM

CUBE can protect the security of SIP connections with TLS. One or both of the call legs of a SIP-to-SIP call can be individually configured for TLS. No current SIP Trunk offering for PSTN access offers TLS as an option, but the leg to CUCM can be used with TLS, and in the future, perhaps the SP SIP trunk leg.

Example 10-14 shows a TLS configuration between CUCM and CUBE.

Example 10-14 *CUBE TLS Configuration*

```
voice service voip
 allow-connections sip to sip
 sip
   url sips (1)
!
crypto pki trustpoint ca-server (2)
 enrollment url http://10.x.x.x:80
 serial-number
 revocation-check crl
 rsakeypair kkp
!
crypto pki certificate chain ca-server
 certificate 04
  3082020D 30820176 A0030201 02020104 300D0609 2A864886 F70D0101 04050030
  ....
  quit
 certificate ca 01
  30820201 3082016A A0030201 02020101 300D0609 2A864886 F70D0101 04050030
  ....
```

```
  quit
!
dial-peer voice 11 voip
  session protocol sipv2
  session transport tcp tls (3)
!
sip-ua
  crypto signaling default trustpoint ca-server (4)
```

Note the following:

1. The URI scheme **sips:** is used for SIP TLS messages.

2. This command defines the global Public-Key Infrastructure (PKI) trustpoint to the Certificate Authority (CA).

3. The session transport can be configured to TLS with this command at either the global level under **voice service voip** or on a dial-peer.

4. Use this command to configure a default trustpoint for the SIP UA.

Telepresence Business-to-Business Interconnect

CUBE provides an enterprise demarcation point for business-to-business Telepresence traffic as it crosses into the SP network as shown in Figure 10-7.

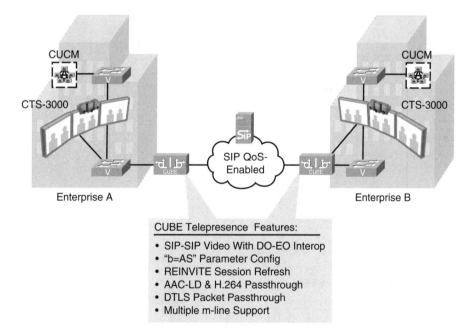

Figure 10-7   *Telepresence SIP Deployments*

Example 10-15 shows the additional configuration to enable Telepresence traffic to flow through the border element.

Example 10-15   *CUBE Telepresence Configuration*

```
voice service voip
  address-hiding
  allow-connections sip to sip
  sip
    rel1xx disable
    header-passing error-passthru
    early-offer forced
    bandwidth audio 640 (1)
    bandwidth video 50000 (1)
!
voice class codec 200 (2)
  codec preference 1 aacld profile 111
  codec preference 2 g711ulaw
  video codec h264 profile 222
!
codec profile 111 aacld
 fmtp "fmtp:96 profile-level-id=16;streamtype=5;config=11B0;mode=AAC-
hbr;sizeLength=13;indexLength=3;indexDeltaLength=3;constantDuration=480"
!
codec profile 222 h264
 fmtp "fmtp:112 profile-level-id=ABCDEF;sprop-parameter-
sets=Z00AKAoWVAPAEPI=,aGFLjyA=;packetization-mode=1"
!
dial-peer voice 240 voip
  destination-pattern 240.......
  rtp payload-type cisco-codec-fax-ind 110 (3)
  rtp payload-type cisco-codec-aacld 96 (3)
  rtp payload-type cisco-codec-video-h264 112 (3)
  voice-class codec 200
  session protocol sipv2
  session target ipv4:x.x.x.x
  incoming called-number 367.......
  codec transparent (4)
!
dial-peer voice 367 voip
  destination-pattern 367.......
  rtp payload-type cisco-codec-fax-ind 110
  rtp payload-type cisco-codec-aacld 96
  rtp payload-type cisco-codec-video-h264 112
  voice-class codec 200
  session protocol sipv2
  session target ipv4:x.x.x.x
  incoming called-number 240.......
```

Note the following:

1. These commands define the bandwidth attributes of Telepresence traffic streams.

2. These commands define the audio and video codec preferences for Telepresence.

3. These commands redefine payload types as Telepresence redefines some payload types set by default in Cisco IOS.

4. This command enables codec streams not supported natively by CUBE to pass through it. CUBE does not do codec filtering on these streams.

Miscellaneous Helpful Configurations

This chapter has offered numerous useful deployment configurations and variations to those deployments. There are additional small helpful configuration snippets that are not deployments but might be useful to enable you to customize certain aspects of the already covered deployment scenarios. This section contains a selection of these, including the following:

- Collocated MTP

- SIP IP address bind

- SIP Out-of-Dialog OPTIONS ping

- Multiple Codecs Outbound from CUCM on a SIP trunk

- SIP header manipulation

- Dual digit drop

- SIP registration

- SIP transport choices

- QoS remarking

- SIP user agent parameters

Collocated MTP

A MTP for CUCM is needed for some call flows. An MTP can be collocated with CUBE on the same IOS router (although CUBE never uses an MTP—unlike a transcoder, an MTP is a pure CUCM service that just happens to be collocated on the same router as CUBE).

Example 10-16 shows a basic MTP configuration.

Example 10-16 *Media Termination Point Configuration*

```
sccp local GigabitEthernet0/0
sccp ccm x.x.x.x identifier 5 priority 1 version 6.0 (1)
sccp
!
sccp ccm group 10 (2)
  associate ccm 5 priority 1
  associate profile 10 register MTP111222333
!
dspfarm profile 10 mtp (3)
  codec g711ulaw
  maximum sessions software 5
  associate application SCCP
```

Note the following:

1. This command defines the IP address of the CUCM that uses the MTP.

2. These commands define the registration of the MTP resources with CUCM.

3. These commands define the number and type of MTP resources the Cisco IOS services offer to CUCM. In this example, a software MTP of five sessions is defined. A software MTP does not require DSP resources on the router (a hardware MTP does).

SIP IP Address Bind

CUBE uses the IP address egress interface to populate the source address of SIP or H.323 messaging it originates. In many cases, this default behavior is the desired operation. However, you can *bind* the source address CUBE uses to a specific interface, such as a loopback, if needed.

The *bind* capability is currently a global command only and therefore binds all SIP messaging (regardless of whether the messaging travels over the inside or outside interface) to the configured address. A future CUBE capability makes this configurable on a dial-peer basis so that inside and outside traffic can be bound to individual addresses.

Example 10-17 shows how to bind SIP messaging to a loopback interface address.

Example 10-17   *Bind Command*

```
voice service voip
  sip
    bind control source-interface Loopback0
    bind media source-interface Loopback0
```

SIP Out-of-Dialog OPTIONS Ping

The out of dialog (OOD) SIP OPTIONS ping command can be used to monitor the status of a SIP trunk.

Example 10-18 shows how to configure CUBE to originate a SIP OPTIONS ping toward the SP on a global basis.

Example 10-18   *Global SIP OOD Options Ping*

```
voice service voip
  sip
    options-ping 1200
```

Example 10-19 shows how to do the same but selectively on a per dial-peer basis.

Example 10-19   *Dial-peer SIP OOD Options Ping*

```
dial-peer voice 100 voip
  voice-class sip options-ping 65
```

Multiple Codecs Outbound from CUCM on a SIP Trunk

CUCM with an MTP can offer only one of G.711 or G.729 codecs on a SIP Early Offer; it cannot offer both. If CUCM instead does a Delayed Offer and CUBE does the Delayed-Offer-to-Early-Offer interworking, CUBE can offer several codecs in the outgoing SIP INVITE on behalf of CUCM. Codecs might be ordered as desired to suit preferences.

Example 10-20 shows a sample configuration for offering different codecs on different calls.

Example 10-20   *Multiple Codecs on Outgoing Early Offer SIP INVITE*

```
voice service voip
  sip
    early-offer forced
!
voice class codec 1  (1)
  codec preference 1 g729r8
  codec preference 2 g711ulaw
voice class codec 2  (2)
  codec preference 1 g711alaw
```

continues

Example 10-20   *continued*

```
dial-peer voice 100 voip (3)
  destination-pattern 9011T
  voice-class codec 2
!
dial-peer voice 101 voip (4)
  destination-pattern 91T
  voice-class codec 1
```

Note the following:

1. This codec class defines G.729A as the preferred codec and G.711 as a second preference alternative.

2. This codec class defines G.711 as the only codec to be negotiated.

3. International calls with starting dialed digits of 9-011- trigger both G.729A and G.711 to be sent to the SP as codec choices for negotiation.

4. National calls with starting dialed digits of 91 trigger only G.711 to be sent to the SP as a codec choice for negotiation.

SIP Header Manipulation

It is often helpful to manipulate SIP messaging when trying to achieve interworking between two systems. The SIP standards are flexible enough that many interoperability difficulties exist even if all equipment is standards-compliant. CUBE offers tools to manipulate SIP messages: headers and fields can be added, deleted, or changed (match and replace) using regular expression syntax. These rules can be applied globally to all messaging or on a per dial-peer basis for directional traffic.

Example 10-21 shows how to remove the timer support indication from an INVITE and instead advertise that the timer feature is not supported.

Example 10-21   *SIP Header Manipulation*

```
voice service voip
   sip
     sip-profiles 100 (1)
!
voice class sip-profiles 100 (2)
  request INVITE sip-header Supported remove
  request INVITE sip-header Min-SE remove
  request INVITE sip-header Session-Expires remove
  request INVITE sip-header Unsupported modify "Unsupported:" "timer"
!
dial-peer voice 555 voip
   voice-class sip-profiles 100 (3)
```

Note the following:

1. This command applies the rules to all SIP traffic on a global basis.

2. This block of commands defines the SIP header manipulation rules.

3. This command applies the rules to SIP traffic passing through a particular dial-peer. Because the rules were already applied on a global basis in (1), this command has no effect here, but if multiple profiles were defined in (2), for example 100 and 101, then profile 100 could be applied globally, as done in (1), and profile 101 could be applied on the dial-peer.

Dual Digit Drop

RFC-2833 DTMF relay travels in the media (in-band) path of the call, unlike most other DTMF relay mechanisms that travel in the signaling (out-of-band) path. To avoid sending both in-band and out-of band DTMF relay indications to the outgoing leg when CUBE converts from in-band to out-of band methods, use the **dtmf-relay rtp-nte digit-drop** command on the incoming SIP dial-peer.

Example 10-22 shows how to configure dual digits to be dropped.

Example 10-22 *Dual Digit-Drop Configuration*

```
dial-peer voice 100 voip
    dtmf-relay rtp-nte digit-drop
```

SIP Registration

Some SIP trunk providers require a SIP registration sequence to be initiated before any calls are routed. CUBE can be used to do the registrations on behalf of the CUCMs or other IP-PBXs in the enterprise. Example 10-23 shows how to configure CUBE to initiate a SIP registration.

Example 10-23 *SIP Trunk Registration*

```
sip-ua
  registrar ipv4:10.x.x.x
or
  registrar dns:csps.cisco.com
  authentication username xyz password xyz realm cisco.com
```

SIP Transport Choices

SIP traffic can use TCP or UDP as the transport protocol. Cisco IOS uses UDP by default, but the desired transport protocol can be configured as shown in Example 10-24.

Example 10-24   *SIP Session Transport Configuration*

```
voice service voip
  sip
    session transport tcp
```

QoS Remarking

One of the functions of an SBC is to control the QoS markings on the voice flows between networks. It might be that the default markings are sufficient, but if a translation is required between your network and the SP's network, CUBE provides handy tools to remark the packets as they pass through the border.

Example 10-25 shows how to do this on the outgoing dial-peer.

Example 10-25   *QoS Packet Remarking*

```
dial-peer voice 2 voip
  ip qos dscp cs5 media
  ip qos dscp cs3 signaling
```

SIP User Agent Parameters

Many global SIP parameters are configurable under the *sip-ua* portion of the Cisco IOS configuration. This is also where you can tune the retry timers to control overall post-dial delay imposed on calls failing over from one dial-peer to another. Example 10-26 shows how to configure this.

Example 10-26   *SIP User Agent Parameters*

```
sip-ua
  retry invite 2
  retry bye 2
  retry cancel 2
```

Troubleshooting

Helpful **show** and **debug** commands for general SIP call-related information include

- show call active
- show sip call
- show voip rtp conn
- debug ccsip message/all
- debug voip ccapi inout
- debug voip rtp session named events

Helpful **show** and **debug** commands for CAC related information include

- show call threshold config
- show call threshold stats
- show call threshold status
- debug call threshold detail
- debug call threshold core
- debug call treatment action

Summary

This chapter provided a significant amount of information on how to deploy and implement SIP trunk termination into an enterprise or SMB network. Two specific SP connection examples were given that can be customized for other providers who might have slight variations in their offerings.

Additional configurations were given for various common deployment variations such as older CUCMs or IP-PBXs capable only of H.323 (and not SIP), Telepresence traffic, collocated SRST, and firewall configurations. For the SMB, integrated single-device IP-PBX, firewall, and SIP trunk configurations were given, and an IAD config for connecting to a traditional key system or PBX.

The last section of the chapter provided short configuration extracts as *helpful hints* for further customization of the more basic configuration given earlier in the chapter.

The implementation information in this chapter with the architectural, design, and functionality discussions in earlier chapters should enable you to deploy and implement a SIP trunk into your network.

The next chapter summarizes overall best practices, and that is followed by a case study providing further information on how best to go about deploying SIP trunks.

Further Reading

The following documents and references provide additional information on the topics covered in this chapter.

Service Provider SIP Trunk Interconnectivity

SIP trunk interoperability configuration examples between various SPs' offerings and the CUBE are provided at www.cisco.com/go/interoperability > Cisco Unified Border Element.

Configurations examples are posted as they become available and provide guidance for ease of configuration and installation. Some documents reflect testing done in Cisco labs with access to the SP's SIP trunk; other documents reflect testing done by the SP in its own labs.

CUCM Connectivity to SIP Trunks

The CUCM Solution Reference Network Design (SRND) document provides coverage of CUCM SIP trunks both for interenterprise connectivity and for connectivity to CUBE for external SIP trunks for PSTN access:

■ **Document:** Cisco Unified Communications SRND based on Cisco Unified Communications Manager 7.x

■ **Location:** www.cisco.com/go/srnd > Unified Communications > Unified Communications Manager > View Design Guide

■ **Chapter:** Cisco Unified CM Trunks > SIP Trunks

■ **Chapter:** Cisco Unified CM Trunks > Cisco Unified Border Element

Contact Center Connectivity to SIP Trunks

The Cisco Voice Portal Solution Reference Network Design (SRND) document provides coverage of SIP trunk connectivity with gateways.

■ **Document:** Cisco Unified Customer Voice Portal (CVP) 7.x Solution Reference Network Design (SRND)

■ **Location:** www.cisco.com/go/srnd > Unified Communications > Voice Portal > View Design Guide

■ **Chapter:** Gateway Options > Cisco Unified Border Element

The CUBE documentation also provides additional configuration details of its features and deployment with Cisco Voice Portal contact center environments.

■ **Document:** Cisco Unified Border Element for Contact Center Solutions

■ **Location:** www.cisco.com/go/cube > Configure > Configuration Examples and TechNotes

Chapter 11

Deployment Steps and Best Practices

This chapter covers the following topics:

■ Deployment steps

■ Best practices

You might already have decided that you want to or should use Session Initiation Protocol (SIP) trunking on your network. Maybe you have read some reports in the industry that indicate that enterprises can save costs by moving from traditional Public Switched Telephone Network (PSTN) to SIP trunking, but they often fail to provide the details necessary to determine exactly how this might be calculated or estimated. You might have a directive in your organization to determine if SIP trunking should be deployed, and if yes, how and when—be it for the purposes of technological transformation or cost savings or both. And you might not be convinced these directions or directives are practical or can be implemented. You might simply be grappling with where to start to get some concrete answers that specifically apply to your company.

The previous five chapters examine several aspects to consider as you investigate SIP trunking. Chapter 4, "Cost Analysis," provides guidance to compare the costs of implementing SIP trunking versus the cost of your current PSTN trunking. Chapter 6, "SIP Trunking Models," Chapter 7, "Design and Implementation Considerations," and, Chapter 8, "Interworking," discuss what SIP trunking might mean to your network design and implementation. Chapter 9, "Questions to Ask of a Service Provider Offering and an SBC Vendor," covers evaluating SIP trunk service providers (SP).

This chapter pulls all the detailed information covered in these chapters into the following:

■ An easy-to-use, step-by-step guide to implementing SIP trunking

■ A summary of best practices to follow during the implementation

Deployment Steps

Although different deployment steps might be necessary to meet your individual business needs and may vary from one implementation to another, some typical deployment steps are common. These include

Step 1. Plan for migrating to SIP trunking.

Step 2. Evaluate available SIP trunk offerings.

Step 3. Conduct a Pilot Trial.

Step 4. Begin production service.

A summary of these steps and the major activities involved in each one is provided in Figure 11-1. Each step is explored in greater depth in the following sections.

① Planning	② Evaluation	③ Pilot	④ Production
• Cost analysis • Assess traffic volumes and patterns • Assess network design implications • Emergency call policy • Define production user community phases • Define user community to pilot • Evaluate future new services • Assess security precautions	• Assess SIP trunk provider offerings • Availability of TDM-equivalent features • Geographic coverage • Investigate DID porting • Call load balancing and failover routing • Emergency call handling • Determine physical delivery • Determine network demarcation • Agree on monitoring and troubleshooting procedures	• Define clear success criteria • Assess organizational responsibility • Determine length of trial • Installation and configuration • Define a clear test plan including all required production call flows • Test failover and redundancy • Address problems that come up • Test monitoring procedures	• Revise the phases of production based on pilot learning • Educate/prepare user community • Port DIDs

Figure 11-1 *Deployment Steps*

Planning

The planning step has two major goals:

■ Complete an analysis to determine the benefits of installing a SIP trunk,

■ Determine the various impacts to your network so that each issue can be objectively evaluated and a plan put in place to address any areas of concern.

Even though a decision might already have been made or directed to implement a SIP trunk in your network, it is still recommended you keep an open mind until completing Step 3, which is to execute a Pilot Trial. After you execute the trial, you will have all the necessary information to make an informed decision on whether to continue with a production implementation in your network. To ensure a smooth and predictable implementation that meets initial expectations, the planning step is of the utmost importance. As already pointed out in earlier chapters, the SIP trunking industry is not yet at the same maturity level as installing a Primary Rate Interface (PRI) from a SP. Hopefully the industry will reach this level of predictability soon, but until then, success might largely depend on the thoroughness of your planning and preparation.

During the planning step, work through the following activities and address each to the satisfaction of your organization's expectations:

- Analyze the cost.

- Assess traffic volumes and patterns.

- Assess network design implications.

- Determine an emergency call policy.

- Define a pilot user community.

- Define the production user community phases.

- Evaluate future new services.

- Assess security implications.

Cost Analysis

Do a thorough cost analysis using the material presented in Chapter 4. Compare the results of this analysis to an objective view of your current PSTN access expenditures and expected future costs.

Keep in mind that providers in certain geographies might drop their traditional PSTN PRI prices in the short term to maximize revenue on infrastructure already in place, whereas in the long term, prices might go up as the providers find it difficult to maintain older equipment in parallel with the newer network technologies.

Assess Traffic Volumes and Patterns

Ensure that you understand what your current PSTN traffic patterns constitute. Understand what call flows are necessary to sustain your business and what the traffic volumes of particular types of calls are, for example, international calling, long distance calling, and local calling. Understand inbound and outbound traffic patterns, office user and home or remote user traffic patterns, and traffic patterns of your different departments or organizations. When you reach the step at which you start using the SIP trunk for the pilot user community, this analysis can help you determine which user communities or which call types (and in what sequence) to place into production SIP trunking.

In a large network you cannot (and should not) migrate your entire network to SIP trunking overnight. It is both impractical and risky. You should define discrete steps and different user communities or call types to start using SIP trunking at a certain stage.

Assess Network Design Implications

Review quality of service (QoS) and call admission control (CAC) policies in the network to ensure coverage of new call flows. Potentially, some calls from remote sites can now cross your WAN to use a centralized unified communications SIP trunk at a campus site. Ensure that SIP trunk codecs and bandwidth needs are understood. Schedule upgrades or reconfigurations of your network prior to Step 3 of the SIP trunk implementation plan.

Determine how traffic from traditional Time Division Multiplexing (TDM) applications, such as fax, modem, point-of-sale credit card authorization, alarm monitoring, and telemetry will be handled while more common voice calls use a SIP trunk. These applications might continue to use your existing PSTN gateways until SIP interconnection offerings reach greater maturity.

Chapter 6 and Chapter 7 provide extensive coverage of network design implications to assess.

Emergency Call Policy

Determine call routing for emergency calls from all sites that will start to use SIP trunk access to ensure that the number and location information is correctly delivered to emergency authorities within the local laws of each site. Discuss the routing of these calls with your SIP trunk provider and, if appropriate measures are not in place, continue to use your traditional PSTN gateways to provide emergency call access.

When the SIP trunk is down, mobile phone access for emergency calls to the PSTN might be acceptable in certain geographies. If not, your traditional PSTN gateways might continue to provide service to these call types. The outcome of this assessment might determine the user communities chosen to participate in the pilot and the initial phase of production service.

Define Production User Community Phases

There are different ways to approach production roll out of SIP trunk service to your network, and there are different reasons for starting with a particular call pattern or user community. This is probably the hardest step to provide a single direction of guidance to because there simply is not a single *best* way of doing it.

Some enterprises start with their contact center operations; others leave those for the last phase. Determining where to start might depend on the information provided by your cost/benefit analysis. The contact center tends to have the most complex call flows to accommodate, but the contact center also tends to be an easier area to cost-justify a change such as SIP trunking.

When rolling out a SIP trunk production service, a common call pattern to start with is outbound long distance and international calls. The reason for starting here is that it is often easy to cost-justify. Also, the more thorny issues, such as Direct Inward Dial (DID) porting for inbound calls, can be delayed until a later phase allowing for more time to work through potential issues.

Another common approach is to start with geographic sites. For example, choose a corporate user community at a campus site and handle all its calls with SIP trunking while other sites continue to use traditional TDM trunks. This simplifies working through geographical differences between SIP trunk providers and handling emergency calls. (They're all in one location.) It also limits the number of DIDs that need to be ported before production service can start.

In summary, the most common user communities for first-phase production roll-out tend to be one of the following:

■   Contact center

■   A specific call type, such as outbound long distance calls

■   A single site or a small collection of sites in a specific geographic area

Define the User Community to Pilot

After you determine the user community to target for the first phase of production roll-out, it is time to focus on the call flows and patterns to test during the pilot phase. Ensure all the call types and patterns important to the chosen user community are adequately exercised and tested during the pilot phase.

The pilot should not involve porting of any DIDs or changing toll-free contact center numbers. Rather, parallel services should be installed during the pilot and the call patterns over these "non-production" numbers tested before the production numbers are changed from TDM PSTN access to SIP trunk.

Evaluate Future New Services

Video and services, like high-fidelity wideband codecs for rich-media collaboration applications such as Cisco Telepresence, currently are not available on general commercial SIP trunk offerings. At some point, though, they will be and you should put some thought into how and when such services, when available, would make sense to your network. This can influence some of the choices you make now regarding:

■   Selecting SPs

■   Reviewing your network for bandwidth, QoS, and CAC

■   Selecting the equipment to terminate a SIP trunk into your network

■   Designing the network architecture (for example, centralized or distributed trunking as discussed in Chapter 6)

Assess Security Implications

A SIP trunk is physically an IP feed coming into your network. For most mid-sized and larger enterprises, this is most likely delivered over an Ethernet medium. It often means that the physical connection into the network might not fall within the purview of the *voice* group as a PRI would, but instead is managed by the traditional *data* group. If you do not have these organizational challenges, count yourself lucky and move on. If you do, be sure to involve all affected groups as soon as possible so that they feel as if they have ownership of the planning and execution of the deployment.

Another potential wrinkle, due to the IP connectivity of a SIP trunk, is making sure that your security group is involved in ensuring the connection is adequately secured. This can mean choices regarding deploying new firewalls or reusing existing ones, and the placement of border elements inside the demilitarized zone (DMZ) of your data center (either in front of, or behind, the firewall). Be sure to work through the physical network design of the SIP trunk terminations with your security group long before you get to the installation of the trunk.

Evaluating a SIP Trunk Offering

Following are three major goals of the second step, evaluating a SIP trunk offering:

- Determine what SP SIP trunk offerings are available.

- Determine the exact capabilities and terms each SP SIP trunk offering includes.

- Determine how your network interacts or interconnects with the SP network.

At the moment, SIP trunk offerings vary considerably more than PRI offerings; therefore, they require careful evaluation. It is good practice to do a side-by-side comparison of your existing PRI offering to the features that would be available on a SIP trunk. These will not be equal, but they will give you the information to decide what features are most important and what you can live without.

During the evaluation of a SIP Trunk offering step, work through the following activities and address each one to the satisfaction of your organization's expectations:

- Assess SIP trunk provider offerings.

- Determine the availability of TDM-equivalent features.

- Determine geographic coverage.

- Assess DID porting realities.

- Determine call load balancing and failover routing.

- Determine emergency call handling.

- Determine the physical delivery of the SIP trunk.

- Determine network demarcation.

- Agree on monitoring and troubleshooting procedures.

Assess SIP Trunk Provider Offerings

Approach SPs with offerings in your geographical area and, based on their responses, rank the top one or two providers to engage in the next round of discussions. Finally, select the top contender (or sometimes two contenders for larger enterprises that require either redundancy or alternate least-cost options for their traffic).

Chapter 9 details Request for Proposal (RFP) type questions to use to evaluate an SPs offering. Use this information as a guide to draw up your own list of questions to evaluate different offerings.

Determine the Availability of TDM-Equivalent Features

At this time in the industry, you cannot assume that SIP trunks offer the exact same features as you would expect on a PRI, even though current SIP trunk offerings are marketed primarily as PSTN replacement access. SIP trunks generally offer fewer features than PRIs, and even where they offer equivalent features, the features might work differently or be less consistent than on a PRI. This is simply an indication of the immaturity of the SIP trunk market. As time passes, the expectation is that SIP trunk services will mature, closing the gap in features with PRIs and then surpass them with features that are not, and never will be, available on PRIs.

Table 11-1 summarizes some of the current, important differences between SIP trunk and PRI services.

Determine Geographic Coverage

Depending on the countries, or regions within a country, where your network has sites targeted to connect to a SIP trunk, you may have to do several evaluations and select several different providers to cover the different geographic areas where you operate.

Assess DID Porting Realities

Routing outbound calls over SIP trunks is often easier than routing inbound calls to the enterprise. And for this reason, it is sometimes where a SIP trunk trial starts—with outbound calls only.

If you target inbound calls to arrive via the SIP trunk, you must determine which DIDs in your organization are affected, which current provider these DIDs belong to, and whether the DID numbers can be reassigned to the SIP trunk. If the DID number belongs to the same provider you are considering for a SIP trunk, this might be eminently achievable, but if they belong to different providers, it will be more difficult.

For a SIP trunk trial, a few new numbers are usually assigned and porting existing DID numbers typically does not take place until you are ready to roll out production services.

Table 11-1   *Current SP SIP Trunk Services Compared to TDM Services*

Consideration	SIP Trunk Services	TDM Services
Basic call completion.	Well defined	Well defined
Supplementary services (Caller ID, Call Waiting, Transfer, Forward, Hold, Conference).	Requires validation testing	Well defined
Fault monitoring and isolation.	Options PING monitoring	Yellow/Red Alarms
Emergency call (911) handling.	Special handling per service provider	Well defined
Malicious Call-ID (MCID).	Not defined	Well defined
Multi-Level Priority and Preemption (MLPP).	Not defined	Well defined
Caller-ID delivery.	Inconsistent	Consistent
Voice band data.	Modems/Baudot TDD ill defined or unsupported	Well defined
Fax technology.	Requires validation testing	Well defined
Deterministic traffic engineering. How are bursts handled? Who generates equipment busy indications, the enterprise, or SP? Who provides announcements?	SP-dependent	Well defined
Porting DID numbers.	Within single SP control	Well defined
Geographic and legal dependencies of call routing.	Independent of geography but not of legislation	Geographically dependent
Future rich media services.	Great potential	No potential
Cost to enterprise for service.	Inconsistent	Well defined
Flexibility of call routing; site aggregation.	Very flexible	SP dependent
Security considerations.	IP considerations; toll fraud	Toll fraud

However, you must evaluate and assess the feasibility of DID number porting before or during your trial. And, if possible, include at least a few ported DID numbers in your trial to ensure services operate per your expectations.

Determine Call Load Balancing and Failover Routing

Large sites of enterprise networks usually have a bank of PRIs coming in from the PSTN and the SP load balances or rotates DIDs across all these interfaces. A SIP trunk has a much larger and flexible capacity, but when the SIP trunk is out of capacity or down, it is still necessary to understand what happens to calls arriving during this time: Are these calls deflected to a secondary SIP trunk at a different site, or are they deflected to the PRIs that likely still exist on this site, or do these calls fail as unreachable?

When multiple SIP trunks come into the same site, or even different IP addresses belonging to the same SIP trunk, you need to understand how calls will be load-balanced or failed-over between them. There are different possible schemes, and the algorithms available vary by SP. How to detect or determine a failure of a SIP trunk might also be provider-specific.

Determine Emergency Call Handling

Many enterprises choose to maintain TDM interfaces for their emergency calls, at least initially. If you decide to place emergency calls on the SIP trunk along with normal business calls, make sure you understand the following:

- How calls are routed to the appropriate emergency responder location. (This is especially important in centralized trunking architectures where the SIP trunk entry point might be geographically distant from the emergency responder location.)

- What location information is delivered for the call and where that information comes from (for instance, from your enterprise network or from the SP's information on your DIDs).

- Whether jurisdiction boundaries are crossed (such as country boundaries) between the SIP trunk location and the emergency site location. These boundaries might render the emergency location information useless or illegal because different systems are in place in the different locations.

Determine the Physical Delivery of the SIP Trunk

With your provider, discuss whether the SIP trunk can be delivered on existing fiber or wiring that already exists to your location, or whether a new physical connection must be put in place. This determination can play a factor in:

- The timeframe for installing the SIP trunk

- The cost of installation

- The security policy or protections you might (or might not) have on this connection

Exercise great caution in accepting services from a SIP trunk provider that does not also provide the physical delivery to your location. Only the provider who owns the physical medium has control over QoS settings.

Determine Network Demarcation

As with data networks, determine the exact equipment that provides the demarcation between your network and the SP's network. Most business-grade SIP trunk services come with a customer-premise equipment (CPE) unit from the SP.

It is best if this CPE device is a full session border controller (SBC) that provides Layer 7 application-level protection and session management features. In some cases these CPE units are merely firewall/network address translation (NAT) devices that offer Layer 3 services or perhaps some application layer gateway (ALG) features. Although this might suffice for small business offerings, it typically is not sufficient for medium or larger enterprises.

Also consider redundancy and failover call routing. For a SIP trunk of 500 or more sessions (500 sessions is the equivalent of approximately 20 T1s or 16 E1s), it is strongly recommended to have a redundant architecture in the CPE devices and network demarcation equipment.

Agree on Monitoring and Troubleshooting Procedures

Discuss with the SP what methods and tools you will use to troubleshoot voice-quality complaints from your user community and how you will isolate problems to determine if they are present in your network or the provider's.

It is also necessary to determine how you, or the provider, will determine if the SIP trunk is overloaded or down and how alternative routing will take place. You also need to agree to how it will be determined that the condition has cleared and normal routing can resume.

Also, determine how you will assess billing information and how you will reconcile the provider's billing records with those from your own network. It might be useful to enable billing at the demarcation point for these purposes.

Pilot Trial

By the time you reach this stage, you have completed all the planning steps, selected your provider, and you are ready to install a SIP trunk, configure the equipment, and start running test calls to see how it operates in your environment.

During the Pilot Trial step, work through the following activities to test the operation of the SIP trunk:

- Define clear success criteria.

- Assess organizational responsibility.

- Determine the length of the trial.

- Install and configure the service.

- Define a clear test plan and execute it.

- Start the pilot user community on the SIP trunk.

Define Clear Success Criteria

You need to be clear on the goals of the Pilot Trial and what conditions would constitute success or failure to your organization. Usually cost benefits are not realized in the trial phase because:

- The installation is new and can be amortized over only a short period of time by a small number of users.

- The call volume is extremely low.

- TDM backup trunking cannot yet be removed.

- If production service is not implemented after the trial, call traffic might need to be directed back to TDM trunks again, which might add to the trial costs.

However, enough information should be available from the results of the pilot to validate the initial cost analysis to determine any adjustments necessary for expected cost savings during production service.

Assess Organizational Responsibility

Before making arrangements to have the SP install a SIP trunk, ensure that you understand organizationally who owns the hand off of traffic from the demarcation point. If you belong to a medium or large enterprise and run the SIP trunk into a data center, there is likely various security policies and equipment and a DMZ, the point any outside connectivity has to pass through before it can terminate on your UCB element for secure hand off to your call agent. Ownership of the SIP trunk CPE equipment, and its placement relative to the DMZ, varies from one enterprise to the next depending on individual policies and network architectures. If you are a small business that gets an integrated data and SIP trunk service from a provider, installed and delivered by a partner or value-added reseller, this step might be much simpler or nonexistent.

Determine the Length of the Trial

Decide how long the trial should run. You need a sufficient amount of time to get through the test plan, address any issues found, and allow a reasonable period of use by the pilot user community to provide valid results on which to base your production service decision. It is recommended that this time is at least 3 months.

Install and Configure the Service

Work with your selected SP to install the physical delivery and CPE for the SIP trunk. Do the configuration changes on your call agent and border element to enable a test call capability to and from the SIP trunk. Ensure that monitoring tools and capabilities are turned on to determine the outcome of the tests that are to follow.

Define a Clear Test Plan and Execute the Test Plan

Write an explicit test plan for the capabilities and services that you expect the SIP trunk to perform correctly before live calls from your pilot community can be placed on the trunk. A suggested outline of such a test plan is provided in the following list:

- Circuit acceptance test cases
  - SP Layer 2 connection
  - SP Layer 3 connection
  - SP reachability and routing
- Connectivity test cases
  - Registration sequence
  - Session refresh
  - Basic outbound/inbound call completion
  - QoS
  - CAC
  - Management access
  - Call accounting
  - Voice quality
  - Stability and duration
  - Restart
- SIP application (call flow) test cases
  - Caller ID
  - Codec negotiation
  - Call hold/resume
  - Call forward to voice mail
  - Call forward back to the PSTN
  - Call transfer
  - Single number reach

- Call modifications due to mobility features

- Ad-hoc conference

- IVR interaction

- DTMF

- FAX, Mode, TTY

- Emergency/911

- Call types (local, long distance, international)

- Monitoring and failover test cases

  - SIP trunk monitoring and alerting on overload or failure

  - Layers 1, 2, 3, 4 failover scenarios

Execute the test plan and address any issues that arise. Make the necessary configuration changes. Make troubleshooting changes to determine where the fault lies. It is often good practice to collect IP call traces of working call flows. This might reduce debugging time later during production service if call behavior changes or problems crop up.

After a satisfactorily working setup is reached, document the configurations of your call agents, firewalls, and border elements as these configurations need to be replicated when you implement production SIP trunk services in your network.

When the test plan has been successfully completed and all serious issues resolved, you are ready to bring your pilot user community's live calls onto the SIP trunk.

Start Using the SIP Trunk for the Pilot User Community

During the planning step, you identified the user community that is to participate in the trial. While the SIP trunk installation and testing take place, prepare this user community for the date on which test calls will start and train them on the procedures you want them to follow to report problems or inconsistencies they might notice.

Provide any training you might deem necessary to these users. Ensure that they have backup calling access and procedures if the SIP trunk should be down or unable to complete the calls they initiate. After you define a clear test plan and execute the test plan satisfactorily, the Pilot Trial user community can start using the SIP trunk actively for normal business calls. You can consider adding a prefix (such as an 8) to the dial plan so that the user community can easily choose whether they use the SIP trunk trial or production TDM trunks.

Another technique to stress test the SIP trunk is to arrange call bursts by the user community where every caller has a script of test calls to execute during a given 5–10 minute time period.

Production Service

In the Pilot Trial step, you defined clear success criteria and the length of the Pilot Trial. When you complete these steps to your organization's satisfaction, and the driving factors for migration to SIP trunk service still hold true (such as cost savings), you are now ready to move into production service.

Before production service can start, you need to educate the larger user community who will now join SIP trunk service in the same way you did the pilot user community. Initially you might still want to maintain TDM backup access for these users until such time that you are satisfied the SIP trunk service is stable and that possible failures are taken care of in your network design.

At this time your SP needs to port the DIDs of the new user community to join the SIP trunk. This might be a single phase of porting, or potentially several phases, depending on the plan you have formulated during the planning step.

Best Practices

This chapter concludes with a summary of best practices for planning, preparing, and deploying SIP trunking in enterprise and SMB networks, giving clear and practical advice on how to approach a SIP trunk deployment in your network.

Providers

Best practices in the area of choosing a provider include

- Look for a provider that owns the physical delivery medium (last mile) to your premises along with the service. The last-mile provider is the only one who can guarantee QoS.

- If keeping your existing DID numbers is important to your business, your most likely provider is the same one with whom you get your current PSTN service.

- Evaluate SIP trunk service offerings carefully—it's an unregulated service and offerings and pricing can vary greatly.

- Always do a proof-of-concept trial before installing a SIP trunk into your production business network.

- Evaluate SIP trunk offering features against your current TDM service and make sure you get all the features that are important to you.

Deployment

Best practices in the area of deployment include the following:

- Plan carefully and don't rush into a production deployment until you're certain of what you're getting. Use the earlier part of this chapter to help you through the planning steps.

- Define the user communities or sites you will deploy in the different phases of the deployment. For all but the smallest of networks composed of no more than a single or a handful of sites, this is a multiphased rollout plan.

- Decide on the call flows included in each phase of deployment, for example inbound, outbound, long distance, contact center, or general business calls.

- SIP trunk provider readiness and cost can vary significantly between countries and continents. Your rollout plan might need geographical phases.

Network Design

Best practices in the area of network design include the following:

- Carefully consider the benefits and challenges of the centralized or distributed SIP trunk designs, even if the choice seems obvious. Centralized designs almost always look more attractive because of their cost savings. However, they have network design implications that might increase the overall cost. A distributed design might be viable especially if you already have a distributed multi-protocol label switching (MPLS) network for your data.

- Most SIP trunk providers enable only two IP addresses with the service, either as primary/secondary or in a load balancing setup. If you need to load balance your calls over more than two devices for either scalability or redundancy reasons, you might need to insert a SIP proxy or load-balancer device to distribute the traffic.

- Most SIP trunk providers currently do not use domain name system (DNS) but instead use absolute IP addressing. This can influence your redundancy and load-balancing considerations.

- Load balancing over the two IP addresses the provider provides is generally a more dynamic and flexible call routing configuration than a primary/secondary algorithm.

- Use a Layer 7 SIP OPTIONS ping to monitor SIP trunk status in addition to one of several Layer 3 mechanisms that might be available, such as Internet Control Message Protocol (ICMP) ping or IP service level agreements (IP SLA).

- Investigate troubleshooting tools and methods to determine the source of any voice-quality issues. If one is reported, decide how to determine if it is present in your network or in the SP's network. Discuss with your provider how such problems will be investigated and resolved.

■ Turn on CAC features on your SBC regardless of whether the provider offers an SLA—especially if your provider does not offer an SLA.

Protocols and Codecs

Best practices in the area of protocol choices include the following:

■ Use SIP end-to-end in your network if you can. Interoperability is easier and more flexible on SIP-to-SIP connections than translating to other protocols.

■ If adhering to the previous guideline is not possible, use a SBC to interoperate H.323 with your SIP trunk.

■ Use RFC-2833 dual-tone multi-frequency (DTMF) relay throughout your network if possible. If not possible, make sure you understand where in your network translations occur between out-of-band signaling methods (such as the traditional H.323 methods) and RFC-2833, which travels in the media stream. The device (such as a call agent on an SBC) that does this conversion must have access to both the signaling and the media streams to do so.

■ Investigate RFC-2833 DTMF payload type value assignments on your own call agents, endpoints, applications, and the values used by the SP. Conversion or inter-working between these values might need to be configured on your border element to ensure proper interoperation of calls.

■ Using T.38 fax relay for fax over IP transmission is technically a more robust method of faxing and works better than other methods where available. But it is not available on all networks and to all endpoints so that fax passthrough (or fax via G.711) is still widely used as it interoperates easier and with more endpoints. If the provider offers T.38, investigate if failover to G.711 fax is offered as a secondary call negotiation service to connect calls to destinations that might not yet support T.38. Consider keeping fax on TDM trunks for a while longer if this is a critical part of your business.

■ Similar to the previous point, keep modem, point-of-sale (POS), and telecommunications devices for the deaf (TDD) traffic on TDM trunks for the time being. SIP trunk technology is not ready to carry these traffic types in a reliable and predictable manner.

■ Seriously consider getting G.711 service on your SIP trunk. Although it uses more bandwidth than G.729, it does not compromise voice quality. (After all, the promise of a SIP trunk is to improve PSTN services, not worsen them.) It also eases fax issues, obviates the need for transcoding at your SBC, and better positions you for new SIP trunk services that will almost certainly include increasingly bandwidth intensive applications such as high-fidelity wideband codecs and video.

■ Although SIP is a *standard* protocol, it actually consists of a large number of individual standards (Internet Engineering Task Force [IETF] Request for Comments [RFC]), and there are many optional components to these RFCs and alternative ways to implement the same call flow. SIP interoperability is not mature enough that all applications predictably interwork with other SIP applications, even though they all might be standards-compliant. This means you might need tools to *normalize* (that is, manipulate) SIP messages as they flow through your network from your applications across the SIP trunk to the PSTN.

Cisco Unified Communications Manager (CUCM)

Best practices in the area of CUCM deployment include the following:

- Generally, the decision between using H.323 and SIP on CUCM depends on the features, your preference, protocol maturity, and the degree of interoperability between the applications you have in your network.

  - CUCM 6.x or 7.x is recommended for SIP trunking, using a SIP-to-SIP configuration.

  - If older versions of CUCM are used and cannot be upgraded to 6.x or 7.x, use H.323 trunking to the call agent and H.323-to-SIP conversion on your SBC.

- The recommended CUCM Configuration for SIP trunking includes

  - Delayed offer (with no media termination point [MTP]) for Cisco UCM outbound calls

  - Early offer (with no MTP) for CUCM inbound calls

  - Use delayed offer to early offer interworking on your session border controller (CUBE)

- Avoid MTP designs if possible; if not, colocate the MTPs with your SBC (CUBE) to optimize the media path.

- Older releases of CUCM prefer higher bandwidth codecs to lower ones, so configure this carefully to get the optimum negotiation with endpoints in your network and across the SIP trunk. Newer releases might support codec preference ordering configuration options.

- Configure alternate (redundant) PSTN routing if the SIP trunk is down. It is best not to remove TDM PSTN trunking and gateways from your network until after a SIP trunk has been proven in. Generally, a CUCM configuration for alternative PSTN routing includes

  - Trunks contained in route groups

  - Route groups contained in route lists

  - Route lists used to cycle through alternative trunk destinations, as illustrated in Figure 11-2

  - Retry timers and counters tuned to optimize failover time to alternative trunks

  - Return code mapping (SIP codes to Q.850) used to stop CUCM trunk selection when needed

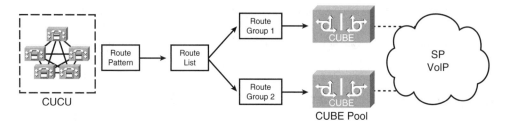

Figure 11-2 *CUCM Alternative Routing*

SBC Best Practices

Best practices in the area of session border controller deployment include the following:

■ For small site, remote office, or SBC deployments that carry low traffic, use a single Cisco router with integrated services such as CUBE, MTP, VoiceXML, firewall, and SRST features.

■ For larger site, campus, data center or SBC deployments that carry high traffic, use a dedicated router for CUBE and other dedicated routers for MTP or VoiceXML or any other service you might need at that site.

■ Pay careful attention to performance engineering of SIP trunks into your network because they most likely change the call flow and the bandwidth allocation to calls.

■ Whether you use H.323-SIP or SIP-SIP on CUBE makes no difference to its session capacity.

■ DTMF interworking or delayed offer to early offer adds no significant extra load to CUBE.

■ Using SIP profiles for normalization on CUBE can have a performance effect depending on the number and complexity of the rules.

■ Configuring MTPs on the same platform as CUBE or using transcoding are CPU-intensive tasks and must be carefully engineered.

If you use CUBE platforms terminating less than 500 sessions (calls) per platform, most of the performance engineering needed is likely on the CUBE platform itself and not elsewhere in your network. But if you use high-end CUBE platforms terminating 2000 or more sessions per platform, the bottleneck moves to your CUCM servers and most of your engineering work is there instead.

■ On SIP-to-SIP CUBE configurations, do not use the **bind** command if topology hiding is required (that is, if only one global IP address is available). Instead use the default CUBE configuration, which is to pick up the egress interface address on outbound SIP packets. For H.323-to-SIP configurations, the **bind** command can be used because there are two addresses available, one for H.323 and one for SIP.

- Define explicit incoming and outgoing dial-peers on your CUBE device. SBC calls have two IP call legs (as opposed to a TDM gateway that has only one), so it is often necessary to have both dial-peers to control the characteristics of each individual call leg—the default settings might not be what you need in your network. This practice also gives you additional control points to combat toll fraud attacks.

Security

Best practices in the area of security include the following:

- In a single-site or small network, a firewall or NAT device might be sufficient as the enterprise demarcation and security border device. In larger networks, use a Layer 7 SBC device with additional protection, configuration, and traffic control.

- If you deploy both a firewall device and an SBC (as most large enterprises do in their campus sites), it is generally recommended to put the firewall on the outside as a first line security defense for all traffic and put CUBE behind it as a second line of defense optimized for unified communications traffic.

- Use SIP registration on the SIP trunk if it is offered by the SP. Also use Digest Authentication on both SIP registrations and INVITEs if available as part of the service.

- Deploy toll fraud features on your CUBE or SBC. Hackers target SIP deployments and SIP ports more so than other VoIP network architectures.

- Consider changing the SIP port from the standard port 5060 for additional protection against Internet sweeps for open SIP ports. Both your border element and the SP SBC must make this change to interoperate successfully.

- Always put ACLs on your CUBE to ensure only the SP SBC can initiate calls to it from the PSTN side, and only your enterprise call agents (CUCM or IP-PBXs) can initiate calls from the internal network side.

Redundancy

Best practices in the area of redundancy include the following:

Consider centralized and distributed trunking network designs carefully. An advantage of distributed trunking is inherent redundancy as you had with your TDM PSTN gateways. If one site's SIP trunk is down, calls from that site can temporarily be routed via the SIP trunk of a different nearby site until service returns.

For SIP trunks under 500 sessions, redundant termination is generally not necessary, although you can always design it that way if you prefer. But for SIP trunks of 1000 or more sessions, redundancy becomes imperative.

Generally SIP trunk SPs offer two IP addresses with a SIP trunk, which you can use to terminate onto two different devices. Either one can handle the full load of the SIP trunk if necessary. The SP can load balance over these two destinations. If you want to load balance across more than two destinations for either scalability or redundancy or both reasons, you might need to put in a SIP Proxy such as Cisco Unified SIP Proxy (CUSP) or another load balancer in between to help distribute the load.

If the SIP trunk is down, outbound calls from the enterprise can easily be routed using traditional TDM PSTN gateways. However, inbound traffic to your DID numbers is not so easily rerouted to traditional TDM trunks. Discuss inbound traffic alternative routing possibilities with your SIP trunk SP.

Summary

This chapter covers an easy-to-use, step-by-step guide to deploying SIP trunks in your network—pulling together for practical use much of the material discussed in more detail in preceding chapters on SP evaluation and network design considerations. It guides you through the stages of planning, evaluating a SIP trunk offering, setting up and running a Pilot Trial, all the way to deploying production service in your network.

The last section of the chapter provides a summary of best practices when implementing a SIP trunk, including practices in the areas of choosing an SP, general deployment, network design, choosing protocols and codecs, CUCM and SBC-specific practices, security, and redundancy.

Chapter 12

Case Studies

This chapter covers the following topics:

- An enterprise connecting to a service provider

- Distributed SIP trunking to connect PSTN

This chapter examines two case studies of real-life Session Initiation Protocol (SIP) trunking deployment scenarios.

- Enterprise connecting to a Service Provider (SP)

- Distributed SIP trunking to connect Public Switched Telephone Network (PSTN)

You learn about the different challenges customers face to make a successful deployment. To maintain the confidentiality of the customer network, we cannot mention the actual names of the customers and their networks, but we try to sketch solutions where possible.

Enterprise Connecting to a Service Provider

In this case study, we show you how a large enterprise (Company P) tried to interconnect its unified communications network through SIP trunking with an SP (Company Q) that provided a conferencing solution for Company P. We also try to explain the complexity and the overall solution of the network.

Initially, Company P's internal conferencing calls were routed over PSTN to Company Q's media gateway. Company P has operations all over the world. When any user from Company P dialed from any of Company P's locations to Company Q, that call came to a centralized location (say, headquarters), and then was terminated to Company Q over the PSTN network. Internal employees used an internal MPLS/WAN link to reach the headquarters. This is similar to our centralized trunking solution.

Company P used 3 million minutes a month, costing millions of dollars for PSTN phone bills. The new SIP trunking solution provides a lower cost routing solution for Company Q's Meeting Center audio participants over the internal IP Telephony infrastructure. They have saved a huge amount of money per month having this enabled over Internet Protocol (IP).

Figure 12-1 shows the PSTN trunk network connection topology between Company P and Company Q.

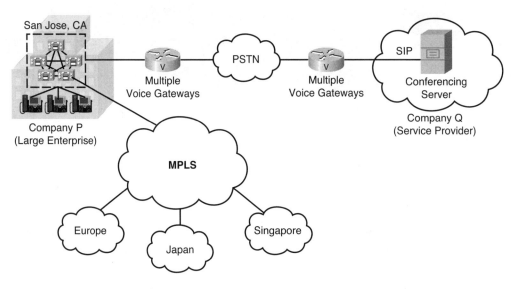

Figure 12-1   *PSTN Trunk Connectivity*

The conferencing servers are hosted in company Q's data center located in a different city. To process a meeting/conference, the service provider uses an Interactive Voice Response (IVR) system to authenticate the dialer and route the call to the appropriate meeting. Moreover, any employee can schedule a meeting and invite other people to join that meeting. So, when the company has 10,000 to 50,000 employees, it should be well designed to support many active users.

When the enterprise migrated from Time Division Multiplexing (TDM) trunking to SIP trunking, its voice network became end-to-end IP-enabled. The calls are originated from IP phones, travel through the Cisco Unified Border Element (CUBE), and then connect to the conference server sitting in the service provider's cloud. The enterprise was using H.323 trunking to connect their Cisco Unified Communications Manager (CUCM) clusters and campuses. It uses a gatekeeper to make the proper routing of the calls in the H.323 network. It has not changed their existing H.323 network as part of this migration process. It changed only the PSTN part of the network. So, within the call flow, you see some parts are in H.323 and some parts are in SIP. Figure 12-2 shows the complete network diagram with SIP trunk connectivity between Company P and Company Q.

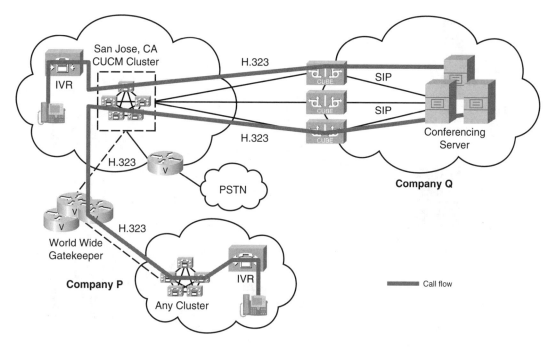

Figure 12-2 *SIP Trunk Connectivity*

We talked to Company P to find out the motivation of this migration process. Initially we thought it wanted to replace the PSTN links to save toll costs, but money was not the only factor. It also wanted to achieve the following things from this migration process:

■ One conferencing platform for all employees. It has multiple conferencing servers in different locations. It wanted to shut them down and use a single unified solution for everyone.

■ Multiple failover sites. The SP offered redundant services all over the world. So, the enterprise wanted to connect more than one location via SIP trunk, which is convenient for it.

■ Active. Active Voice Cluster between conferencing servers located in Mountain View, California and London, England.

■ Audio failover between the two locations.

■ Global disaster recovery capabilities for main sites.

■ Create user distribution based on load and the proximity to a conferencing server.

Figure 12-3 shows the redundancy between two locations.

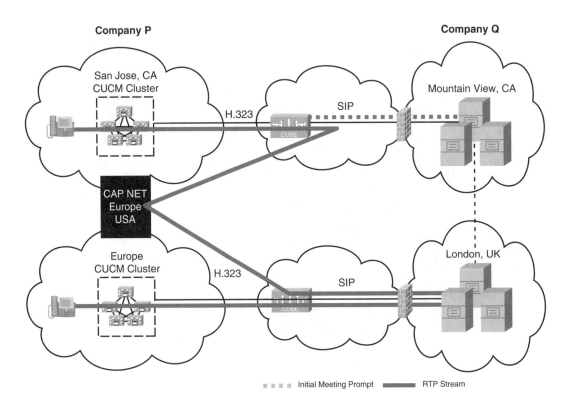

Figure 12-3   *SIP Trunk Redundancy*

Migrating a small system from few T1s/E1s to a SIP trunk is easy; but, when you need to handle thousands of users, it becomes challenging. Although it planned for many things, it could not achieve the target within the given time frame. It planned the whole migration in multiple phases, and the process is still going on. Here are the few things it could not achieve while we interviewed employees to get the status of the project:

■   Did not fit all internal users. The size of the company is so big that it could not bring everyone under the same platform. So, it has to keep internal conferencing servers to accommodate the rest of the employees and meetings.

■   Initially deployed for one location (Mountain View, California), although they also planned to deploy SIP trunks in London, England.

■   One conferencing audio platform.

Next, we look at the detailed configuration of Company P's voice network.

Creating Different Route Groups

Initially Company P started with five CUBEs to observe the performance. Based on what it learned, it gradually added more CUBEs into the network. Basically, they stacked CUBE into its data center located in San Jose, California.

It created multiple dial plans and distributed them into different CUBEs. Here is the sample dial plan based on the dial pattern, where 8 is the prefix for internal dialing:

- Route Pattern 8-421-xxxx goes to CUBE#1

- Route Pattern 8-422-xxxx goes to CUBE#2

- Route Pattern 8-423-xxxx goes to CUBE#3

- Route Pattern 8-424-xxxx goes to CUBE#4

- Route Pattern 8-425-xxxx goes to CUBE#5

Then, it created the main route pattern 81545600 and created the route list into CUCM. This created call-load balancing, redundancy, and failover to Remote CUCM Cluster.

Figure 12-4 shows the dial-plan design for Company P.

MTP Configuration

Media Termination Point (MTP) is required in this call flow, because:

- Company Q's media servers require Early Media (SIP INVITE with SDP) to interoperate with CUBEs.

- To accommodate Early Media (SIP)/Fast Start (H.323), CUCM dictates MTPs for each call, regardless of the direction.

Example 12-1 shows the standard MTP configuration in IOS (into CUBE). A call using the MTP has two call legs, so 600 sessions means 300 calls.

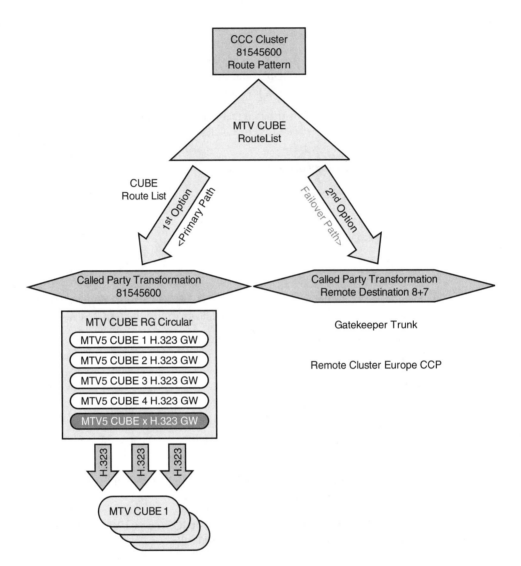

Figure 12-4 *Dial Plan in CUCM*

Example 12-1 *MTP Configuration in CUBE*

```
sccp local Loopback0
sccp ccm 171.xx.xx.101 identifier 1 version 5.0.1
sccp ccm 171.xx.xx.102 identifier 2 version 5.0.1
sccp
!
sccp ccm group 1
 description SJC-CUCM-CLUSTER
 associate ccm 1 priority 1
 associate ccm 2 priority 2
 associate profile 30 register mtv5-pop-sbc1
!
dspfarm profile 30 mtp
 codec g711ulaw
 maximum sessions hardware 600
 associate application SCCP
```

As you know, CUBE works as a demarcation point between two networks. In this deployment, CUBE communicates with Company P's internal devices over H.323 protocol; and it communicates with Company Q's devices over SIP protocol. Therefore, the communication between CUBE and CUCM is done over H.323, whereas the communication between CUBE and Company Q's conference server is done over SIP.

Because the router (CUBE) has multiple Ethernet interfaces a Loopback interface is configured to communicate with the CUCM. In Example 12-2, you can also see how the H.323 gateway is configured under that loopback address. It ensures the single IP address is used while communicating with CUCM over H.323 protocol. In the following example, EIGRP is also configured to enable the routing within the network. But, if you use a static route, you don't need to configure EIGRP.

Example 12-2 *Loopback Interface Configuration for H.323*

```
interface Loopback0
 ip address 10.18.225.17 255.255.255.255
 h323-gateway voip interface
 h323-gateway voip bind srcaddr 10.18.225.17
!
interface GigabitEthernet0/0
 description Connection to mtv5-rbb-gw1 4/1
 ip address 10.18.225.66 255.255.255.252
 duplex auto
 speed auto
 media-type rj45
```

continues

Example 12-2   *Loopback Interface Configuration for H.323 (continued)*

```
!
interface GigabitEthernet0/1
 description Connection to mtv5-rbb-gw2 4/1
 ip address 10.18.225.98 255.255.255.252
 duplex auto
 speed auto
 media-type rj45
!
router eigrp 109
 passive-interface default
 no passive-interface GigabitEthernet0/0
 no passive-interface GigabitEthernet0/1
 network 0.0.0.0
 distribute-list 10 out
 no auto-summary
 eigrp stub connected
```

Interconnect Between H.323 and SIP

In a preceding section, we mentioned that Company P operates H.323 internally and uses SIP to connect to an external entity such as Company Q. CUBE works as the interconnecting point between these two networks. While on the subject of interconnection between H.323 and SIP, you need to consider a few issues:

- H.323 was chosen by Company P as the trunk protocol for calls from CUCM.

- Company Q's system works only with SIP and requires Early offer (SIP INVITE with SDP).

- This implies the H.323 side must be H.323 Fast Start.

- For Company P, CUCM must be configured inbound and outbound H.323 Fast Start, which requires the use of an MTP.

- MTP is a co-resident on the same router. PVDM2-64 Digital Signal Processor (DSP) is used to facilitate MTP resources.

- A side effect for using Early Offer (MTP) is that IVR Greetings are played instantly; no waiting for the far end to finish setup for the RTP media path.

- 500 ms delay is introduced at the initial prompt Welcome to Meeting.

- CUBEs are over-provisioned with MTP resources for redundancy.

Example 12-3 shows the configuration in the CUBE that ensures the interworking between H.323 and SIP network.

Example 12-3 *H.323—SIP Interworking Configuration*

```
voice service voip
 no notify redirect ip2ip    <<< Needed for SIP LoadBalancer
 allow-connections h323 to sip <<< Calls from Company-P to Q
 allow-connections sip to h323 <<< Calls from Company-Q to P
 redirect ip2ip                      <<<< Allows redirects w/o drops
 h323
  ip circuit max-calls 500 <<<< Loop protection H323
  ip circuit default only
 sip
  redirect contact order best-match <<< Needed to pass extra Session Digits
```

DTMF Interworking

Dual-Tone Multi-Frequency (DTMF) plays an important role in the IVR system. Company Q's conferencing server does not have speech recognition technology. You need to press the meeting number from your telephone key pad to join a specific meeting. When we have multiple call-legs in a single conversation, DTMF code does not flow end to end. It hops call-leg to call-leg. So, if the DTMF does not work in any of the call-legs, the pressed digits will never reach the destination.

Different methods exist to carry DTMF digits. You can set up in-band or out-of-band techniques to pass DTMF. Moreover, H.323 and SIP have their own implementations to transmit DTMF codes. So, to make the DTMF interworking between two different networks, the appropriate DTMF type must be configured at the incoming and outgoing dial-peers. Company Q's backend systems use RFC-2388 (Named Telephony Event [NTE] Inband DTMF), so Company P needs to configure its system in such a way that every digit passes without any error.

Table 12-1 lists possible options of DTMF interworking between H.323 and SIP signaling.

Table 12-1 *DTMF Interworking Between H.323 and SIP*

H.323	SIP
H.245-Alphanumeric	NOTIFY
H.245-Signal	NOTIFY
RFC-2833	NOTIFY
H.245-Alphanumeric	RFC-2833
H.245-Signal	RFC-2833
H.245-Alphanumeric	KPML
H.245-Signal	KPML
RFC-2833	RFC-2833

In this specific case, it used H.245-Alphanumeric and RFC-2833 (the fourth row in Table 12-1), and it worked fine.

Example 12-4 shows the dial-peer configuration at the H.323 side. The IP address is taken out for privacy purposes.

Example 12-4   *DTMF Configuration in H.323*

```
dial-peer voice 3 voip
 description Dial-back to CUCM - Company-P
 destination-pattern 91.
 session target ipv4:xx.xx.xx.xx
 dtmf-relay h245-alphanumeric
 codec g711ulaw
 ip qos dscp cs5 media
 no vad
```

Example 12-5 shows the dial-peer configuration at the SIP side. The IP address is taken out for privacy purposes.

Example 12-5   *DTMF Configuration in SIP*

```
dial-peer voice 88532929 voip
 description Connected to Company-Q's Server
 destination-pattern 88532929
 session protocol sipv2
 session target ipv4:xx.xx.xx.xx
 session transport udp
 dtmf-relay rtp-nte
 codec g711ulaw
 ip qos dscp cs5 media
 no vad
```

Dial-Peer Configurations Example

In the previous section, we showed the configuration of two dial-peers that establish the basic communications between Company P's CUCM and Company Q's conference server. This conference server has a web conferencing feature where people can join a meeting through a web browser and then ask the conference server to dial-back to attendee's telephone number to establish the voice session. So, the call comes to CUBE from Company Q's conference sever over SIP, and then CUBE passes that call to Company P's CUCM to locate the final destination of the call.

Figure 12-5 shows the call flow between Company P's CUCM and Company Q's conference server.

Here the conference server assigns nte (rfc2388) to use payload 96. This is needed for the media servers at Company Q. Example 12-6 shows the RTP pay-load configuration.

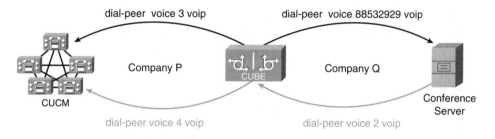

Figure 12-5 *Dial-Peer Configuration Example*

Example 12-6 *RTP Payload Configuration*

```
dial-peer voice 2 voip
 description **Incoming SIP Dial-Peer **
 rtp payload-type cisco-codec-fax-ack 114
 rtp payload-type cisco-codec-fax-ind 112
 rtp payload-type nte 96
 session protocol sipv2
 session transport udp
 incoming called-number .
 dtmf-relay rtp-nte
 codec g711ulaw
 ip qos dscp cs5 media
 no vad
```

Example 12-7 shows another configuration of an H.323 dial-peer that connects to Company P's CUCM and handles all the international calls initiated by the prefix 9011.

Example 12-7 *Dial-Peer Toward Company P's CUCM*

```
dial-peer voice 4 voip
 description Dial-back CUBE to ccm-sjc
 destination-pattern 9011.
 session target ipv4:xx.xx.xx.xx
 dtmf-relay h245-alphanumeric
 codec g711ulaw
 ip qos dscp cs5 media
 no vad
```

Call Admission Control

When we took the snapshot of the solution, Company P was running 4700 active calls during peak hours and close to 34,000 users, all G.711 traffic. It forecasted that call volume for the combined sites would never exceed 6000 calls, but during the economic downturn, the company instituted travel restrictions. Therefore, employees would not need to fly to have face-to-face meetings, and they were asked to use web-based conferencing to save money. It increased the maximum hit at 6641 calls.

To manage the call admission control (CAC) in many CUBE boxes, Company P tried following CAC options in CUBE, including:

- Total calls

- CPU

- Memory

- IP call capacity

- Max-connections

- Resource ReSerVation Protocol (RSVP)

Company P used the total calls control mechanism for CAC. Example 12-8 shows the configuration from the router.

Example 12-8 *Call Admission Control*

```
call threshold global total-calls low 280 high 300
call treatment cause-code busy
call treatment on
```

Distributed SIP Trunking to Connect PSTN

In this case study, we cover the SIP trunking solution of one of the largest banks in the United States. This is a financially strong and well-capitalized bank that customers have entrusted with their money for more than 130 years. Its current position is as one of the top 25 commercial banks in the nation with assets of $66.2 billion. The bank now serves more than 4 million business and household accounts in hundreds of communities in 19 western and midwest states.

This bank selected Cisco to provide the communications infrastructure to ensure that the SIP trunking service would meet its security, compliance, and architectural requirements.

The bank's existing Unified Communication Setup includes

- Two CUCM clusters

- Unity cluster

- IP Contact Center Express (IPCCX)

- More than 700 commercial and retail banking locations

- Approximately 10,400 employees

The bank wanted to move its legacy PRI/Analog voice traffic onto a SIP trunking SP so that it could achieve the following goals:

- Reduce telephony operating expenses

- Make the transition without ripping and replacing the existing telephony infrastructure

- Ensure interoperability with its existing CUCM clusters

- Provide a single, integrated management view of voice services and enable the use of existing IT systems and staff to administer voice across the enterprise

- Enable the rapid deployment of SIP trunk on its remote gateways by using the UCSPT tool

The results were

- Moving remote sites from traditional PRI/Analog trunks to SIP trunks enabled the bank to reduce its monthly telephony costs.

- These savings came from a reduction in access charges, the elimination of local calling fees, and a significant reduction in long distance fees.

- Approximately $1 million/year saving due to SIP trunk migration.

Enterprise Architecture

The distributed SIP trunking solution was deployed with CUBE at each site, SIP trunk IP address per site, and call flow directly from remote site to the SP. Figure 12-6 shows the overall SIP trunking architecture of the bank.

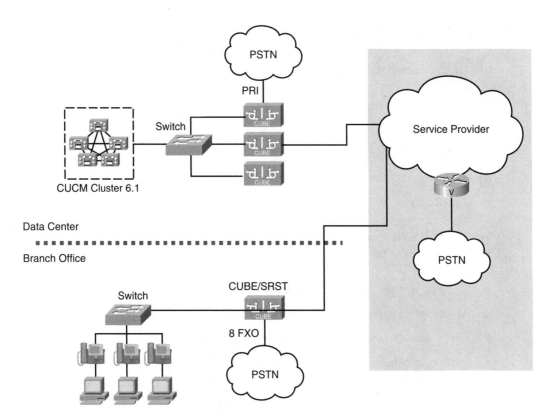

Figure 12-6 *Distributed SIP Trunking Connectivity*

Bank Requirements

The bank had the following requirements:

- PSTN Access: The bank was asking for the following PSTN services from the SP:
    - Emergency services
    - Local numbers
    - Long distance
    - International calling
- Codec Default codec of G.729 on both call legs, that is, CUCM and SP:
    - CAC.
    - The bank wanted to use threshold values of CPU, memory, and total call for the CAC on the remote gateway.

■ Multiple protocols on single remote site gateway: CUBE, SRST, and MGCP in a single router.

SP Requirements

The SP had the following requirements:

■ SIP Signaling: SP requires the usage of Early Offer over SIP trunk.

■ SIP trunk registration: No credentials required for SIP trunk registration from the SP.

■ CAC: The SP's requirement is to send it a 486 Busy Here SIP error code when the threshold is reached so that the SP issues a standard busy indication back to the caller.

■ Calling number: The SP is to allow calls only into the SP's network that have the allocated Direct Inward Dial (DID)—numbers either in the Remote Party ID or Diversion header of the SIP INVITE message.

Configurations

You need to configure two components to enable the SIP trunk at the enterprise side:

■ CUCM configuration

■ CUBE configuration

In the following sections, we show you the step-by-step configurations of CUCM and CUBE. But, we do not cover the configuration of the SP side.

CUCM Configuration

You need to log in into the CUCM administrative interface and configure the following things to enable the SIP trunking with CUBE.

Step 1.   Configure a SIP Trunk Security Profile: The SIP Trunk Nonsecurity Profile is defined.

Step 2.   Create a new SIP Profile. The Standard Profile is created.

Step 3.   Configure a Region and Device Pool: To accommodate the G.729 codec and MTP requirement, you must configure the Region and Device Pool.

Step 4.   Create the SIP trunk: The Outbound Calls option needs to be adjusted to accommodate Call Forward All.

Step 5.   Route List and Route Groups: The SIP trunk is to be part of this Route Group.

Now, let's see the step-by-step configuration with screenshots:

Step 1.   To set the TCP/User Diagram Protocol (UDP) settings, configure a SIP Trunk Security Profile and choose the following options from the CUCM

Administrative user interface menu system: **System > Security Profile >S IP Trunk Security Profile.** Figure 12-7 shows the menu system in the CUCM Administrative interface to select the SIP Trunk Security Profile.

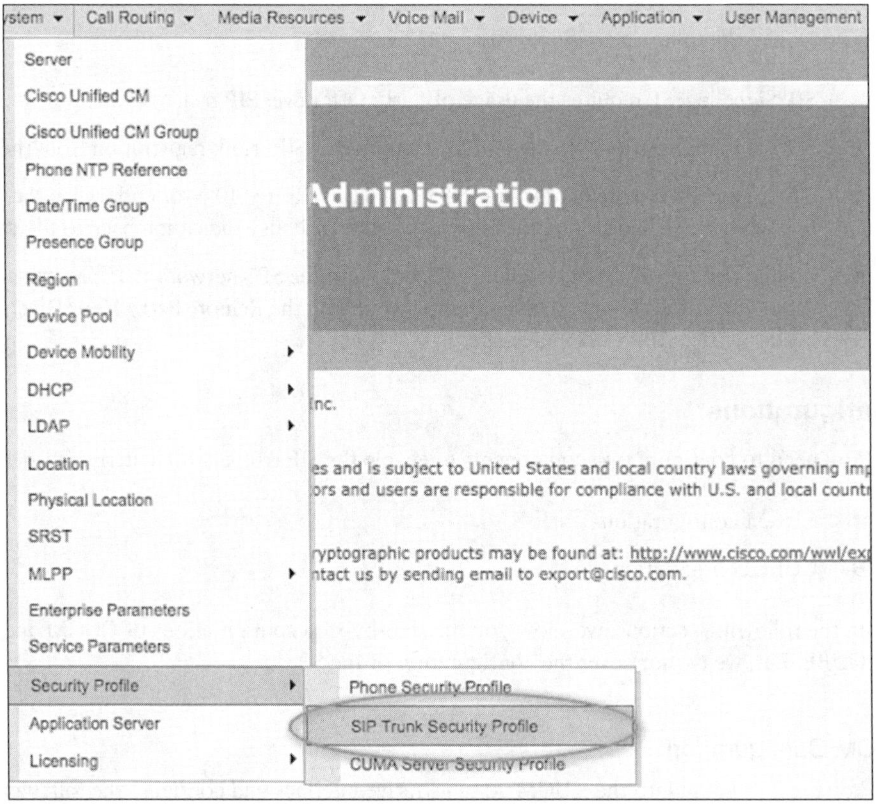

Figure 12-7   *SIP Trunk Security Profile*

Step 2.   After you select **SIP Trunk Security Profile** in the previous step, a screen displays where you can choose **Find** and **Copy**, the Default SIP Trunk Nonsecurity Profile. The screen in Figure 12-8 displays. Fill in the following two values under Name and Description, respectively, and then click **Save**.

Name: **CUBE_SIP_Trunk_Sec_Profile**

Description: **SIP Trunk to CUBE Security Profile**

Step 3.   Now, you need to create a SIP profile. To create a new SIP Profile, choose **Device > Device Settings > SIP Profile** from the top menu bar. Figure 12-9 displays the SIP Profile menu system under the Device menu.

Step 4.   Click **Find** and **Copy** the Standard SIP Profile, or click on the existing profile and then select **Copy**, as shown in Figure 12-10.

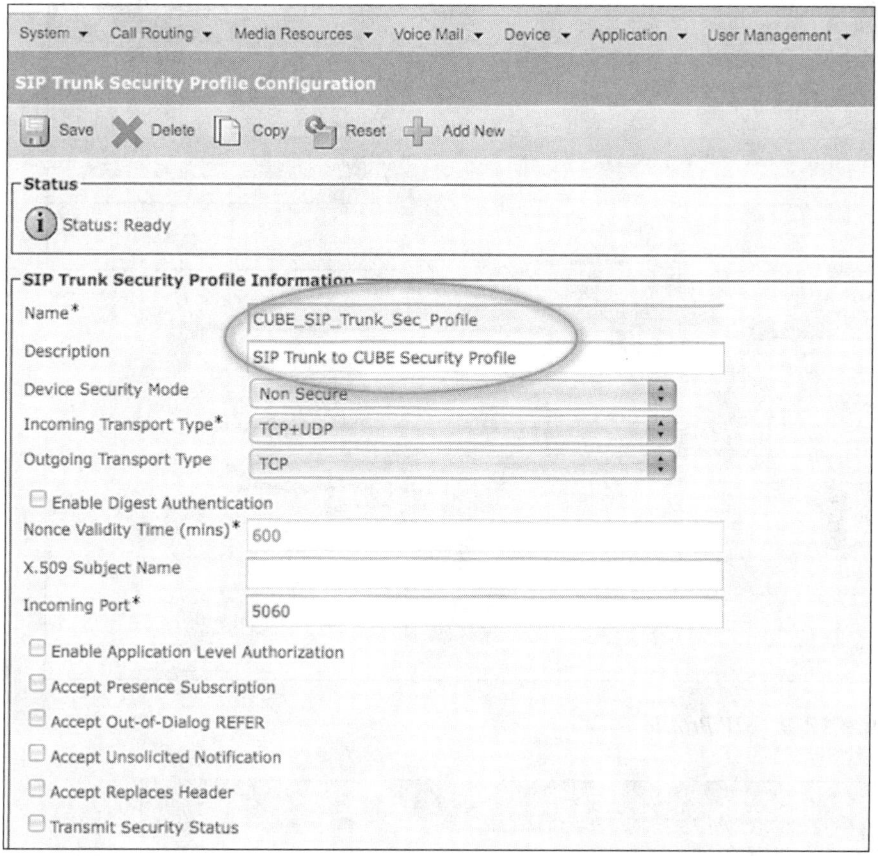

Figure 12-8   *SIP Trunk Security Profile Information*

Step 5.   Next, you define the SIP profile (see Figure 12-11). Fill in the values as follows for "Name" and "Description," respectively, and then click **Save**:

Name: **CUBE_SIP_Trunk_Profile**

Description: **SIP Trunk to CUBE Profile**

Step 6.   Now you need to create a device pool in the CUCM. Device pools are used to define sets of common characteristics for Unified Communications (UC) devices. When a user in Branch1 moves to Branch2 and calls via SIP trunks, the CUCM must know characteristics of that device. The device characteristics you can specify for a device pool are Region, Date/Time group, Cisco Communications Manager Group, and Calling search space for auto-registration.

Step 7.   Before you can define the device, Figure 12-12 and Figure 12-13 show how to configure a region and device pool. Note that the bank decided to create a Region that would use G.729 codec within the region and with other regions to make the outbound and inbound calls. Figure 12-12 displays the screen to create a region named CUBE_Region.

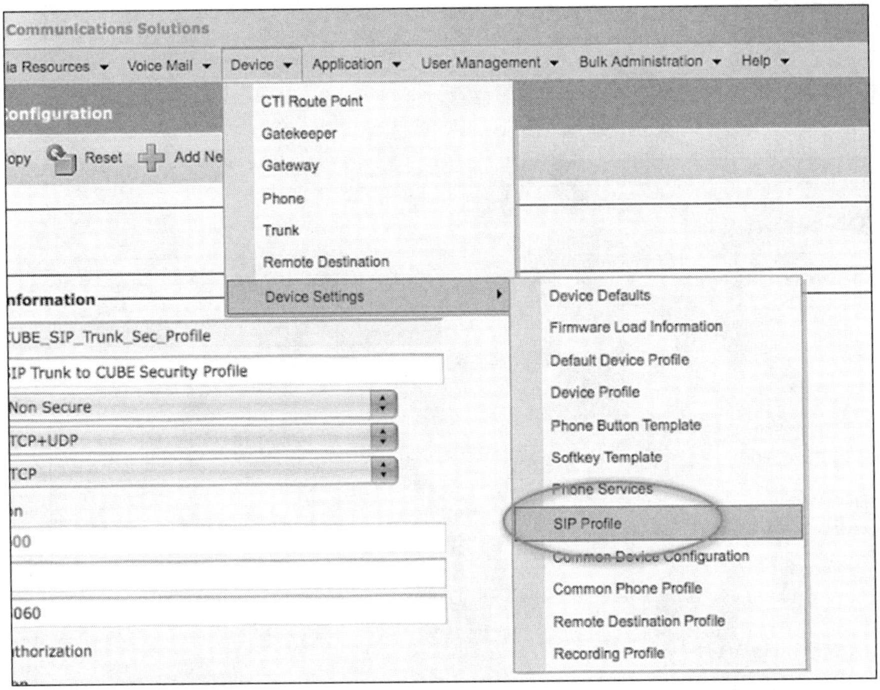

Figure 12-9   *SIP Profile*

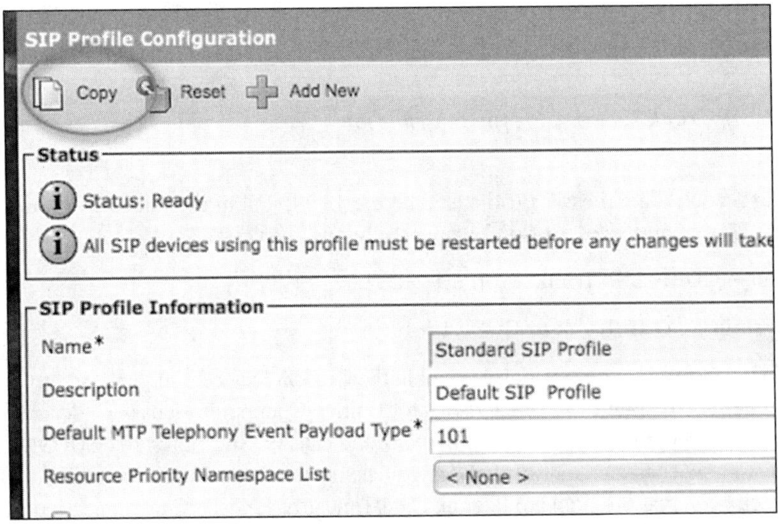

Figure 12-10   *SIP Profile Configuration*

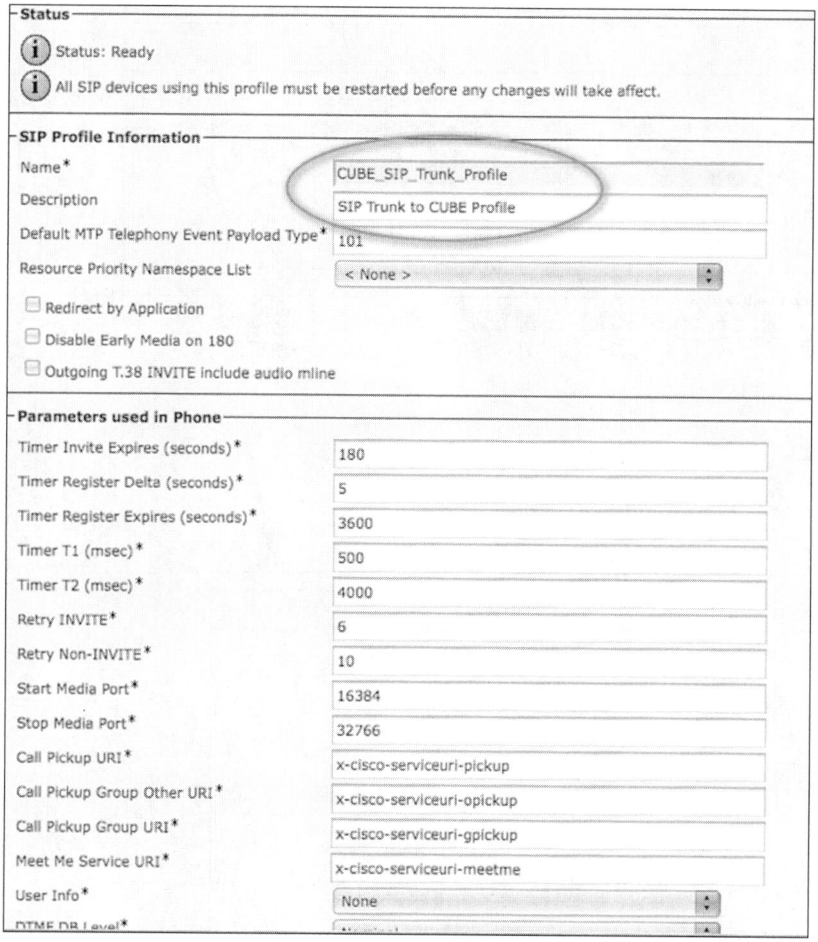

Status

(i) Status: Ready

(i) All SIP devices using this profile must be restarted before any changes will take affect.

SIP Profile Information

Name*	CUBE_SIP_Trunk_Profile
Description	SIP Trunk to CUBE Profile
Default MTP Telephony Event Payload Type*	101
Resource Priority Namespace List	< None >

☐ Redirect by Application

☐ Disable Early Media on 180

☐ Outgoing T.38 INVITE include audio mline

Parameters used in Phone

Timer Invite Expires (seconds)*	180
Timer Register Delta (seconds)*	5
Timer Register Expires (seconds)*	3600
Timer T1 (msec)*	500
Timer T2 (msec)*	4000
Retry INVITE*	6
Retry Non-INVITE*	10
Start Media Port*	16384
Stop Media Port*	32766
Call Pickup URI*	x-cisco-serviceuri-pickup
Call Pickup Group Other URI*	x-cisco-serviceuri-opickup
Call Pickup Group URI*	x-cisco-serviceuri-gpickup
Meet Me Service URI*	x-cisco-serviceuri-meetme
User Info*	None
DTMF DB Level*	

Figure 12-11 *CUBE SIP Trunk Profile*

Step 8. Now, you can configure a Device Pool for a SIP trunk that uses the predefined region CUBE Region. Figure 12-13 shows how to create a new device pool. In this example, device pool CUBE_DP is created.

Step 9. So far, you have configured to enable the SIP trunk. Now, you configure the actual trunk. Choose **Devices > Trunk** from the Cisco Unified CM Administration page. Figure 12-14 shows how to select the Trunk option from the main menu.

Step 10. In the screen that displays, choose **Add New**, and then select the trunk type SIP Trunk and select the device protocol SIP from the drop-down list (see Figure 12-15). Click the **Next** button.

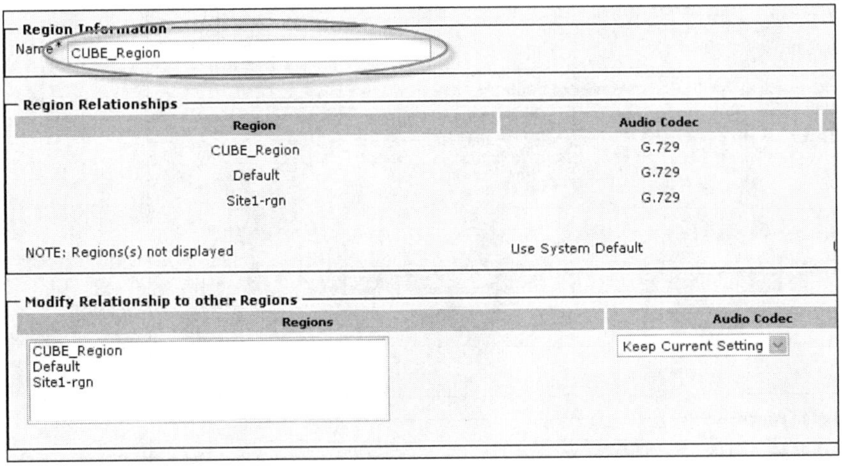

Region Information
Name* CUBE_Region
Region Relationships
Region
Audio Codec
CUBE_Region
G.729
Default
G.729
Site1-rgn
G.729
NOTE: Regions(s) not displayed
Use System Default
Modify Relationship to other Regions
Regions
Audio Codec
CUBE_Region
Default
Site1-rgn
Keep Current Setting

Figure 12-12 *Configure Region*

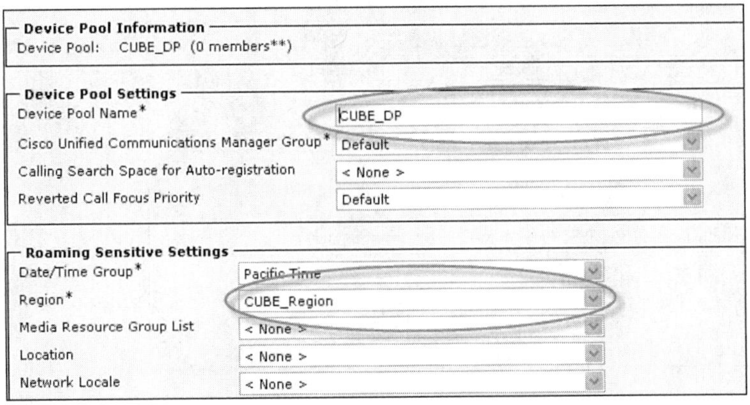

Device Pool Information
Device Pool: CUBE_DP (0 members**)
Device Pool Settings
Device Pool Name* CUBE_DP
Cisco Unified Communications Manager Group* Default
Calling Search Space for Auto-registration < None >
Reverted Call Focus Priority Default
Roaming Sensitive Settings
Date/Time Group* Pacific Time
Region* CUBE_Region
Media Resource Group List < None >
Location < None >
Network Locale < None >

Figure 12-13 *Configure Device Pool*

Cisco Unified CM Administration
For Cisco Unified Communications Solutions
System
Call Routing
Media Resources
Voice Mail
Device
Application
User Management
SIP Profile Configuration
Save
Delete
Copy
Reset
CTI Route Point
Gatekeeper
Gateway
Phone
Trunk
Remote Destination
Device Settings
Status
Status: Ready

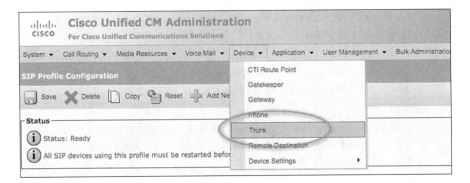

Figure 12-14 *Configure Trunk*

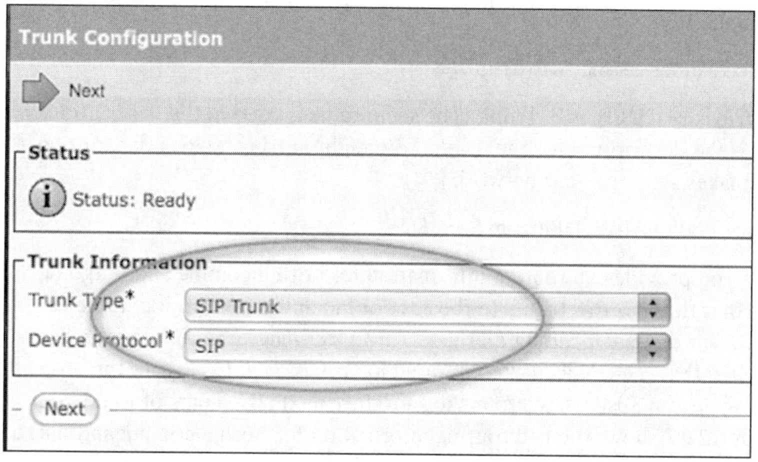

Figure 12-15 *Select Trunk Type: SIP Trunk*

Step 11. After you press the **Next** button in the previous screen, a list of parameters to configure the trunk displays. This list is divided into the following sections:

- Device Information

- Call Routing Information (Inbound Calls and Outbound Calls)

SIP Information (where to connect the trunk) as shown in Figure 12-16, you need to enter the parameters for the Device Information screen. In this case study, the bank has provided the values for Device Name, Description, and Device Pool. The other parameters are default values.

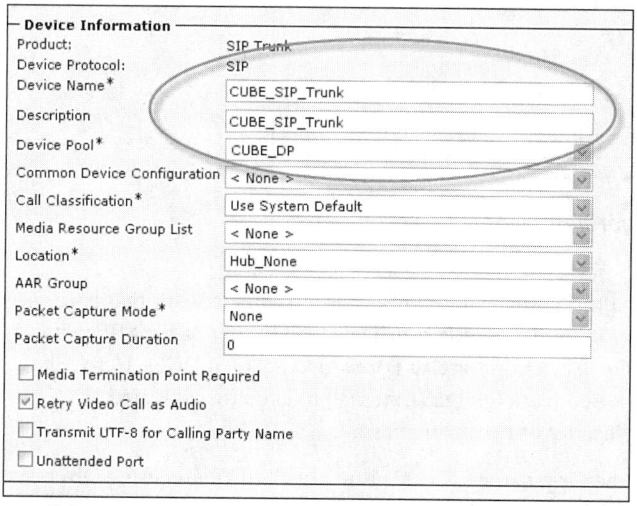

Figure 12-16 *SIP Trunk Information*

Fill in the following values:

Device Name: **CUBE_SIP_Trunk**

Description: **CUBE_SIP_Trunk** (The same value is used in the description. This is the description for the trunk. You might need to write a description that makes sense to your network.)

Device Pool: **CUBE_DP** (from Step 6)

Step 12.   Now, you provide call routing information for both incoming and outgoing calls that flow via this trunk. In the case of incoming call routing, there can be significant digits depending on the CUCM DN's length. In this case, it is assumed that the DN length configured in CUCM is 4. Configure the proper Calling Search Space (CSS) to make sure the called DN is part of that CSS. Figure 12-17 shows the call routing information for both incoming and outgoing calls.

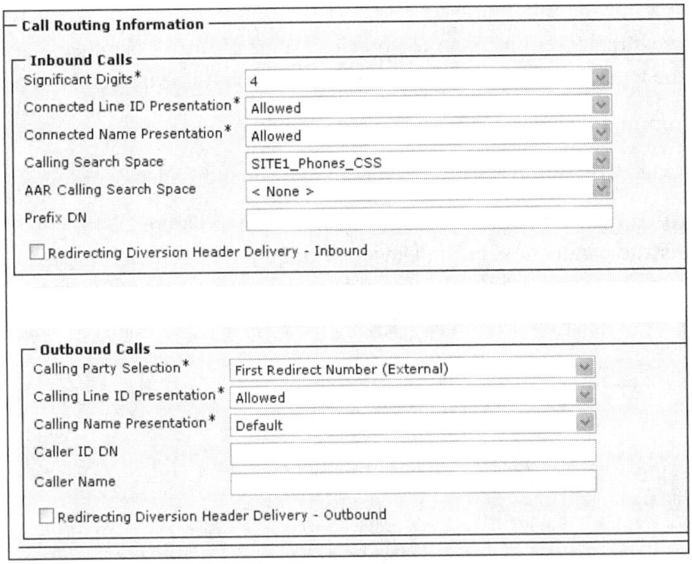

Figure 12-17   *Call Routing Information*

For outbound calls, the SP (in this case) enables only calls into the network that have the allocated DID numbers either in the Remote Part or Diversion header of the SIP invite message. To accommodate the restriction for Call Forwarded All on a DN, select Calling Party Selection with the First Redirect Number (External) to keep the allocated DID number in the Remote Party header of the invite message.

Another option to preserve the Originator Caller ID is to check the Redirecting Diversion Header option. In this case, a Diversion header is inserted in the SIP INVITE message, which is used to authenticate the calling party DID. The problem with this approach is that the Diversion header has the original four-digit DN as the calling party and is not recognized by the SP.

You need to tell the CUCM where to send the SIP INVITE, or the IP address of the CUBE (as the CUBE is the connecting point for this trunk). To do this, you need to provide the information shown in Figure 12-18:

■   Destination Address 10.10.1.1 (IP Address of remote site gateway or CUBE)

■   SIP Trunk Security Profile: CUBE_SIP_Trunk_Sec_Profile

■   SIP Profile: CUBE_SIP_Trunk_Profile

After you fill in the previous values, click **Save**.

Figure 12-18 shows the CUBE configuration in the CUCM system.

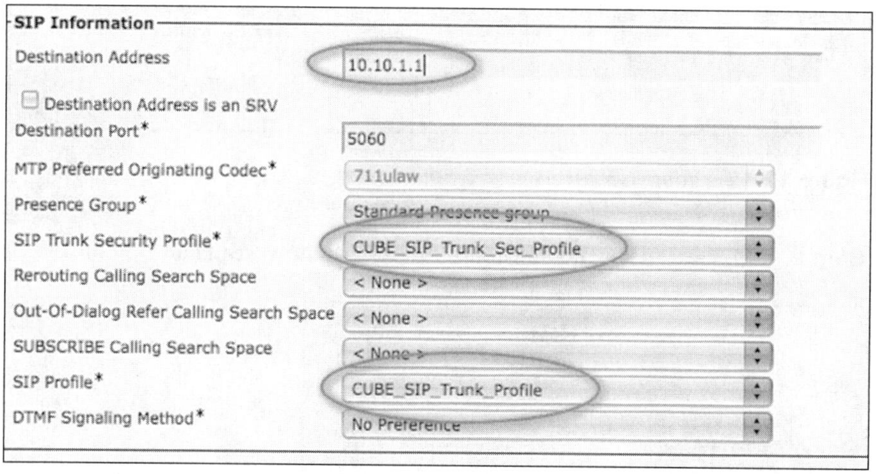

Figure 12-18   *CUBE Address*

Now, we have to tell CUCM how to route the outbound calls via this newly configured trunk. Follow these steps:

Step 1.   First, before you can add the route, you need to create the route group. Choose **Call Routing > Route/Hunt > Route Group** in the CUCM Administration web page. Figure 12-19 shows how to select Route Group from the main menu of Administration web page.

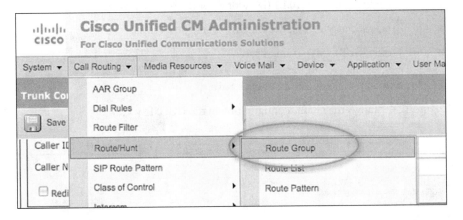

Figure 12-19   *Route Group*

Step 2.   To create a new Route Group, choose **Add New** (see Figure 12-20).

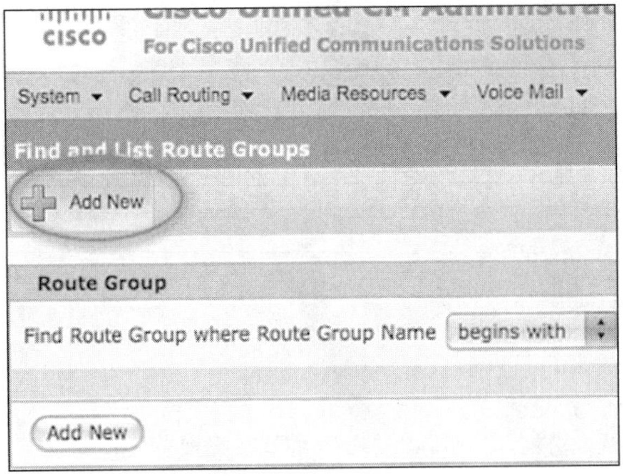

Figure 12-20   *Add New Route Group*

Step 3. Figure 12-21 displays route group information. Here you need to enter the route group information. Enter the value **SIP_Trunk_to_PSTN_RG** for the Route Group Name. You can use other names. Select the CUBE_SIP_Trunk from the list of Available Devices. Click **Add to Route Group**. Click the **Save** button at the top of the page.

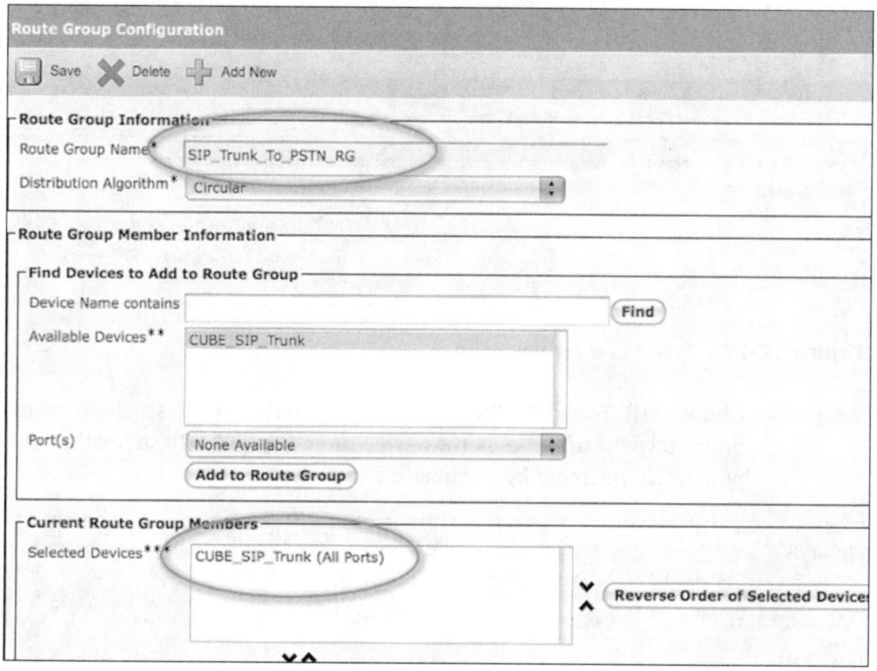

Figure 12-21 *Route Group Information*

Step 4. Create a Route List with SIP Trunk Route Group in it. Choose **Call Routing > Route/Hunt > Route List** from the main menu of the CUCM Administration web page (see Figure 12-22).

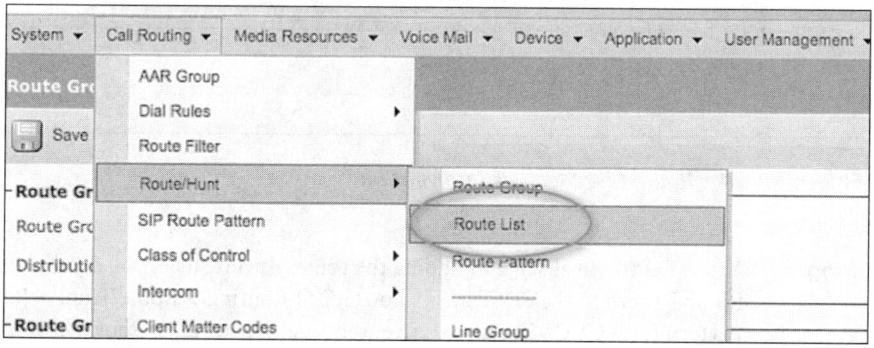

Figure 12-22 *Route List*

Step 5. After selecting the Route List from the main menu, Figure 12-23 displays. Here you define the parameters for that route list. Fill in the value **SIP_Trunks_To_PSTN_RL** under **Name. Click the Add Route Group** button.

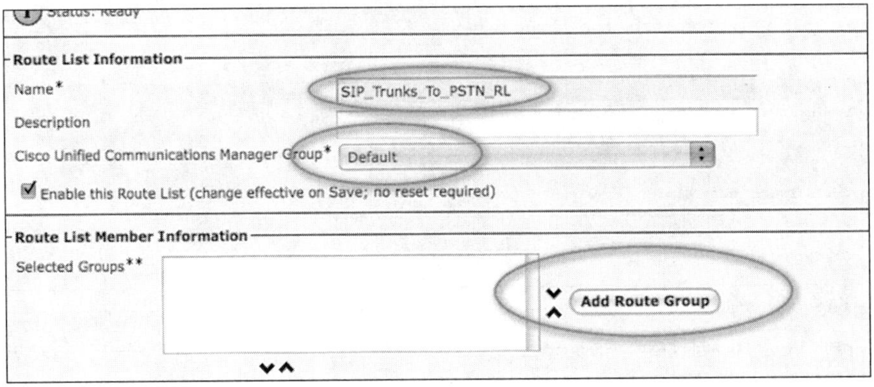

Figure 12-23 *Route List Information*

Step 6. Choose **SIP_Trunk_To_PSTN_RG** (created in the previous step) from the drop-down menu and click the **Save** button. Figure 12-24 shows the selection process for the route list member information.

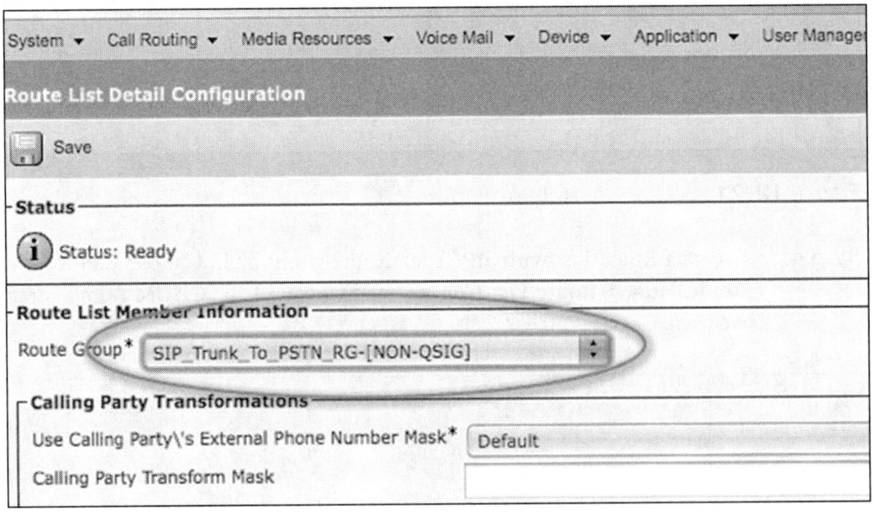

Figure 12-24 *Route List Member Information*

Step 7. You are at the final stage of adding the route. At this stage, you need to add a Route Pattern to the SIP Trunk. Choose **Call Routing > Route/Hunt > Route Pattern** from CUCM administrative webpage. Figure 12-25 shows how to select the **Route Pattern** from the main menu.

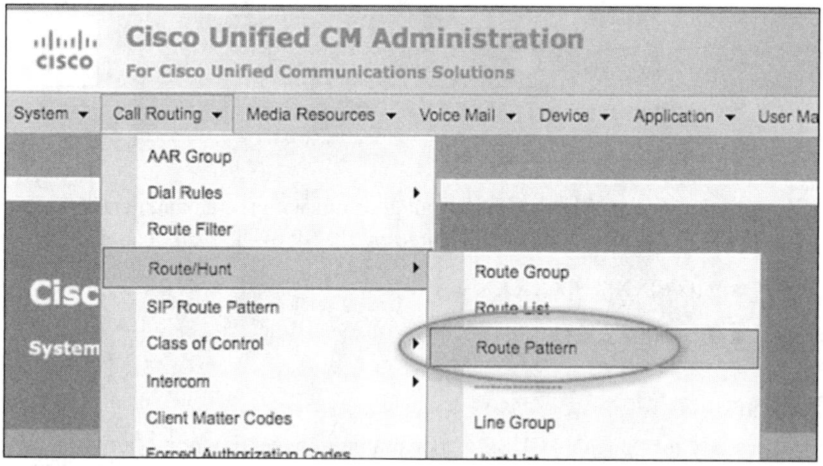

Figure 12-25 *Route Pattern*

Step 8. Choose **Add New**. Then configure the route pattern (see Figure 12-26) for calling the PSTN phone over that SIP trunk. You need to enter information for the following fields here.

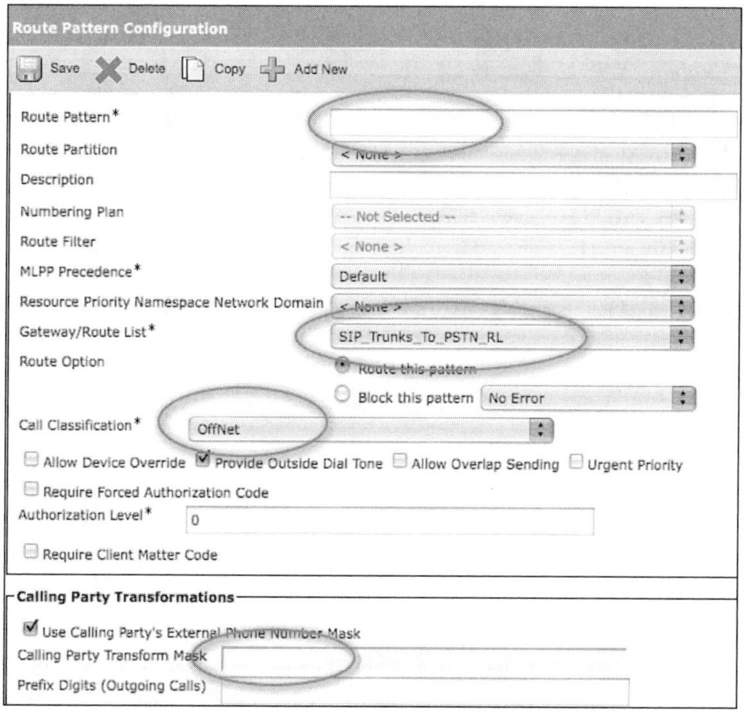

Figure 12-26 *Route Pattern Information*

- Route Pattern

- Gateway/Route List

- Call Classification

- Calling Party Transform Mask

Make sure that the outbound call goes out with the calling numbers matching the DID number range as allocated by the SP to the bank. For example:

- 9.1[2-9]XX[2-9]XXXXXX

- 9. [2-9]XXXXXX

CUBE Configuration

In the case study for the bank, CUBE works as a interconnecting point between internal and external networks. Both the call legs are SIP-enabled. CUBE communicates with an external facing SP network via SIP and an internal-facing CUCM network via SIP. Now let's see the configurations of different sections of CUBE.

Example 12-9 enables SIP-to-SIP calls between two networks. You can also see the comments and explanations of the Cisco IOS commands.

Example 12-9   *Enabling SIP Services in CUBE*

```
voice service voip                    ! Enters voice services configuration for voip
 allow-connections sip to sip             ! (CUBE Feature)
 sip
  bind control source-interface Loopback0        ! SIP source address
  bind media source-interface Loopback0
  early-offer forced                      ! SIP Signaling
  midcall-signaling passthru           ! Is needed for G.711 and G.729 call hold
 !
sip-ua
 retry invite 2              ! This is important when the gateway is in SRST mode
 retry bye 2
 retry cancel 2
 g729-annexb override
 !
```

When the employees of the bank dial PSTN or mobile numbers from their desk phones, they dial 9 as a dialing prefix. We need to set up translation rules to strip this prefix so that it does not go to SP network with the called number.

Example 12-10 shows the translation rule configuration to strip the dialed prefix.

Example 12-10   *Configuring Translation Rules*

```
voice translation-rule 1
 rule 1 /^9\(.*\)/ /\1/
!
voice translation-profile DIGITSTRIP_9
 translate called 1
!
interface Loopback0                     ¦ Make sure, this Loopback interface is
routable from your network.
 ip address 10.255.125.36 255.255.255.255
!
! For Call Admission Control
call treatment cause-code busy           ! This will translate to SIP 486 message
call treatment on
call threshold global cpu-avg low 68 high 75
call threshold global total-mem low 75 high 85
call threshold global total-calls low 8 high 10 treatment
```

The router hosting CUBE functionality has DSP, and the bank wanted to use it as the MTP device. Moreover, the same box can be used for transcoding and conferencing purpose.

Example 12-11 shows the details configuration of MTP, transcoding, and conferencing capabilities into CUBE.

Example 12-11   *MTP, Transcoding, and Conferencing Configuration*

```
voice-card 0
 dspfarm
 dsp services dspfarm

sccp local Loopback0
sccp ccm 10.103.144.70 identifier 1 version 4.1
sccp
!
sccp ccm group 1
 bind interface Loopback0
 associate ccm 1 priority 1
 associate profile 1 register XDR-NE27605
 associate profile 2 register CFB-NE27605
 associate profile 3 register MTP-NE27605
 keepalive retries 5
 switchover method immediate
```

continues

Example 12-11   *MTP, Transcoding, and Conferencing Configuration (continued)*

```
 switchback method graceful
 switchback interval 15
!
dspfarm profile 1 transcode
 description Transcoder
 codec g711ulaw
 codec g711alaw
 codec g729ar8
 codec g729abr8
 codec g729r8
 maximum sessions 3
 associate application SCCP
!
dspfarm profile 2 conference
 description conference bridge
 codec g711ulaw
 codec g711alaw
 codec g729ar8
 codec g729abr8
 codec g729r8
 codec g729br8
 maximum sessions 2
 associate application SCCP
!
dspfarm profile 3 mtp
 codec g729r8
 maximum sessions software 20
 associate application SCCP
```

Note   Make sure the profiles in Example 12-11 are part of Media Resource Group and the Media Resource Group List that are assigned to the SIP Trunk and IP Phones.

Finally, we need to configure dial-peers pointing toward SP and CUCM network. In Example 12-10, we created translation rules. Now, you can see how those rules are applied under different dial-peers. To maintain the privacy of the SP network, we have masked the IP addresses.

Example 12-12 shows the configuration of dial-peers in CUBE pointing toward SP's SBC.

Example 12-12 *Dial-Peers Pointing to the SP's SBC*

```
dial-peer voice 1000 voip
  translation-profile outgoing DIGITSTRIP_9
! For striping 91 from the called Number
    destination-pattern 91[2-9]........
! For outbound call to the SP
    voice-class sip early-offer forced
    session protocol sipv2
! Sets the protocol for call to SIP
    session target ipv4:172.xx.xx.xx:5297
! IP address/port of the SP's SBC
    incoming called-number 402715....
! To identify the inbound dial-peer
    dtmf-relay rtp-nte
! For DTMF tones
!
dial-peer voice 1001 voip
    translation-profile outgoing DIGITSTRIP_9
    destination-pattern 9[2-9]......
    voice-class sip early-offer forced
    session protocol sipv2
    session target ipv4:172.xx.xx.xx:5297
! IP addresses are masked for privacy reason
    dtmf-relay rtp-nte
!
dial-peer voice 1002 voip
    translation-profile outgoing DIGITSTRIP_9
    destination-pattern 9911
    voice-class sip early-offer forced
    session protocol sipv2
    session target ipv4:172.xx.xx.xx:5297
    dtmf-relay rtp-nte
!
dial-peer voice 1003 voip
    destination-pattern 911
    voice-class sip early-offer forced
    session protocol sipv2
    session target ipv4:172.xx.xx.xx:5297
    dtmf-relay rtp-nte
```

Example 12-13 shows the configuration of dial-peers in CUBE pointing toward the bank's CUCM cluster.

Example 12-13 *dial-peers Pointing Toward CUCM*

```
dial-peer voice 2000 voip
   destination-pattern 402715....                    ! DID Phones DNs
   session protocol sipv2
   session target ipv4:10.103.144.70       ! IP add of the first CUCM in CM Group
   incoming called-number 9T               ! To identify the inbound dial-peer
   dtmf-relay rtp-nte

dial-peer voice 2001 voip
   preference 1
   destination-pattern [2-9]..[2-9]......
   session protocol sipv2
   session target ipv4:<secondary CUCM IP Add>
   incoming called-number 9T
dtmf-relay rtp-nte
```

We need to configure a few more dial-peers so that the branch can work during the Survivable Remote Site Telephony (SRST) fallback mode. It is important to match the destination patterns defined here to the dial-peers configured for sending the call to the SP.

Example 12-14 shows the configured dial-peers that will be used during the SRST fallback mode.

Example 12-14 *Configuring SRST Mode*

```
dial-peer voice 200 pots
  incoming called-number .
  direct-inward-dial
  port 0/2/0
!
dial-peer voice 91120 pots
  preference 1
  destination-pattern 911
  port 0/2/0
  forward-digits all
!
dial-peer voice 991120 pots
  preference 1
  destination-pattern 9911
  port 0/2/0
  forward-digits 3
```

```
!
dial-peer voice 100 pots
  description Local-1FB
  preference 1
  destination-pattern 9[2-9]......
  port 0/2/0
  forward-digits 7
!
dial-peer voice 101 pots
  description LD-1FB
  preference 1
  destination-pattern 91[2-9].........
  port 0/2/0
  forward-digits 11
!

call-manager-fallback
  secondary-dialtone 9
  max-conferences 16 gain -6
  transfer-system full-consult
  timeouts interdigit 5
  ip source-address 10.255.126.36 port 2000
  max-ephones 42
  max-dn 144
  dialplan-pattern 1 402715.... extension-length 4
! Should represent the SP expected DIDs
  default-destination 59981
  moh All_in_the_Mind.ULAW.wav
  multicast moh 239.1.1.1 port 16392 route 10.255.126.36 10.125.250.1
```

Summary

In this chapter, we tried to provide a case study from a real-life deployment of a SIP trunk. We tried to capture as much information as possible without violating the confidentiality of the customers and their network. If you notice the problems and their solutions carefully, you should get an idea of the challenges and depth of the SIP trunk deployment.

Chapter 13

Future of Unified Communications

This chapter covers the following topics:

- Meaning of unified communications (UC)

- Components of UC

- UC today

- UC is anytime, anyplace, anywhere

- Mobility provides access anytime

- Telepresence: the future of presence

- UC in healthcare

- The journey ahead

During the past few years, Unified Communications (UC) has revolutionized the services available within a company. People started using Plain Old Telephony System (POTS) a few decades back, then they started communicating through email, file transfer (FTP), Bulletin Boards (BBS), World Wide Web (WWW), and so on. People also started using Instant Messaging (IM) greatly. Then, we have seen the mobile revolution. The web, IM, and smart phone have changed the whole world of communications. Now, we see the evolution of video and social networking. We have so many ways to communicate and collaborate.

This chapter discusses how UC might develop in the coming years based on roadmaps of current products and technologies. Some of the developments seem like part of a science fiction story. A sample day for a business user is provided with that person connecting via new UC technologies such as voice-based communications, push technology, and virtual assistants. Some additional, more futurist parts of this example include how a person can interact with others both physically using virtual robots and logically with interactions to virtual agents that enable a single person to be in multiple places virtually at the same time. These are all possibilities; however, in this chapter, we cover the current status of UC, the components of UC, and how UC can connect anyone, anywhere, at any time based on the available resources. This is a very interesting world to live in. It can change the way we work, live, play, and learn.

Meaning of UC

You need to understand what is meant by UC, which has come into widespread use in the past year or two. In addition to face-to-face communication, three types of communications are used in the real world today:

- **Person-to-person communications:** We mean real-time interactive communications here, such as voice and video. In this specific case, we are not talking about in-person, face-to-face communication. We are talking about person-to-person communication through a device. And we cannot discount IM, Short Messaging Service (SMS), and other text messaging tools either. Email is an asynchronous way of communicating that makes it nonreal time.

- **Person-to-machine communications:** This is purely an interaction with a device or system. It might consist of surfing the web, dialing numbers to pull information (such as Interactive Voice Response [IVR]), checking a Twitter feed, querying the corporate inventory system, or selecting a video-on-demand program.

- **Machine-to-machine communications:** This stream of communication is the entire background processing taking place between networking devices, routers, servers, cloud computing, databases, and so on. It might include call setup and teardown. It's made up of streaming XML SOAP for web services, tracking some remote devices through mobile networks, reading the electric meters automatically by another machine, batch file transfers, and machine transactions.

UC is not telephony. It's more than that. Telephony is just one component of the whole picture. UC interacts with a person or network resource anywhere on the network (the corporate network, home network, the Public Switched Telephone Network (PSTN), or the Internet).

Components of UC

UC is a concept that describes how multiple modes of communications can be seamlessly integrated. UC is not a single product. It is a solution consisting of several elements, including (but not limited to) the following:

- Call control and multimodal communications

- Conferencing—audio, web, and video

- Collaboration tools (such as WebEx)

- Mobility

- Presence

- IM

- Unified messaging

- Speech access and personal assistant

- Business process integration (BPI)

- Software to enable business process integration

You can connect all these together through presence.

A typical UC session might start with an IM between two parties that escalates to a phone call or web conference through the click of a button on the PC screen. That click connects the parties via audio, and another turns the call into video, if desired. If other people need to be added to the conversation, a look at the presence status of people on your buddy list lets you simply click-to-conference to bring them into the call.

Presence has an important role in UC. It helps to know where one's intended recipients are and whether they are available in real time. To put it simply, UC integrates all the systems a user might already be using and enables those systems to work together in real time. Most people associate presence with IM (IM "buddy lists"). But, in many business process applications, what is important is finding someone with a certain skill. In these environments, presence identifies available people with certain skills or capabilities.

For example, a customer service representative (CSR) receives a call from a customer who has a question that is outside of the CSR's area of expertise. UC can enable the CSR to access a real-time list of available expert colleagues and then make a call that would reach the necessary person. This would enable the customer to receive an answer faster and eliminate rounds of back-and-forth emails and phone tag. Enterprises find that they can achieve an even greater impact by using UC capabilities to transform business processes. This is achieved by integrating UC functionality directly into business applications.

UC Today

UC has evolved over the last decade. *Convergence* took hold as a concept in the late '90s. Internet Protocol (IP) became the most widely accepted transport technology for data traffic. Around the same time VoIP came on the scene as a potentially disruptive technology for telecommunications. This convergence of voice and data networks has continued around the globe for the past several years. Today there are many networks that still haven't fully converged. The process continues.

In addition, in the last few years, the word convergence has given way to the UC. For most people, UC simply means the fully converged network, supporting data, voice, and video. UC also refers to a trend to offer business process integration, that is, to simplify and integrate all forms of communication to optimize business processes and reduce the response time, manage flows, and eliminate device and media dependencies. There are mission-critical business applications that integrate more tightly through Communications Enhanced Business Processes (CEBP). These include the following:

- Enterprise Resource Management (ERP) Sales Force Automation (SFA)

- Supply Chain Management (SCM)

- Customer Relationship Management (CRM)

- Human Resource Management (HRM)

There is always room to further integrate for efficiency.

UC enable an individual to send a message on one medium and receive a message on another. In most situations, it is possible to transfer any activity or message to another medium.

For example, you can receive a voice mail message and choose to access it through email or a cell phone. If the sender is online according to the presence information and accepts calls, the response can be sent immediately through text chat or video call. Otherwise, it might be sent as a nonreal-time message that can be accessed through a variety of media.

UC Is Anytime, Anyplace, Anywhere

Voice used to be a silo application. However, products are moving toward unifying the multiple types of communications currently deployed separately by both companies and individual users.

Some of our preferred mode of communications is email; however, some people use IM to check on somebody's presence or availability or even send an instant message to say, "Do you have a minute to talk?" With UC, you'll know where the other person is physically located so you can meet in person if they are nearby. The system is also aware of the different modes of communication available to them—perhaps they are in a Telepresence room equipped with high-quality video, in a conference call and cannot accept any phone call, in car and can talk only via cell phone, or in a remote office near a desk phone. If multiple modes are available, the system knows which way of communicating the person prefers or is most appropriate at any particular time.

The system can also be capable of working with other applications. For example, it can set up a collaboration session on a document you are developing with another person. It can also seamlessly access back-office data. The productivity increase comes from doing things more quickly, no matter where other people are located. Another thing that can make UC special is that it can work over any type of IP network—if there is enough bandwidth.

End users will like UC because connectivity will be simplified. Specifically, it can offer users a single logon and authentication to access all the various modes of communication. It also can change the whole paradigm of communicating with people, moving away from the idea that there are multiple ways of reaching you. To contact you, someone can select your name, and the communication is mapped to whatever is available to you.

Cisco CEO John Chambers says, "That's the future. It's a hard concept [to understand], but it goes right to the issue of increased productivity. I clearly communicate at 200 words a minute, and I'm much better with the video capability that goes with it." The way young people communicate now, through video, text messaging, and social networking sites, is how enterprises will communicate in the next few years, he added.

Mobility Provides Access Anytime

The networks that will handle the increased IP traffic due to UC are still. Fast wireless networks are only the beginning of the sea of changes in mobile communications.

According to pundits, we'll soon live in a world in which the network will locate anyone for you, tell you how best to make contact, and, after making contact, support collaboration and access to data from anywhere. UC will speed business processes dramatically, resulting in more responsive companies and significant increases in productivity.

The shape of our communication tools has been undergoing change for some time. The form factor we work with today is quite different from the early days of computing and cellular communications. Computers have shrunk from desktop to laptop to notebook to what is now being called a netbook. At the same time, smartphones incorporate more and more computing features, and with the addition of wireless broadband capabilities, they have become the primary tool of business for many. Don't forget the new segment of handheld tablet devices that are filing in the gaps between the two extremes.

The shape of computing has changed. The desktop box or mini-tower alongside the desk is rarely the first choice for users buying a new communications system today. Just as computers have changed in shape and size, mobile telephones have shrunk. What were once bulky devices in a shoulder bag became handhelds. Today they're miniscule electronics that fit in a shirt pocket or purse. Wristwatch mobile phones also exist today.

We are expecting some wireless technology to provide a constantly morphing Personal Area Network (PAN) that automatically joins all the resources within range. Here are some resources you may think about:

- Keyboards

- Display units

- Microphones

- Cameras

- Scanner

- Printers

- Processors

- Automobiles

- Workplace

- Home

- Airplane resources for travelers

Because the network resources can automatically connect, new service convergences that are possible but impractical today will become routine in the future. UC delivers the convergence point where these devices will integrate into one single portable tool that performs a myriad of functions.

With the ever-changing workday, it no longer lasts from 9 a.m. to 5 p.m.; people work differently. They work at home, in the office, in a waiting room, in the car, in the plane. Soon, a telephone call may follow this scenario.

We might easily make a phone call in the early morning from our device using our business office number, but connected to some communications devices in our home office. While we're getting ready to work, the phone call can be transferred to our headset. When we start driving to work, the phone call can pass from home to automobile. When we arrive at the office, the phone call might transfer from the cellular carrier to the corporate WiFi network, and eventually wind up on our computerized workstation in a cubicle.

All these things go through growth curves with early adopters and then take off more broadly. It will be a number of years before we achieve ubiquity.

Telepresence: the Future of Presence

There is a tremendous upsurge in the use of personal video calling. In the future of network-connected homes, there will be an entertainment wall that can be configured into a number of virtual screens and video cameras in every room of the house, for both video calling and security.

Cisco Telepresence is a product developed by Cisco that provides high-definition 1080 p video, spatial audio, and a setup designed to link two physically separated rooms so they resemble a single conference room even though the two rooms might be on opposite sides of the world.

Cisco Telepresence creates a live, face-to-face communication experience over the network that empowers you to collaborate like never before. Telepresence helps people meet, share content, create high-quality video recordings and events, consult with experts, and deliver powerful personalized services, all using the power of the network for an immersive in-person experience.

With Cisco Telepresence:

- Scheduling is easy—no IT support required.

- Launching a meeting is as simple as making a phone call.

- People appear life-like and life-size.

- In-room controls are intuitive.

- Collaboration applications are plug and play.

- Participants can meet in many rooms at once—up to 48 locations in one meeting.

- Users can meet, record high-quality video, or participate in impactful special events.

- Users can easily bring in collaboration applications such as WebEx.

- Existing SD or HD videoconferencing systems can be easily integrated.

PAN inside homes will recognize who the inhabitants are and where they are in the house (through Bluetooth and RFID-like technologies). The system can deliver a video call to whichever room they are in. As they move from room to room, the video can easily transfer from one camera to another, and a new virtual screen will light up on the wall of the room being entered. Rooms also can be designated off-limits for privacy, and video will not be transmitted from those locations.

The journey of the Telepresence has just started. We expect a huge wave to take the experience to the next level within the next few years.

UC in Healthcare

UC will have a huge impact on the healthcare system. It will change the way healthcare is delivered today and create better tools to manage caregiver communication and collaboration in healthcare.

For way too long the doctors, hospitals, and insurance companies have focused almost solely on the telephone system. Granted, the phone was a great invention for doctors, and they couldn't practice medicine without it. When telephones went mobile, physicians were among the first professionals to use cellular because it delivered real business value in an informative intensive environment.

But society has moved well beyond the limitations of synchronous voice communication. There are times when waiting for a phone call to relay information doesn't make sense. In plenty of situations, the telephone isn't optimal for human collaboration involving complex work flows and information-rich content.

However, just as the telephone has its limitations, reading about UC can only get you so far.

UC ultimately leads to improved communication and collaboration across the healthcare ecosystem and eventually right into the home. The patient could connect to the doctor from home; the doctor could pull all the records of that patient and prescribe the medicine; or the session could instantly be connected to an available specialist for expert opinion, and then the patient could be get admitted into the hospital (if needed) without disconnecting the session. And after the patient is hospitalized, he could collaborate with family members in distant locations by simply lying in the hospital bed. Usually, visitors are restricted in the patient's rooms in the hospital. But next generation hospitals will allow patient's family members and friends to collaborate with the patient from anywhere of the world. It is not far away when the grandchildren living at home will be playing with their grandparents in the hospital room.

Journey Ahead

The proliferation of communications options has become a burden that often makes it more difficult to reach people, rather than easier. Rapid advances in hardware, networks, and the software that powers them are laying the foundation for groundbreaking innovations in communications technology that will revolutionize the way we share information and experiences with the people who are important to us at work and at home.

Microsoft founder Bill Gates said, "A fundamental reason that communicating is still so complex is the fact that the way we communicate is still bound by devices. In the office, we use a work phone with one number. Then, we ask people to call us back on a mobile device using another number when we are on the go or reach us on our home phone with yet another number."

People also have different identities and passwords for their work and home email accounts and for IM, he said, noting that this would all change in the very near future as more communications and entertainment is transmitted over the Internet by email, IM, videoconferencing, and the emergence of Voice over IP (VoIP), IPTV (IP television), and other protocols.

A new wave of innovations will eliminate the boundaries between the various modes of communications we use throughout the day. Soon, you will have a single identity that spans all the ways people can reach you, and you will move a conversation seamlessly between voice, text, and video and from one device to another as your location and information-sharing needs change.

Longer-Term Technological Changes

To realize many of the goals for UC, three major areas need to change:

- Immersive experiences outside of controlled environments
- Ability to connect to experiences across a wide variety of devices at different fidelities
- The capability to initiate connections between any device with a pervasive methodology to connect

Each of these three areas will have a dramatic effect on the future of communications. The year 2050 can be assumed as a reasonable proxy for "Longer Term," and as such, is used here as a date proxy to describe how UC experiences will occur in the longer term. Table 13-1 outlines the impact, possible timeline, and technology advancements required for these changes.

Table 13-1 *Future UC Experiences and the Technology Changes Required to Enable Them*

Time Frame/Change	Today	Year 2050	Technologies Required
Immersive experiences	Immersive experiences are possible today under controlled environments. 3D audio and full-screen video calls in Telepresence rooms provide the richest capabilities today.	Immersive experiences must occur without a controlled environment. The same senses of sight and sound will be utilized in these pervasive experiences, but these experiences will occur at the same fidelity without the environmental constraints imposed with today's solutions.	The capability to miniaturize cameras and microphones nd the capability to project images and sounds under uncontrolled environments will be required to fulfill this future.
Ability to experience UC across a wide variety of devices	Voice is the ubiquitous lowest common denominator with many different media and devices, from desk phones, to PC with Skype to cell phones all having the capability to send audio.	The most basic telecom devices will include the capability to support both voice and video. This change in the lowest common form of communications from voice-only-to-voice, video, and data will bring in a new social norm of what is considered a "basic call" in both the business and personal worlds.	The capability for all devices to support video will be required to support this dramatic change. Today's networks are on the cusp and are having more video traffic than any other, and the future will be realized when even the most basic devices support video. The technology to accomplish this is the continued decline in cost and improvement in features for video-enabled endpoints.

continues

Table 13-1   *Future UC Experiences and the Technology Changes Required to Enable Them (continued)*

Time Frame/Change	Today	Year 2050	Technologies Required
Capability to initiate connections from any device to any device	There are two major unique identifiers that people use for connecting across communications providers: email addresses and phone numbers. Other identifiers, such as an iCHAT service screen name or SKYPE username can provide rich experiences, but those identifiers are not owned by the individual and are not routable across providers.	There will be a unique identifier that will be composed of some easy to remember tag, such as an email address, that will be owned by the end users. This tag will then be associated with an IPv6 address space that will enable end users to have a myriad of devices that can be connected with a few common identifiers that they have control over.	A new top-level identifier for name resolutions will need to occur. This will likely be based on Domain Name System (DNS), because it has proven to be scalable for finding services. The expansion of DNS to assist in the resolution of routing information for individuals does not require any technological changes but would require a change in the business models for funding such services. The other dramatic change required is the widespread adoption of IPv6. With IPv6, the problems running out of available IP addresses is resolved with the dramatic increase in routable IP addresses and the dramatic increases in features.

The current state-of-the-art technologies for immersive experiences are Cisco Telepresence technologies that were described in early sections. Telepresence deployments currently require a controlled environment and controlled endpoints and are typically deployed on an IPv4 network.

IPv6 and Its Effect on the Future of UC

IPv6 is a technology that has been "almost" ready to deploy for several years. As of the publishing of this book in 2010, it still has not been successful. However, as a basis for additional enhancements to UC, the importance of IPv6 cannot be understated. There are significant benefits IPv6 brings to both the consumer and the operator of networks.

Consumers will use a myriad of devices without the inherent problem with connectivity issues. With Ipv6, each user can have a large number of devices and will not have as many issues that exist today with using private addressing schemes and mapping the schemes, in sometimes awkward ways, to public IP addressing schemes to access the rich content of the Internet. With IPv6, each end user could literally have a million devices and each of them would access rich Internet content in a secure, flexible, and reliable way.

This change does imply that in the next 40 years all consumer IP devices will be changed. It is not an unrealistic expectation. Today's consumer devices are designed for a 3-to-5-year lifecycle. Within the next 40 years, there is little chance that any device created today would be on the network. However, IPv6 has a great capability for backward compatibility, so accessing older content for consumers and some older devices will not be a problem. In 40 years it will not be uncommon to look at an iPhone or a Cisco Desktop IP Phone with the same nostalgia that is reserved for looking at candlestick phones today.

SPs see a great benefit in their capability to see across all their assets with IPv6 networks. Today, as networks have evolved from multiple protocols and transports to a more homogenous set of protocols, SPs can better diagnose and monitor their network. The end result is increased efficiency as fewer resources are needed to monitor large networks; for instance, it is easier to troubleshoot one routing protocol than multiple ones.

Unfortunately, due to the inherent limitations in IPv4 networks, there is little or no capability to see the routing and underlying infrastructure and health between networks. Each private 10.x.x.x address space must be examined and monitored independently. IPv6 can resolve this for SPs by creating a routable address space across a large network. This large address space can be monitored in a holistic way enabling SPs to see what is going on throughout their network with a single set of extensive monitoring tools. This increase in efficiency will enable them to lower their costs and pass the decrease on to the consumer in the form of lower prices. This, in turn, will enable for the expansion of bandwidth and enhancement of the UC experience.

The Power of Revolution: The Greening of Unified Communications

An important revolution that will have a major impact on UC is the Green revolution. There are many definitions of what the Green revolution means and where it will go; however, one thing is clear: UC solutions in the next 40 years will have to consume less power for the same experience as UC solutions today.

The primary component of voice communications, the phone, has a reasonable power consumption profile. The sheer volume of production led companies to innovate in the area of battery life. However, the primary components of UC include video, and it has not yet had the same focus for power optimization as voice has undergone. Improved screen technology that will consume less power and be more pervasive will be the key to "greener" video. One possibility is that screen technology will not necessarily travel with the end device; instead, the display screen and video recording device will become a fixed resource that end devices participating in UC can manipulate. In this future, screens will be used for multiple purposes, from advertising to public announcements and will also double as screens to be used for personal UC in some type of pay per use or shared environment. The device that was initiating the call will also start a connection with the display device and utilize the hardware with the SP charging a small additional fee to utilize this previously public device. When the device was not utilized for personal calls, the device would revert to being used for public announcements or advertising to help recover the cost.

The ramifications are that display and recording devices could be optimized to use low power without being dependent on battery technologies. The devices that move with the customers, much like today's traditional cell phones, would be optimized for long battery life, but would take advantage of other devices. The devices that are fixed resources at specific locations can be used for multiple purposes, such as public displays, and could take advantage of passive power sources such as solar energy for outdoor devices. This more efficient utilization of resources will result in lower power consumption and be a major component of the greening of UC.

Summary

The future of UC in the *short term* will not have the speed and dramatic changes that have occurred in other areas such as personal computing; however, in the *long term*, the changes will be dramatic and have more of an impact than any other technology change in the 21st century. The revolution in communications will fundamentally change the nature of people's lives. The capability to share rich personal experiences across vast distances with the aid of immersive telecommunications equipment will enable cultures to continue to thrive and communities to continue to exist across wide physical divides that were not possible in the past. The capability to have those rich communications experiences, albeit at a lower level of fidelity, across a wide variety of platforms that can be mobile or low cost, will enable individuals to experience different cultures at a much more dramatic rate than is possible today.

A glimpse at the future of UC can often be seen in science fiction novels. A good example is the first vision of the cellular "flip phone" that was shown in Gene Rodenberry's Star Trek series as the "communicator." Some extreme examples of possibilities of the future of communications can be seen in the science fiction genre called cyberpunk. A popular novel in this genre is *Neuromancer* by William Gibson. This is recommended reading to anyone who would like to take a glimpse at a possible future of what the Internet could be.

Imagine the capability to remotely experience Mardi Gras in Brazil or a Japanese tea ceremony in a rich immersive, personal, and real-time experience. This revolution will occur as a combination of advancements in technologies and business models enable consumers and businesses to experience a level of interconnectedness that is not possible today. The future of UC is bright and will occur faster than most people expect, but perhaps, not as fast as most people dream.

Index

I

J-K-L

P

Q

QA (quality assurance), 184-185
QoS, 127
  congestion management, 128
  delay, 128
  echo, 128
  jitter, 128
  remarking, configuring, 240
  traffic marking, 111, 127
quality control
  certification, 185
  QA, 184-185

R

real-time billing servers, SIP trunking
  for SP networks, 61
recording services, 30
redundancy, 131
  best practices, 261
  on border elements, 132
  PSTN TDM gateway failover, 137
registration, 122-123
regulatory design considerations, 102
RFPs (Request for Proposal), 35
  preparing for SBC
    delivery issues, 181-182
    demarcation issues, 171-173
    documentation and training issues, 182
    internetworking support issues, 169-171
    operations and management issues, 176-178
    performance/sizing issues, 178-180
    security issues, 173-175

    session management issues, 162-168
    support issues, 182-183
    systems specification issues, 178

S

SBC (Session Border Controllers).
  See also SBC vendors
  deploying, best practices, 260-261
  SIP trunks for Enterprise networks
    application interconnection SBC, 78-79
    interconnecting SBC, 76
  SIP trunks for SP networks
    edge SBC, 58-59
    peering SBC, 71-73
SBC vendors
  technical requirements
    certification issues, 185
    QA issues, 184-185
  technical requirements for SIP deployment
    delivery, 181-182
    demarcation, 171-173
    documentation and training, 182
    internetworking support, 169-171
    operations management, 176-178
    performance/sizing, 178-180
    security, 173-175
    session management, 162-168
    support, 182-183
    system specification, 178

T

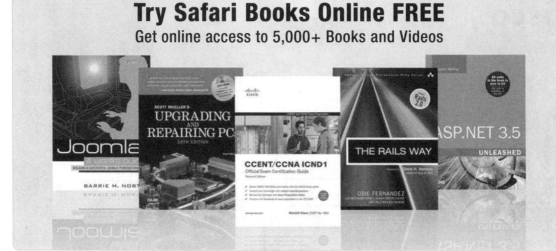

IP COMMUNICATIONS

SIP Trunking

Migrating from TDM to IP for Business to
Business Communication

Christina Hattingh
Darryl Sladden
ATM Zakaria Swapan

ciscopress.com

FREE Online Edition

Your purchase of **SIP Trunking** includes access to a free online edition for 45 days
through the Safari Books Online subscription service. Nearly every Cisco Press book
is available online through Safari Books Online, along with more than 5,000 other
technical books and videos from publishers such as Addison-Wesley Professional,
Exam Cram, IBM Press, O'Reilly, Prentice Hall, Que, and Sams.

SAFARI BOOKS ONLINE allows you to search for a specific answer, cut and paste
code, download chapters, and stay current with emerging technologies.

Activate your FREE Online Edition at
www.informit.com/safarifree

> **STEP 1:** Enter the coupon code: CGWCIWH.

> **STEP 2:** New Safari users, complete the brief registration form.
> Safari subscribers, just log in.

If you have difficulty registering on Safari or accessing the online edition,
please e-mail customer-service@safaribooksonline.com